PENGUIN BOOKS

THE PENGUIN BOOK OF BUSINESS WISDOM

Stephen Dando-Collins was born at Launceston, Tasmania, in 1950. After training as a graphic artist, he worked in advertising in Australia and Britain as a graphic designer, copywriter, creative director, and senior advertising agency executive. An independent marketing consultant for some years, he ran the Australian operations of an American market research company before moving to Noosa, Queensland, where he now writes full-time. He is the author of a number of books, including the novel *Finklestein's Miracle* (1989), the business book *The Customer Care Revolution* (1996) and, most recently, the novel *Cobbers* (1997) and the children's novel *Chance in a Million* (1998).

D1362876

THE PENGUIN BOOK OF
BUSINESS
WISDOM

A MUST-HAVE COLLECTION OF BUSINESS
QUOTATIONS, THOUGHTS AND ANECDOTES
FOR EVERY BUSINESS SITUATION

COMPILED & EDITED BY
STEPHEN DANDO-COLLINS

PENGUIN BOOKS

Penguin Books India (P) Ltd., 11 Community Centre, Panchsheel Park, New Delhi 110 017, India
Penguin Books Ltd., 27 Wrights Lane, London W8 5TZ, UK
Penguin Putnam Inc., 375 Hudson Street, New York, NY 10014, USA
Penguin Books Australia Ltd., Ringwood, Victoria, Australia
Penguin Books Canada Ltd., 10 Alcorn Avenue, Suite 300, Toronto, Ontario, M4V 3B2, Canada
Penguin Books (NZ) Ltd., Cnr Rosedale and Airborne Roads, Albany, Auckland, New Zealand

Published by Penguin Books Australia Ltd 1998
First published in India by Penguin Books India 2000

10 9 8 7 6 5 4 3 2 1

Cover design by Scott Williams, Penguin Design Studio
Text design by Leonie Stott, Penguin Design Studio
Printed at Chaman Offset Printers, New Delhi

Contents

Acknowledgements

My heartfelt thanks to Louise, my wife and partner and assistant in all things, who has, as usual, supported and endured above and beyond the call of duty.

My thanks also to the team at Penguin, in particular Bob Sessions, Clare Forster, Peg McColl, and Helen Pace.

And a special thankyou to the many people around the world who have gone out of their way to help source the material in this book, and who kindly gave permission for its reproduction. There are too many to list here.

Introduction

The Penguin Book of Business Wisdom was conceived as a business library in one volume: a book for anyone involved in or interested in business, in all its facets, be they a businessperson, student, university professor or business writer; a book that will inform, advise, enthuse, inspire and amuse.

I have endeavoured to collect quotations ranging from pithy and amusing one-liners to sage anecdotes that run to several paragraphs. There are contributions from worldly-wise men and women of yesterday to business gurus of today; from citizens of the ancient world to members of contemporary academia; from players in big business to performers in show business. Many of the contemporary wisdoms have never before been published in collected form, and several were penned especially for inclusion in this book.

Categories were established with a view to their relevance to business generally and to business practice in particular. In the same way, quotations were selected that could be applied to a business environment. Individual quotations were chosen using several main criteria: the quotation either expressed a key point or was worded in such a way as to make it stand out and be worthy of repetition; or the person making the quote was of such note that a reader might be interested in their view; or any combination of these factors.

Few books of collected quotations have such a high representation of quotes from women as does this volume. However, we do not take responsibility for the fact that many contributors have used 'he' rather than 'she' or 'he and she' when giving examples. This was the case even with many female writers quoted. On the other hand, the reason that the 'Women in Business' category is dominated by quotes from females is possibly that women appear more willing than men to speak about this subject.

While every effort has been made to clarify the attribution details accompanying the quotations, it is not unlikely that some corrections may be required. Readers who are able to correct any attribution errors are requested to write with the details to me c/o the publishers. Corrected details will be included in future revised editions.

How to use this book

To help readers find quotations relevant to their needs, the quotations in this book are arranged alphabetically in thematic sections; for example Accuracy, Achieving, Advertising, Advice, and so on. The quotations within each thematic section are arranged in alphabetical order according to the person or persons to whom the quotation is attributed.

To help readers further, there are two indexes at the back of the book. The first is a compilation of the names of the people to whom the quotations have been attributed. This is particularly useful for readers looking for the ideas of a particular person. The second is a key-word index that identifies the key word or words within a quotation so that, again, readers will find it easy to locate the most useful quotation or quotations on any given subject.

Running heads refer to section name and number

2 If you want to accomplish something, you can't eliminate all risk.
> MALCOLM FORBES, American publisher. Quoted in Edward de Bono, *Tactics: The Art and Science of Success* (Collins, London, 1985). Reprinted by permission of HarperCollins Publishers Limited.

3 Back of every achievement is a proud wife and a surprised mother-in-law.
> BROOKS HAYS, American lawyer, educator, presidential aide and congressman. Attrib.

4 Who begins too much accomplishes little.
> GERMAN PROVERB.

5 To achieve great things we must live as though we were never going to die.
> MARQUIS DE LUC DE CLAPIERS VAUVENARGUES (1715–47), French moralist. *Reflections and Maxims* (1746).

6 The greatest pleasure in life is achieving things that people say can't be done.
> SCOTT VOLKERS, Australian swimming coach and coach of Olympians Susie O'Neill and Samantha Riley. Part of a message contained in a note handed to O'Neill the night before her gold-medal swim at the 1996 Atlanta Olympics. *Australian Magazine*, 11 January 1997.

advertising 3

See also: brands 6; marketing 58; publicity 84; products 80; selling 93

1 Advertising can get people into a store, but it can't make them buy.
> ANON.

Section name and number

Cross-references refer to other relevant sections by their section number, not page number

A note on sources

The sources for the quotations in this book are many and varied. However, they tend to fall into several main categories: books; newspapers, magazines, and journals; stage plays; speeches and addresses; written communications; and television broadcasts.

Where a book may still be in print, the full name and location of the publisher is shown, as is the year of publication. This should enable a reader who wishes to read more from a particular author to locate the book or books concerned at a bookshop. Book publisher details appear in parentheses.

The source is identified after each quotation. Where the source has not been confirmed, it is shown as 'Attrib.'.

Source abbreviations

Anon.   Anonymous
Attrib.   Attributed
CWE   A quotation provided in correspondence with the editor of this volume

'It is much easier to follow a pioneer
than to be a pioneer . . .'
RICHARD BRANSON

advice 4:4

1 accuracy
See also: details 22

1 I do not mind lying, but I hate inaccuracy.

> SAMUEL BUTLER (1835–1902), British scholar, translator and novelist. 'Truth and Convenience', *Note-Books* (1912).

2 This insistence on photographic accuracy, so unusual in a poet, may have been the one loose bearing in the otherwise perfect machinery of his mind; or it may have been that his training as a sub-editor had bitten so deeply into his system that he looked upon inaccuracy as the cardinal sin. There was no satisfaction for him in a majestic march of words if any of the words were out of step.

> A. B. 'BANJO' PATERSON (1864–1941), Australian author, poet, journalist and newspaper editor. Comments made about Rudyard Kipling, after visiting him at his home in England. Originally in 'Rudyard Kipling', a newspaper article, and reprinted in *A Literary Heritage: Banjo Paterson* (Octopus, Melbourne, 1988).

3 It is not enough to aim. You must hit.

> ITALIAN PROVERB.

2 achieving
See also: goals & goal-setting 36; success 98; winners & winning 106

1 Nothing great was achieved without enthusiasm.

> RALPH WALDO EMERSON (1803–82), American philosopher, poet and essayist. 'Circles', *Essays; First Series* (1841).

2 If you want to accomplish something, you can't eliminate all risk.

> MALCOLM FORBES, American publisher. Quoted in Edward de Bono, *Tactics: The Art and Science of Success* (Collins, London, 1985). Reprinted by permission of HarperCollins Publishers Limited.

3 Back of every achievement is a proud wife and a surprised mother-in-law.

> BROOKS HAYS, American lawyer, educator, presidential aide and congressman. Attrib.

4 Who begins too much accomplishes little.

> GERMAN PROVERB.

5 To achieve great things we must live as though we were never going to die.

> MARQUIS DE LUC DE CLAPIERS VAUVENARGUES (1715–47), French moralist. *Reflections and Maxims* (1746).

6 The greatest pleasure in life is achieving things that people say can't be done.

> SCOTT VOLKERS, Australian swimming coach and coach of Olympians Susie O'Neill and Samantha Riley. Part of a message contained in a note handed to O'Neill the night before her gold-medal swim at the 1996 Atlanta Olympics. *Australian Magazine*, 11 January 1997.

advertising 3

See also: brands 6; marketing 58; publicity 84; products 80; selling 93

1 Advertising can get people into a store, but it can't make them buy.

> ANON.

2 To win the battle for market share, make the product the hero of your advertising.

ANON.

3 Just when you think advertising has scraped the bottom of the barrel of indecency, they lower the bottom.

MICHAEL ANTEBI, American advertising executive. Robert Gustafson, Johan Yssel & Lea Witta, 'Ad Agency Employees Give Views on Calvin Klein, Benetton Ads', *Marketing News* (American Marketing Association), 23 September 1996, page 16. Reprinted with permission.

4 The advertisements in a newspaper are more full of knowledge in respect to what is going on in a state or community than the editorial columns are.

HENRY WARD BEECHER (1813–87), American clergyman, lecturer and author. *Proverbs from Plymouth Pulpit* (1887).

5 Advertising isn't a science. It's persuasion. And persuasion is an art.

BILL BERNBACH (1911–82), American advertising expert and co-founder of Doyle Dane Bernbach Advertising. Attrib.

6 There is an inherent drama in every product – our number one job is to dig for it and capitalise on it. Steep yourself in your subject, work like hell, and love, honour and obey your hunches.

LEO BURNETT (1891–1971), American advertising expert and founder of Leo Burnett advertising agency, Chicago. His creative creed for agency staff.

7 One of the conditions of the consumer culture is that it relies upon human insecurities to create aspirations that can be satisfied only by the purchase of some product or service. If all of us said today, 'Okay, I have enough stuff. From now on I will buy

only the bare necessities,' that would be a disaster for our economy. But spurred on by cultural messages that encourage us to feel dissatisfied with what we have and that equate success with consumption – messages fuelled by the advertisements that constantly bombard us – we face the far more likely danger of allowing greed to overshadow moderation, restraint, and the stability that comes from saving and investing for the future rather than satisfying short-term desires.

HILLARY RODHAM CLINTON, American lawyer, and First Lady of the United States of America 1993– . *It Takes a Village* (Simon & Schuster, New York, 1996).

8 It is easier to write ten passably effective sonnets than one effective advertisement.

ALDOUS HUXLEY (1894–1963), British novelist and critic, and one-time advertising copywriter. Attrib.

9 Advertising, though certainly not free from criticism, is an economic asset and not a liability.

RICHARD D. IRWIN, American academic, economist and author. *The Economics of Advertising* (Chicago, 1942).

10 Promise, large promise, is the soul of an advertisement.

SAMUEL JOHNSON (Dr Johnson; 1709–84), British poet, essayist, critic, journalist and lexicographer. *The Idler* (c. 1758–60).

11 Advertising may be described as the science of arresting the human intelligence long enough to get money from it.

STEPHEN LEACOCK (1869–1944), British-born Canadian humorist, educator, lecturer and author. 'The Perfect Salesman', *The Garden of Folly*.

12 Half the money I spend on advertising is wasted, and the trouble is I don't know which half.

LORD LEVERHULME (William Hesketh Lever, 1st Viscount Leverhulme of the Western Isles; 1851–1925), British soap and detergent entrepreneur, and founder of the Lever Brothers manufacturing empire. Attrib.

13 Ads shouldn't just sell products, they should change the world.

GEORGE LOIS, American advertising creative executive and author. Bob Lamons, 'Research Won't Yield The Big Idea', *Marketing News* (American Marketing Association), 18 November 1996, page 18. Reprinted with permission.

14 A lot of clients, especially the younger ones, have been trained to think advertising is a science. If advertising is a science, I'm a girl.

GEORGE LOIS, American advertising creative executive and author. Bob Lamons, 'Research Won't Yield The Big Idea', *Marketing News* (American Marketing Association), 18 November 1996, page 18. Reprinted with permission.

15 *Creative Advertising Guidelines*
   1. **Break the pattern.**
   2. **Position the product clearly and competitively.**
   3. **Reflect the character of the product.**
   4. **Appeal to both heart and head.**
   5. **Generate trust.**
   6. **Speak with one voice.**

USP NEEDHAM, Australian advertising agency. Corporate guidelines for the creation of advertising (1970s–80s).

16 It is often charged that advertising can persuade people to buy inferior products. So it can – *once*. But the consumer perceives that the product is inferior and never buys it again. This causes grave financial loss to the manufacturer, whose profits come from *repeat* purchases.

DAVID OGILVY, British-born American advertising expert, founder of Ogilvy & Mather international advertising group, New York, and author. *Ogilvy on Advertising* (Pan, London, 1983).

17 *What's Wrong with Advertising?*
   1. Whether economists are right or wrong in proclaiming that advertising is an 'economic' waste, manufacturers do not regard it as a *commercial* waste.
   2. Apart from political advertising, which is flagrantly dishonest, advertising is now far more honest than consumers realise.
   3. The world would be a safer, prettier place without billboards.
   4. The majority of campaigns fail to give consumers enough information.

DAVID OGILVY, British-born American advertising expert, founder of Ogilvy & Mather international advertising group, New York, and author. *Ogilvy on Advertising* (Pan, London, 1983).

18 Truth in Advertising. A whole new business with someone like Ralph Nader as CEO. Finally, ads and commercials so truthful that you can believe every word that is written. The Truth in Advertising agency will even sign off on them – and be held accountable for the claims . . . If Truth in Advertising sounds too bare, too spare, too honest, for American companies today, understand that it will be here tomorrow. The consumer has finally peeled off the glitz and grime of the 80s and is ready to hear the truth – to buy the truth, whether business is ready or not.

FAITH POPCORN, American business consultant, co-founder and CEO of BrainReserve, and author. *The Popcorn Report* (Doubleday, New York, 1991). Copyright 1991 by Faith Popcorn. Used by permission of Doubleday, a division of Bantam Doubleday Dell Publishing Group, Inc.

19 One Ad is worth more to a paper than forty Editorials.

WILL ROGERS (1879–1935), American actor, performer and humorist. 'Well, Who is Prunes?', *The Illiterate Digest* (1924).

20 If I were starting life over again, I am inclined to think that I would go into the advertising business in preference to almost any other.

> FRANKLIN D. ROOSEVELT (1882–1945), American statesman, and 32nd President of the United States of America 1933–45. Attrib.

21 There seems to be a realisation in England that maybe, just maybe, the product being sold is *not* the most important thing in the consumer's mind. The decision as to which dishwashing liquid to buy, which beer to drink or which toaster to purchase, is *not* a life-and-death decision. Realising this, the British are able to present their product to the consumer in perspective. They joke about it, sing about it, and often underplay it. In short, they have a sense of proportion.

> BILL TAYLOR, American advertising executive and partner in Ogilvy & Mather international advertising group, New York. Quoted in David Ogilvy, *Ogilvy on Advertising* (Pan, London, 1983).

4 advice

See also: listening 54

1 Advice: many offer it, but few can take it.

> ANON.

2 Death is nature's way of advising you to slow down.

> ANON.

3 Take my advice – I never use it myself.

> ANON.

4 We can all learn more by examining other people's failures, successes and general philosophy. I am the first to admit that it is much easier to follow a pioneer than to be a pioneer – in

business or in everyday life – and that it should always be possible to avoid the pioneers' pitfalls by taking their advice. Even if the advice is as simple as 'If they get you down, sue the bastards!' as Sir Freddie Laker said to me ten years ago when we were starting Virgin Atlantic.

RICHARD BRANSON, British entrepreneur, and founder and CEO of Virgin Group. In 'Entrepreneurship', a foreword to Tom Cannon (ed.), *How to Get Ahead in Business* (Virgin, London, 1993).

5 It's a pity that the people who should be running the country are too busy driving taxicabs and cutting hair.

GEORGE BURNS (1897–1996), American comic, actor and entertainer. Attrib.

6 He who does not seek advice is a fool. His folly blinds him to Truth and makes him evil, stubborn, and a danger to his fellow man.

KAHLIL GIBRAN (1883–1931), Lebanese–American philosophical essayist, mystic poet, novelist and artist. *A Third Treasury of Kahlil Gibran* (Citadel, Secausus, New Jersey, 1965).

7 The advice shared at the watercooler or the tip shared over an impromptu lunch is a benefit to workers that often isn't measured when companies talk about the advantages of the virtual office.

JULIANNE MALVEAUX, American newspaper columnist. *San Francisco Examiner*, 25 September 1994. © 1994 King Features Syndicate Inc. Used with permission of King Features Syndicate.

8 In order to establish in the Prince's mind that the Servant is a specialist, it is important for him to comment only on his subject, and to assert, when asked of other matters, 'I know too little to be of help.' . . . Eventually, the constant Servant is in a position to influence the Prince on subjects on which he says he knows too little to be of help.

ALISTAIR McALPINE (Lord McAlpine of West Green), British business leader, political figure and author. *The Servant* (Faber & Faber, London, 1992).

9 Some people don't think taking advice is important. To them it is a sign of weakness rather than a necessary social skill. It is passive rather than active. No-one congratulates you for being good at it. When was the last time someone praised you for 'taking advice well'? In the advice game, we all would rather be perceived as the one dispensing wisdom rather than seeking it.

MARK H. McCORMACK, American sports marketing consultant, founder and CEO of International Management Group, and author. *The 110% Solution* (Villard, New York, 1991). © 1991 by Mark H. McCormack. Reprinted by permission of Villard Books, a division of Random House Inc.

10 He who builds to every man's advice will have a crooked house.

DANISH PROVERB.

11 Everybody knows good counsel except him that has need of it.

GERMAN PROVERB.

12 Good advice is beyond price.

LATIN PROVERB.

13 Everybody cheerily tells a playwright how to repair his script and it takes cool courage and wondrous manners to endure the amateurs' well-meant advice. In Boston during the tryout of *The Odd Couple*, I had been up till four o'clock in the morning rewriting the third act – for the fifth time. Exhausted, I finally fell asleep on my typewriter. At seven A.M. a dentist from Salem, Mass., phoned to tell me how *he* would fix the third act. I thanked him and promised myself I would call him at five the next morning to tell him how I would fix his bridgework.

NEIL SIMON, American playwright and screenwriter. 'RX for Comedy', *Playbill*, January 1966.

ambition 5

See also: achieving 2; getting started 35; goals & goal-setting 36; motivation 63; success 98

1 I don't want to achieve immortality through my work. I want to achieve it by not dying.

> WOODY ALLEN, American screenwriter, film producer and director. Attrib.

2 Ambition is a hard task-master.

> ANON.

3 Those who seek their place in the sun are going to get burnt along the way.

> ANON.

4 What shall it profit a man, if he shall gain the whole world, and lose his own soul?

> THE BIBLE. Mark 8:36.

5 Ah, but a man's reach should exceed his grasp,
  Or what's a heaven for?

> ROBERT BROWNING (1812–89), British poet. 'Andrea del Sarto', *Men and Women* (1855).

6 Ambition can be an overwhelming drive that can send you insane. I have a philosophy – good things come to those who wait and work hard.

> LIZ DAVENPORT, Australian fashion designer. *Australian Women's Weekly*, October 1996.

7 Manners make the fortune of the ambitious youth.

> RALPH WALDO EMERSON (1803–82), American philosopher, poet and essayist. 'Behaviour', *The Conduct of Life* (1860).

8 Nothing is more commonplace as to wish to be remarkable.

> OLIVER WENDELL HOLMES SNR (1809–94), American physician, humorist, poet and author. *The Autocrat of the Breakfast Table* (1858).

9 Most people would succeed in small things, if they were not troubled with great ambitions.

> HENRY LONGFELLOW (1807–82), American poet. 'Table-Talk', *Driftwood* (1857).

10 If you want something bad enough the whole world conspires to help you get it.

> MADONNA (Madonna Louise Ciccone), American singer, dancer and actress. *Vanity Fair*, November 1996.

11 Honourable ambition is one of the finest of qualities – and should be rewarded.

> JOHN MAJOR, British statesman, and Prime Minister 1990–97. 'Trust My Instincts', *Weekly Telegraph*, 8 January 1997.

12 He who would leap high must take a long run.

> DANISH PROVERB.

13 The greatest evil which fortune can inflict on men is to endow them with small talents and great ambition.

> MARQUIS DE LUC DE CLAPIERS VAUVENARGUES (1715–47), French moralist. *Reflections and Maxims* (1746).

14 There is always room at the top.

> DANIEL WEBSTER (1782–1852), American lawyer, politician and orator. His response to being advised not to become a lawyer because the profession was overcrowded. Attrib.

'In show business there are lots of pros and cons in every sense of the word. The problem is, we have more cons than pros!'

CHRISTOPHER LEE

business ethics 7:7

6 **brands**

See also: advertising 3; marketing 58; products 80; selling 93

1 The three key rules of marketing are brand recognition, brand recognition, and brand recognition.

ANON.

2 In a fast-paced world, today's popular brand could be tomorrow's trivia question.

WAYNE CALLOWAY, American industrialist, Chairman of PepsiCo. *PepsiCo Annual Report*, 1989.

3 In an age when consumers need to catalogue and organise huge amounts of information on a daily basis, brands with the strongest positive identities win. They are trusted and familiar brands that have maintained a consistent message and image. They have remained true to a 'brand ethic.'

RUDY MAGNANI and PETER BENKENDORF, American marketing consultants and principals of Magnani & Associates, Chicago. 'Info Glut, or Marketing in The Blur Age', *Marketing News* (American Marketing Association), 20 January 1997, page 4. Reprinted with permission.

7 **business ethics**

See also: corporate culture 15; profits 81; success 98

1 A false balance is abomination to the Lord: but a just weight is his delight.

THE BIBLE. Proverbs 11:1.

2 You can always depend on Americans to do the right thing, once they've exhausted every other possibility.

> WINSTON CHURCHILL (1874–1965), British statesman, Prime Minister 1940–45 and 1951–55, artist, historian, author and Nobel laureate. Attrib.

3 The problem – for the Japanese – is deciding what is a scandal . . . Usually, they'll wait for someone else to decide for them.

> GREGORY CLARK, American academic, a professor teaching comparative culture at Sophia University, Tokyo. 'A Matter of Ethics: Why Japan is Not Like the US', *Industry Week*, 16 March 1992. © Copyright Penton Publishing, Inc, Cleveland, Ohio.

4 You can look at it as an imperative for business survival; you can look at it as a way to build a competitive edge. But ultimately, corporate environmentalists need to flex their considerable muscles for one fundamental reason: because they're the most powerful allies our planet has.

> CRAIG COX, American journalist and editor, Managing Editor of *Business Ethics*, and SALLY POWER, American academic, lecturer at the University of St Thomas, St Paul, Minnesota. 'Executives of the World Unite', *Business Ethics*, September–October 1992.

5 Perhaps the biggest responsibility of any corporation is to own up when it makes a mistake.

> LEE IACOCCA, American automotive industry leader, former CEO of Chrysler Motors, and director of several other auto manufacturing companies, and author. *Talking Straight* (Bantam, New York, 1988). Copyright © 1988 by Lee Iacocca. Used by permission of Bantam Books, a division of Bantam Doubleday Dell Publishing Group Inc.

6 Having been in publishing for over 35 years, the change in attitudes, morality and ethics in the media and journalists themselves is not to be applauded. I would say one should

be true to oneself and to remember that what goes around comes around. You may, sooner than you think, need the person you stab in the back on your frantic way up the ladder.

MAGGIE KOUMI, British journalist and editor, Editor of *Hello!* magazine, London. CWE, 8 October 1996.

7 People gravitate here [Los Angeles] more and there's more money to be made, therefore the greed is greater, therefore the cover-up is greater. Now in show business there are lots of pros and cons in every sense of the word. The problem is, we have more cons than pros!

CHRISTOPHER LEE, British actor. Quoted in Alan Whicker, *Whicker's New World* (Weidenfeld & Nicolson, London, 1985).

8 I'm not willing to look the other way when somebody is off base with regard to integrity on the grounds that they're making such a wonderful technical or professional contribution that we can't afford to live without them. To me it's an easy choice.

PAUL O'NEILL, American industrialist, CEO of ALCOA, Pittsburgh. 'True Innovation, True Values, True Leadership', *Industry Week*, 19 April 1993. © Copyright Penton Publishing, Inc, Cleveland, Ohio.

9 Cheat me in price, but not in the goods I purchase.

SPANISH PROVERB.

10 The behaviour of the community is largely dominated by the business mind. A great society is a society in which its men of business think greatly of their functions. Low thoughts mean low behaviour, and after a brief orgy of exploitation, low behaviour means a descending standard of life.

A. N. WHITEHEAD (1861–1947), British mathematician, philosopher, Professor of Philosophy at Harvard University and author. *Adventures of Ideas* (Harvard University Press, Cambridge, Massachusetts, 1933; reprinted Penguin, London, 1942).

C

'It's better to be a pirate than join the navy.'

STEVE JOBS

corporate culture 15:3

8 challenge

1 Helping talented people blossom and develop is one of management's toughest challenges.

> JAN CARLZON, Swedish business leader, former CEO of Scandinavian Airlines System, speaker and author. *Moments of Truth* (Ballinger, Cambridge, Massachusetts, 1987; revised edition Harper & Row, New York, 1989). Copyright © 1987 by Ballinger Publishing Company. Reprinted by permission of HarperCollins Publishers, Inc.

2 You are more likely to overcome challenges if you have learned, in advance, what to expect and how to respond. That is why training, at all levels, is critical to the success of any organisation.

> ALLEN SHEPPARD, British business leader, Chairman and Group Chief Executive of Grand Metropolitan. In a foreword to Jeremy G. Thorn, *Developing Your Career in Management* (Mercury, London, 1992).

9 change

1 I'm aware of the risks involved with change. But this is a business, not a monument. We have a responsibility to our shareholders.

> ROBYN AHERN, Australian businesswoman and CEO of Aherns department store chain. *Qantas Club*, November 1996.

2 Change for change's sake is not progress.
    ANON.

3 Change is life. Life is change.
    ANON.

4 Change what you can change. Accept what you cannot change.
    ANON.

5 Those who ride the crest of the wave of change will profit from it. Those who resist change will be left behind in its wake.
    ANON.

6 You only get one chance to change the world. Nothing else matters as much – you'll have another chance to have vacations, have kids.
    BILL ATKINSON, American computer industry pioneer and Senior Executive of Apple Computers. Quoted in Steven Levy, *Insanely Great: The Life and Times of Macintosh, the Computer that Changed Everything* (Viking, London, 1994; revised edition Penguin, 1995).

7 It's amazing how many people beat you at golf now that you're no longer president.
    GEORGE BUSH, American statesman, and 41st President of the United States of America 1989–93. Attrib. (1993).

8 Everything, Senators, which we now hold to be of the highest antiquity, was once new. Plebeian magistrates came after patrician; Latin magistrates after plebeian; magistrates of other Italian peoples after Latin. This practice too will establish itself, and what we are this day justifying by precedents, will be itself a precedent.
    CLAUDIUS CAESAR (10 BC–AD 54), Roman emperor, AD 41–54. Address to the Roman Senate, AD 47. Quoted in Tacitus, *The Annals: Book XI* (c. AD 116).

9 change

9 We might think of ourselves as surfers riding the waves of change. The successful surfer is one who stays just ahead of the wave that could wipe him out at any moment. He uses the power of this very same wave, participating with it, not fighting it or trying to control it – interacting with its every nuance in the most intimate manner. In order to ride that ever-changing wave, he must also be in good communication with his own body and feelings. His senses and his emotions must give him accurate, undistorted information. Both his internal communications and his communications with his environment are functioning at a high level of clarity. He is a finely tuned instrument for learning from experience.

> SUSAN M. CAMPBELL, American lecturer and author. *From Chaos to Confidence* (Simon & Schuster, New York, 1995).

10 The character of society, the foundations of politics, the methods of war, the outlook of youth, the scale of values, are all changed, and changed to an extent I should not have believed possible in so short a space without any violent domestic revolution. I cannot pretend to feel that they are in all respects changed for the better.

> WINSTON CHURCHILL (1874–1965), British statesman, Prime Minister 1940–45 and 1951–55, artist, historian, author and Nobel laureate. *My Early Life* (Macmillan, London, 1930).

11 Changes in the economy, such as technological innovations·and the globalisation of commerce, have combined over the past two decades to produce what economists Robert H. Frank and Philip J. Cook call a 'winner-take-all society.' The middle class, the backbone of our nation, is splitting, with more and more falling into the 'anxious class' of honest, hardworking Americans who go in debt every time a child falls ill or the family car breaks down. Midlevel managers and white-collar workers are increasingly vulnerable to becoming what [US] Secretary of Labor Robert Reich calls 'frayed-collar workers in gold-plated times.'

HILLARY RODHAM CLINTON, American lawyer, and First Lady of the United States of America 1993– . *It Takes a Village* (Simon & Schuster, New York, 1996).

12 Anyone who has ever been faced with the task of objective self-evaluation will agree that, while not pleasant, it was enlightening. Once you have completed your self-examination, you must be willing to change your thinking and behaviour to that which is more beneficial. Old habits die hard and change is tough, so you must discipline yourself until the new behaviour becomes old habit. The whole process is one of getting mentally tough with yourself in the short run to make it easier on yourself in the long run.

JACK COLLIS, Australian business lecturer and author, and MICHAEL LEBOEUF, American business consultant, speaker and author, Professor of Management at the University of New Orleans. *Work Smarter Not Harder* (Goal Setting Seminars, 1988; republished HarperBusiness, Sydney, 1995).

13 Probably the only thing that we humans fear more than change is death. Some, perhaps many of your own people will resist the changes in service provision that you envision, so that it will seem that the easiest course is not to rock the boat. The choice is yours. He or she who approaches customer care with a determination to profit from change will succeed.

STEPHEN DANDO-COLLINS, Australian author and editor. *The Customer Care Revolution* (Pitman, Melbourne, 1996).

14 If we have a thinking system that is not intended to produce change, it is not surprising that we do not have much confidence in the change process.

EDWARD DE BONO, Maltese-born British scholar, teacher, lecturer and author. *Parallel Thinking: From Socratic to de Bono Thinking* (Viking, London, 1994). Copyright © McQuaig Group Inc, 1994.

15 The global information market will be huge and will combine all the various ways human goods, services, and ideas are exchanged. On a practical level, this will give you broader choices about most things, including how you earn and invest, what you buy and how much you pay for it, who your friends are and how you spend your time with them, and where and how securely you and your family live. Your workplace and your idea of what it means to be 'educated' will be transformed, perhaps almost beyond recognition. Your sense of identity, of who you are and where you belong, may open up considerably. In short, just about everything will be done differently. I can hardly wait for this tomorrow, and I'm doing what I can to help make it happen.

You aren't sure you believe this? Or want to believe it? Perhaps you'll decline to participate. People commonly make this vow when some new technology threatens to change what they're familiar and comfortable with. At first, the bicycle was a silly contraption; the automobile, a noisy intruder; the pocket calculator, a threat to the study of mathematics; and the radio, the end of literacy.

But then something happens. Over time, these machines find a place in our everyday lives because they not only offer convenience and save labour, they can also inspire us to new creative heights. We warm to them. They assume a trusted place beside our other tools. A new generation grows up with them, changing and humanising them. In short, playing with them.

BILL GATES, American information technology pioneer, founder and CEO of Microsoft Corporation, and author. *The Road Ahead* (Viking Penguin, New York, 1995). Copyright © 1995 by William H. Gates III. Used by permission of Viking Penguin, a division of Penguin Books USA Inc.

16 The way people deal with things that go wrong is an indicator of how they deal with change.

BILL GATES, American information technology pioneer, founder and CEO

17 The 1990s have initiated a wave of political and governmental change of historic proportions: the collapse of the Soviet Empire, the replacement of the post-World War II Italian political structure, the virtual elimination of the Canadian governing party in the 1993 elections – they dropped from 153 seats to 2 in the Parliament – the collapse of the Japanese Liberal Democratic Party after a forty-year virtual monopoly of power – and the rise of a new reform movement – the rise of Ross Perot and the United We Stand movement and the election of 1994 in America. Again and again there are startling changes under way in politics and government.

Politicians, columnists and academics all seem confused by the scale of change. There is an inevitable focus on the pain of those who have been dominant and the disorientation of those who have been powerful. The agony of the past is outweighing the promise of the future.

NEWT GINGRICH, American Republican politician and Speaker of the US House of Representatives. In 'A Citizen's Guide to the Twenty-first Century', a foreword to Alvin & Heidi Toffler, *Creating a New Civilisation* (Turner, Atlanta, 1995).

18 The view of an outsider at a revolution is an odd and slanting one, rather like a pretentious camera-angle; he may sometimes even be unaware that anything is happening around him at all.

GRAHAM GREENE (1904–91), British journalist, critic and novelist. *Ways of Escape* (The Bodley Head, London, 1980).

19 Business reengineering means putting aside much of the received wisdom of two hundred years of industrial management. It means forgetting how work was done in the age of the mass market and deciding how it can be best done now. In business reengineering, old job titles and old organisational

arrangements – departments, divisions, groups, and so on – cease to matter. They are artifacts of another age. What matters in reengineering is how we want to organise work today, given the demands of today's markets and the power of today's technologies. How people and companies did things yesterday doesn't matter to the business reengineer.

MICHAEL HAMMER and JAMES CHAMPY, American academics and authors. *Reengineering the Corporation* (HarperCollins, New York, 1993). Copyright © 1993 by Michael Hammer & James Champy. Reprinted by permission of HarperCollins Publishers, Inc.

20 More difficult than forgiving others is to forgive oneself. That turns out to be one of the real blocks to change. We as individuals need to accept our past but then turn our backs on it.

CHARLES HANDY, British academic, business consultant and author. *The Age of Unreason* (Business Books, London, 1987).

21 To achieve change, we must mobilise our most valuable resource: the talents of the Australian people. This does not necessarily mean working harder; in Germany and Japan, both highly successful competitive countries, working hours are actually falling. But it does mean working smarter – working more effectively, using new materials, new production technologies and new management methods. It means being, like Germany and Japan, a clever country . . . We live in a world of unprecedented, indeed breathtaking, change. Our own region is a crucible for change. We can no longer afford the easy simplicities, the costly complacencies of the fifties and sixties and seventies . . . We need the habit of adaptation – because the lesson of international competitiveness must be constantly learned and relearned.

BOB HAWKE, Australian union leader, politician, and Prime Minister 1983–91. 'Building a Competitive Australia', Parliamentary Statement to the Australian House of Representatives, 12 March 1991.

22 Change is usually what we want the other person to do.

> LOUISE L. HAY, British motivator and author. *The Power is Within You* (Airlift Books, London; Applause Books, New York; Specialist Publications, Concord, New South Wales, 1991).

23 Nothing is permanent but change.

> HERACLITUS (c. 500 BC), Greek philosopher. Quoted in Diogenes Laertius, *Lives and Opinions of Eminent Philosophers* (4th century AD).

24 Change is not made without inconvenience, even from worse to better.

> SAMUEL JOHNSON (Dr Johnson; 1709–84), British poet, essayist, critic, journalist and lexicographer. Quoting Richard Hookes in *Of the Laws of Ecclesiastical Polity*.

25 The more things change, the more they remain the same.

> ALPHONSE KARR (1808–90), French journalist and author. *Les Guêpes*, January 1849.

26 Life is either a daring adventure or nothing. To keep our faces toward change and behave like free spirits in the presence of fate is strength undefeatable.

> HELEN KELLER (1880–1968), American author and educator. *Let Us Have Faith* (1940).

27 Change is the law of life. And those who look only to the past or the present are certain to miss the future.

> JOHN F. KENNEDY (1917–63), American statesman, and 35th President of the United States of America 1961–63. In a speech made in Frankfurt, West Germany, 25 June 1963.

28 As the pace of change increases, it has been estimated that the average American worker, now in his thirties, may have to change occupations two or three times to stay employed during

the rest of his working life . . . To meet this challenge, we have to give those now on the job opportunities equal to those who will be joining the labour force in the future.

ROBERT F. KENNEDY (1925–68), American politician, Senator, US Attorney General and presidential candidate. In a speech made in Indianapolis, 4 April 1968.

29 Leadership is a relationship, founded on trust and confidence. Without trust and confidence, people don't take risks. Without risk, there is no change. Without change, organisations and movements die.

JAMES M. KOUZES and BARRY Z. POSNER, American educators, management and training consultants, and authors. *The Leadership Challenge* (Jossey-Bass, San Francisco, 1995).

30 The most effective change processes are incremental; they break down big problems into small, doable steps and get a person to say yes numerous times, not just once.

JAMES M. KOUZES and BARRY Z. POSNER, American educators, management and training consultants, and authors. *The Leadership Challenge* (Jossey-Bass, San Francisco, 1995).

31 When you're through changing, you're through. Change is a process, not a goal; a journey, not a destination.

ROBERT KRIEGEL, American business consultant, speaker and author, and DAVID BRANDT, American clinical psychologist, organisational consultant, executive coach and author. *Sacred Cows Make the Best Burgers* (Warner, New York, 1996).

32 We are comfortable with a kind of woman that is submissive and subservient, maternal, soft and vulnerable. Not terribly opinionated, not very well educated . . . It's going to be a long time before we're comfortable, as a society, with the opposite. But I feel I'm contributing to that change.

MADONNA (Madonna Louise Ciccone), American singer, dancer and actress. *Sydney Morning Herald,* 4 January 1997.

33 I don't think you change at all. If you look at a school playground you can see all the little judges and bankers and crooks and they're not going to change.

JOHN MORTIMER, British lawyer, screenplay writer, playwright and author. In an interview with Graham Lord, *Weekly Telegraph,* 9 June 1993. Reprinted by permission of the Peters Fraser & Dunlop Group Ltd.

34 A revolutionary confluence of technological change has set the stage for a new environment that will empower individuals as never before.

JOHN NAISBITT, American social forecaster, visiting professor, speaker and author. *Global Paradox* (William Morrow, New York, 1994).

35 The accelerating pace of change, especially in technology, has brought corporations face-to-face with the competitive advantage of speed – getting products to customers faster and thereby increasing market share while reducing inventory costs.

JOHN NAISBITT and PATRICIA ABURDENE, American social forecasters, academics and authors. *Megatrends 2000* (William Morrow, New York, 1990).

36 The world's in a mess – always has been, always will be. You can't change that. You can change yourself.

NICK NOLTE, American actor. *OK! Magazine,* May 1993.

37 Once you bring out all your gifts, you can change anything you need to change:
If you don't like how it is for you now, change it.
If it isn't enough, change it.
If it doesn't suit you, change it.

> If it doesn't please you, change it.
> Remember: YOU CAN CHANGE ALL THINGS FOR THE BETTER WHEN YOU CHANGE YOURSELF FOR THE BETTER.
>
> JIM ROHN, American business philosopher, lecturer and author. *Seven Strategies for Wealth and Happiness* (Brolga, Melbourne, 1994).

38 Every employee is affected by the transformation of business organisations. Everyone who holds a job is taking part in defining the new relationship between the individual and the corporation. The changes are both scary and liberating at once. Remember life-time job security? The demise of corporate paternalism is forcing workers to take responsibility for their own careers. At the same time, the quest for speed and innovation often translates into teamwork and empowerment, which can make jobs richer and more interesting. Anyone challenged by these changes can benefit from a better understanding of the forces that drive them.

> NOEL M. TICHY, American academic and author, and STRATFORD SHERMAN, American journalist and author. *Control Your Destiny or Someone Else Will* (Doubleday, New York, 1993). Copyright © 1993 by Noel M. Tichy and Stratford Sherman. Used by permission of Doubleday, a division of Bantam Doubleday Dell Publishing Group, Inc.

39 Change is essential to man, as essential now in our 800th lifetime as it was in our first. Change is life itself. But change rampant, change unguided and unrestrained, accelerated change overwhelming not only man's physical defences but his decisional processes – such change is the enemy of life.

> ALVIN TOFFLER, American scholar, lecturer and author. *Future Shock* (The Bodley Head, London, 1970).

40 As change accelerates and reaches into more and more remote corners of the society, uncertainty about future needs increases. Recognising the inevitability of change, but unsure as to the

demands it will impose on us, we hesitate to commit large resources for rigidly fixed objects intended to serve unchanging purposes. Avoiding commitment to fixed forms and functions, we build for short-term use or, alternatively, attempt to make the product itself adaptable. We 'play it cool' technologically. The rise of disposability – the spread of the throw-away culture – is a response to these powerful pressures. As change accelerates and complexities multiply, we can expect to see further extensions of the principle of disposability, further curtailment of man's relationships with things.

ALVIN TOFFLER, American scholar, lecturer and author. *Future Shock* (The Bodley Head, London, 1970).

41 It is always easier to talk about change than to make it. It is easier to consult than to manage.

ALVIN TOFFLER, American scholar, lecturer and author. *The Adaptive Corporation* (Gower, Aldershot, Hampshire, 1985).

42 People always ask, 'Is the change over? Can we stop now?' You've got to tell them, 'No, it's just begun.' Leaders must create an atmosphere where people understand that change is a continuing process, not an event.

JACK WELCH, American industrialist, CEO of General Electric Company. *Fortune*, 13 December 1993. © 1993 Time Inc. All rights reserved.

43 We adopt enough of the West to hoist in their science, their technology, their competitiveness. Like the Japanese, we should try to remain as much ourselves as we can.

LEE KUAN YEW, Singaporean statesman and senior minister, Prime Minister 1959–90. In a speech to the Parliament of Singapore, 1 March 1985.

10 civilisation

See also: human nature 39; people 70

1 America is the only country to have gone from barbarism to decadence without going through civilisation.

    ANON.

2 If civilisation has arisen from the Stone Age, it can rise again from the Wastepaper Age.

    JACQUES BARZUN, French-born American educator, critic and author. *The House of Intellect* (Harper & Row, New York, 1959).

3 A good civilisation spreads over us freely like a tree, varying and yielding because it is alive. A bad civilisation stands up and sticks out above us like an umbrella – artificial, mathematical in shape; not merely universal, but uniform.

    G. K. CHESTERTON (1874–1936), British journalist, essayist, poet and novelist. 'Cheese', *Alarms and Discursions* (1910).

4 The true test of civilisation is, not the census, nor the size of cities, nor the crops – no, but the kind of man the country turns out.

    RALPH WALDO EMERSON (1803–82), American philosopher, poet and essayist. 'Civilisation', *Society and Solitude* (1870).

5 The civilised man is a larger mind but a more imperfect nature than the savage.

    MARGARET FULLER (Marquesa Ossoli; 1810–50), American poet, educator, editor and essayist. *Summer on the Lakes* (1844).

6 Human history becomes more and more a race between education and catastrophe.

    H. G. WELLS (1866–1946), British author. *The Outline of History* (1920).

7 Civilisation is constituted out of four elements: 1. Patterns of Behaviour; 2. Patterns of Emotion; 3. Patterns of Belief; and, 4. Technologies.

A. N. WHITEHEAD (1861–1947), British mathematician, philosopher, Professor of Philosophy at Harvard University and author. *Adventures of Ideas* (Harvard University Press, Cambridge, Massachusetts, 1933; reprinted Penguin, London, 1942).

8 The major advances in civilisation are processes that all but wreck the societies in which they occur.

A. N. WHITEHEAD (1861–1947), British mathematician, philosopher, Professor of Philosophy at Harvard University and author. *Adventures of Ideas* (Harvard University Press, Cambridge, Massachusetts, 1933; reprinted Penguin, London, 1942).

communication & communicating 11

See also: change 9; computers 13; information 44; innovation 45; originality 69; technology 101

1 In a decentralised, customer-driven company, a good leader spends more time communicating than doing anything else. He must communicate with the employees to keep them all working towards the same goals, and he must communicate with his customers to keep them abreast of the company's new activities and services.

JAN CARLZON, Swedish business leader, former CEO of Scandinavian Airlines System, speaker and author. *Moments of Truth* (Ballinger, Cambridge, Massachusetts, 1987; revised edition Harper & Row, New York, 1989). Copyright © 1987 by Ballinger Publishing Company. Reprinted by permission of HarperCollins Publishers Inc.

2 Man, she's like the cellular phone. I don't know what I did before I had it.

HARRY CONNICK JR, American entertainer and actor. Comment made about his recently-born daughter in an interview with Richard Wilkins on Nine Network Australia's *Today* program, 25 September 1996.

3 When you are alert to what the people in the lower echelons have to say, and take it into consideration, so that your plans include the rank and file, then all people are your eyes and a multitude of voices helps your ears.

ZHUGE LIANG (2nd century AD), Chinese general of the Han dynasty. *Mastering the Art of War: The Way of the General.*

4 Today, a person's business card might list a phone number for office and home, a fax number, an E-mail number, an Internet number, and car phone number. But in the not too distant future each person will have a lifelong number that goes with him wherever he goes. His personal computer assistant – which is always with him – will sort out what messages go where. Individuals will phone other individuals wherever they are in the world – without knowing where they are.

JOHN NAISBITT, American social forecaster, visiting professor, speaker and author. *Global Paradox* (William Morrow, New York, 1994).

5 The movie business has often proved its resilience and it will do so once more. In these days of super communications, it makes no sense to think that the greatest form of mass entertainment ever invented will just fade away.

DAVID NIVEN (1909–83), British actor and author. *The Moon's a Balloon* (Hamish Hamilton, London, 1971).

6 The greatest compliment a writer can have; to know that he has written a thing so truly that people not only believe that it happened but that it happened to themselves.

A. B. 'BANJO' PATERSON (1864–1941), Australian author, poet, journalist and newspaper editor. Originally in 'Singers Among Savages', a newspaper article, and reprinted in *A Literary Heritage: Banjo Paterson* (Octopus, Melbourne, 1988).

7 Non-verbal research has revealed a correlation between a person's command of the spoken word and the amount of gesticulation that that person uses to communicate his or her message. This means that a person's status, power or prestige is also directly related to the number of gestures or body movements he uses.

ALLAN PEASE, Australian sales and management trainer, 'body language' expert and author. *Body Language* (Pease Training, 1981; republished Camel Publishing, Sydney, and Sheldon Press, London, 1995). Published in the USA as *Signals: How to Use Body Language for Power, Success and Love* (Bantam, New York).

8 The more we elaborate our means of communication, the less we communicate.

J. B. PRIESTLEY (1894–1984), British novelist, playwright and essayist. 'Televiewing', *Thoughts in the Wilderness* (Heinemann, London, 1957). Reprinted by permission of Peters Fraser & Dunlop Group Ltd.

9 The articulate voice is more distracting than mere noise.

SENECA (Lucius Annaeus Seneca, The Younger; c. 4 BC – AD 65), Roman philosopher, playwright, poet, administrator, tutor and chief minister to Emperor Nero. *Letters to Lucilius* (c. AD 30).

10 Until the 1920s, when they could no longer afford the service, phones were more common among farm families than among city ones. So crazed were rural people for the companionship the phone brought that, by the beginning of the twentieth century, over six thousand 'mutuals,' or rural phone cooperatives, had been founded by farmers in isolated communities. Sometimes they transmitted their calls through barbed wire,

and if the resultant service was awful, it was better than nothing. If people want it badly enough, we may see them do the same with videoconferencing through the Internet.

NICHOLAS VON HOFFMAN, American journalist, playwright and novelist. 'Say Hello to Videoconferencing', *Architectural Digest*, May 1996.

11 Have you ever tried talking to a blank wall? Have you ever tried writing a letter to a nonexistent lover? Both experiences are extremely frustrating. Every act of communication presupposes a communicator and an audience, whether the audience be actual or putative. If you want an audience, you have to have enough art to be able to command its attention for a single instant, which is the beginning of your story, and hold it thereafter for the duration of your narrative.

MORRIS L. WEST, Australian author. 'How to Write a Novel', in A. S. Burack (ed.), *The Writer's Handbook* (The Writer, Boston, 1978).

12 If you are an enthusiast, it communicates. And nothing communicates so much as the lack of it.

ROWLAND WHITEHEAD, British baronet, Chairman of the Institute of Translation and Interpreting, and founder and member of various charitable institutions. *Country Life*, 28 November 1996.

12 **competition & competitors**
See also: marketing 58; strategy 97

1 He may well win the race that runs by himself.

BENJAMIN FRANKLIN (1706–90), American statesman, scientist, inventor, printer and author. *Poor Richard's Almanack* (1732–57).

2 The companies which sustain monopolistic market shares do so, paradoxically, by acting as if they were beset by formidable competitors on every side.

3 Tough competitors eat the competition's lunch. Change-Ready competitors eat their own lunch before someone else does. In other words, you've got to cannibalise your own products to stay ahead.

ROBERT KRIEGEL, American business consultant, speaker and author, and DAVID BRANDT, American clinical psychologist, organisational consultant, executive coach and author. *Sacred Cows Make the Best Burgers* (Warner, New York, 1996).

4 A horse never runs so fast as when he has other horses to catch up and outpace.

OVID (real name Publius Ovidius Naso; c. 43 BC – AD 17), Roman poet. *The Art of Love* (c. AD 8).

5 One barber shaves not so close but another finds work.

ENGLISH PROVERB.

6 Yesterday everyone was a competitor. Today everyone is a customer.

DENIS WAITLEY, American personal development counsellor, lecturer and author. *Empires of the Mind: Lessons to Lead and Succeed in a Knowledge-Based World* (William Morrow, New York; Nicholas Brealey, London, 1995). Reprinted by permission of Nicholas Brealey Publishing Limited, London, Tel. (0171) 430-0224, Fax (0171) 404-8311.

computers 13

See also: communication & communicating 11; future, the 33; information 44; innovation 45; originality 69; technology 101

13 computers

1 By 2000 AD computers will be growing restless and demanding the vote.

> PHILLIP ADAMS, Australian broadcaster, columnist and author. Quoted in Stephen Dando-Collins, *2000 AD* (Pan, Sydney, 1986).

2 Computers were invented by Murphy [of Murphy's Law fame].

> ANON.

3 To err is human; to really foul things up takes a computer.

> ANON.

4 • Any given program, when running, is obsolete.
   • Any given program costs more and takes longer.
   • If a program is useful, it will have to be changed.
   • Any given program will expand to fill all available memory.
   • If a program is useless, it will be documented.
   • The value of a program is proportional to the weight of its output.
   • Program complexity grows until it exceeds the capability of the programmer who must maintain it.
   • Make it possible for programmers to write programs in English, and you will find that programmers cannot write in English.

> ANON. Quoted in Tom Cannon, *How to Get Ahead in Business* (Virgin, London, 1995).

5 Computer geeks aren't like you and me. Cyberspace may be a fictional place, but the true geek is trying to move there nonetheless. This probably accounts for the other-wordly aura that surrounds them and explains why they have difficulty communicating through speech. You probably knew a geek in high school or college. You remember, the one with the thick glasses and silly laugh. He who laughs last, laughs best. Now, thanks to the computer revolution, many geeks make ten times as much money as you do.

LAURENCE A. CANTER and MARTHA S. SIEGEL, American lawyers and authors. *How to Make a Fortune on the Information Superhighway* (HarperCollins, London, 1995). Reprinted by permission of HarperCollins Publishers Limited.

6 As new computer systems decentralise control and empower people all along the information chain, they dissolve conventions of ownership, design, manufacturing, executive style, and national identity.

GEORGE GILDER, American academic. 'Into the Telecosm', *Harvard Business Review*, March–April 1991, page 152. Copyright © 1991 by the President and Fellows of Harvard College, all rights reserved.

7 Man is still the most extraordinary computer of all.

JOHN F. KENNEDY (1917–63), American statesman, and 35th President of the United States of America 1961–63. In a speech, 21 May 1963.

8 It has already set a process into motion that will eventually change our thinking about computers, our thinking about information, and even our thinking about thinking. In terms of our relationship with information, Macintosh changed everything.

STEVEN LEVY, American journalist and author. *Insanely Great: The Life and Times of Macintosh, the Computer that Changed Everything* (Viking, New York and London, 1994; revised edition, Penguin 1995). Copyright © Steven Levy, 1994, 1995.

9 A theologian asked the most powerful supercomputer, 'Is there a God?' The computer said it lacked the processing power to know. It asked to be connected to all the other supercomputers in the world. Still, it was not enough power. So the computer was hooked up to all the mainframes in the world, and then all the minicomputers, and to all the personal computers. And eventually it was connected to all the computers in cars, microwaves, VCRs, digital watches and so on. The theologian asked for the final time, 'Is there a God?' And the computer replied: 'There is now!'

RANDAL L. TOBIAS, American industrialist, former Vice Chairman of AT&T. 'In Today Walks Tomorrow', *Vital Speeches of the Day*, McDonough Caperton Lecture Series, University of West Virginia, 1 October 1992.

10 First get it through your head that computers are big, expensive, fast, dumb adding-machine-typewriters. Then realise that most of the computer technicians that you're likely to meet or hire are complicators, not simplifiers. They're trying to make it look tough. Not easy. They're building a mystique, a priesthood, their own mumbo-jumbo ritual to keep you from knowing what they – and you – are doing.

ROBERT TOWNSEND, American business leader, CEO of Avis car rental group, and author. *Further up the Organisation* (Alfred A Knopf, New York, 1970; revised edition Michael Joseph, London, 1984).

14 **consumers**
See also: advertising 3; customers 19; marketing 58; people 70; selling 93

1 Consumers are not stupid. They just act that way.

ANON.

2 What's the difference between a consumer and a customer? One consumes a lot, while the other cusses a lot.

ANON.

3 The urge to consume is fathered by the value system which emphasises the ability of the society to produce.

JOHN KENNETH GALBRAITH, Canadian-born American economist, Emeritus Professor of Economics at Harvard University, former senior White House adviser, diplomat and author. *The Affluent Society* (1958; republished with a new introduction Deutsch, London, 1985).

4 The corporation/consumer relationship is a relationship between human beings. Give consumers credit for knowing what's going on. Listen to what consumers want and say. Tell them what they need to know when they need to know it. Respond to the consumer's concerns and desires. Even in the face of market pressures, a company will find out that decency is not only the only way to behave, but decency can also be profitable.

> FAITH POPCORN, American business consultant, co-founder and CEO of BrainReserve, and author. *The Popcorn Report* (Doubleday, New York, 1991). Copyright 1991 by Faith Popcorn. Used by permission of Doubleday, a division of Bantam Doubleday Dell Publishing Group, Inc.

5 Conspicuous consumption of valuable goods is a means of reputability to the gentleman of leisure.

> THORSTEIN VEBLEN (1857–1929), American economist and philosopher. *The Theory of the Leisure Class* (1899).

corporate culture 15

See also: business ethics 7; goals & goal-setting 36; leadership 51; success 98

1 The 1980s were very speculative, involving borrowings and huge money risks. The types of people who ran companies in the 80s had to be aggressive and risk taking. Tessy or testosterone types, as my wife calls them. But the 90s are about building businesses and making them work. We want to build companies that are durable and healthy. That means worrying about and looking after staff.

> ROBERT FERGUSON, Australian banker, director of Bankers Trust Australia. Quoted in Ruth Ostrow, 'The Taming of the Beast', *Weekend Australian*, 9 September 1995. © The Weekend Australian.

2 A lot of people don't do great things because great things really aren't expected of them and because nobody really demands they try and nobody says, 'Hey, that's the culture here, to do great things.'

> STEVE JOBS, American computer technology pioneer and founder of Apple Computers. Quoted in Steven Levy, *Insanely Great: The Life and Times of Macintosh, the Computer that Changed Everything* (Viking, New York and London, 1994; revised edition Penguin, 1995). Copyright © Steven Levy, 1994, 1995.

3 It's better to be a pirate than join the navy.

> STEVE JOBS, American computer technology pioneer and founder of Apple Computers. Quoted in Steven Levy, *Insanely Great: The Life and Times of Macintosh, the Computer that Changed Everything* (Viking, New York and London, 1994; revised edition Penguin, 1995). Copyright © Steven Levy, 1994, 1995.

4 Nothing is sacred – challenge everything. Sacred cows roam in every conference room, office, and hallway. Don't just round them up, develop a hunting organisation.

> ROBERT KRIEGEL, American business consultant, speaker and author, and DAVID BRANDT, American clinical psychologist, organisational consultant, executive coach and author. *Sacred Cows Make the Best Burgers* (Warner, New York, 1996).

5 Anything worth doing is worth doing to excess.

> EDWIN LAND (1909–91), American physicist and inventor, creator of the Polaroid Land Camera, and founder of Polaroid Corporation. Attrib.

6 Love your neighbour is not merely sound Christianity; it is good business.

> DAVID LLOYD GEORGE (1863–1945), British statesman, and Prime Minister 1916–22. Attrib.

7 Make sure you have a Vice-President in charge of Revolution, to engender ferment among your more conventional colleagues.

DAVID OGILVY, British-born American advertising expert, founder of Ogilvy & Mather international advertising group, New York, and author. *Ogilvy on Advertising* (Pan, London, 1983).

8 From bank to boilermaker, the typical US firm's response to the economic revolution engulfing us has been hardware first, people and organisation second. The wisest heads, usually ignored, have warned that this was a perilous course.

TOM PETERS, American academic, consultant, lecturer and author. In a foreword to Jan Carlzon, *Moments of Truth* (Ballinger, Cambridge, Massachusetts, 1987; revised edition Harper & Row, New York, 1989). Copyright © 1987 by Ballinger Publishing Company. Reprinted by permission of HarperCollins Publishers, Inc.

9 I never wanted a traditional corporation, with each employee sitting robotically in his or her office. I tried to create a community for thinking – for I believe what inspires productivity the most is freedom – and freedom begets creativity. Having a free and flexible environment provides a place where people can work together to focus on the future.

FAITH POPCORN, American business consultant, co-founder and CEO of BrainReserve, and author. *The Popcorn Report* (Doubleday, New York, 1991). Copyright 1991 by Faith Popcorn. Used by permission of Doubleday, a division of Bantam Doubleday Dell Publishing Group, Inc.

10 We don't have receptionists. We don't think they are necessary, despite all our visitors. We don't have secretaries either, or personal assistants. We don't believe in cluttering the payroll with ungratifying, dead-end jobs. Everyone at Semco, even top managers, fetches guests, stands over photocopiers, sends faxes, types letters, and dials the phone. We don't have

executive dining rooms and parking is strictly first-come, first-served. It's all part of running a 'natural business.' At Semco we have stripped away the unnecessary perks and privileges that feed the ego but hurt the balance sheet and distract everyone from the crucial corporate tasks of making, selling, billing, and collecting.

-RICARDO SEMLER, Brazilian industrialist, CEO of Semco, Brazil, and author. *Maverick!* (Century, London, 1993). Copyright © 1993 by Tableturn Inc. Reproduced by permission of the author c/o Rogers, Coleridge & White Ltd, 20 Powis Mews, London W11 1JN.

11 American capitalism needs a heart transplant. The financial traders who have become the heart of American capitalism need to be taken out and replaced by real capitalists who can become the heart of an American industrial rebirth. What America lacks is genuine, old-style capitalists – those big investors of yesteryear who often invested the technologies they were managing and whose personal wealth was inextricably linked to the destiny of their giant companies. It misses them. Men like Henry Ford; Thomas J. Watson, of IBM; and J. P. Morgan were at the heart of the system that produced the greatest economic power and the highest standard of living in history.

LESTER C. THUROW, American sociologist, professor at Massachusetts Institute of Technology, and author. *Head to Head* (William Morrow, New York, 1992).

12 Don't try to get your wild geese to fly in formation.

THOMAS J. WATSON (1874–1956), American industrialist, founder of IBM. Attrib.

13 What we are trying relentlessly to do is get that small-company soul – and small-company speed – inside our big company body.

JACK WELCH, American industrialist, CEO of General Electric Company. *USA Today*, 2 February 1993.

14 Service, quality and a highly motivated workforce depend on the culture of the organisation, and when one of the business units fails to get the balance right – it might be profit ahead of service, or it might be productivity ahead of human resources – the image of the organisation will deteriorate. The check, at that point, is the intervention of the CEO.

> BOB WHITE, Australian banker, former CEO of Westpac Banking Corporation, and CECELIA CLARKE, Australian author. *Cheques and Balances* (Viking, Victoria, 1995).

15 I couldn't care less about business, other than the fact that I feel it's like boarding a ship, robbing all the men and raping all the women. It's an adventure, as long as it's fun. It *has* to be fun if you're going to tilt against the Establishment.

> GORDON WHITE, British-born American-based businessman, Chairman of Hanson Industries, New York. Quoted in Alan Whicker. *Whicker's New World* (Weidenfeld & Nicolson, London, 1985).

courtesy 16

See also: consumers 14; customers 19; selling 93; service 94; sincerity 95

1 Courtesy costs nothing but reaps rich rewards.

> ANON.

2 Manners don't exist any more ... Manners have changed so much that sometimes it's almost like being on another planet.

> JOAN COLLINS, British actress, producer and author. *Hello!*, 23 September 1995.

3 Manners require time, as nothing is more vulgar than haste.

> RALPH WALDO EMERSON (1803–82), American philosopher, poet and essayist. 'Behaviour', *The Conduct of Life* (1860).

4 All doors open to courtesy.

> THOMAS FULLER M.D. (1654–1734), British physician and author. *Gnomologia* (1732).

5 The knowledge of courtesy and good manners is a very necessary study.

> MICHEL DE MONTAIGNE (1533–92), French moralist and essayist. 'The Ceremony of the Interview of Princes', *Essays* (1580–88).

6 Manners maketh the man.

> ENGLISH PROVERB.

7 The greater man the greater courtesy.

> ALFRED, LORD TENNYSON (1809–92), British poet. 'The Last Tournament', *Idylls of the King* (1871).

17 creativity

See also: imagination 42; innovation 45; inspiration 46; originality 69

1 There is a great deal of rubbish written about creativity because – like motherhood – it is automatically a good thing. My preference is to treat creativity as a logical process rather than a matter of talent or mystique ... I invented the term 'lateral thinking' many years ago because the term 'creativity' is too general, too vague, too full of artistic connotations and too value laden. Indeed many creative people are not creative at all. Some artists are no more than productive stylists inasmuch as they produce within a defined style. Some creative people are also very rigid. They may have an unusual, and valuable, idea but remain rigidly within that idea.

> EDWARD DE BONO, Maltese-born British scholar, teacher, lecturer and author. *Conflicts* (Harrap, London, 1985).

2 When creativity is regarded as a magic gift, there is nothing that can be done about it if you are not lucky enough to have the gift. But everyone can develop some skill in lateral thinking and those who develop most skill will be the most creative.

EDWARD DE BONO, Maltese-born British scholar, teacher, lecturer and author. *Lateral Thinking for Management* (McGraw-Hill, London, 1971).

3 It is clear that his impetuosity has not yet allowed him to settle on any particular style of his own. In fact, his personality lies in that very impetuosity, in that young and furious spontaneity. It is said he is not yet twenty, and that he covers three canvases a day. But there is danger here. This same impetuosity could lead him to a kind of facile virtuosity and to even more facile successes: the prolific and the fecund are two different things, just like energy and violence. It would be a shame, when he has such brilliant virility.

FELICIEN FAGUS, French writer and critic. Comments made about the young Picasso. 'L'invasion espagnole: Picasso', *La Revue Blanche*, Paris, 15 July 1901.

4 Creative minds have always been known to survive any kind of bad training.

ANNA FREUD (1895–1982), Austrian-born British psychoanalyst, youngest daughter of Sigmund Freud and founder of child psychoanalysis. Annual Freud Lecture to the New York Psychoanalytic Society, 1968.

5 Your work serves as your expression of creativity. You need to go beyond your feelings of not being good enough or not knowing enough. Allow the creative energy of the Universe to flow through you in ways that are deeply satisfying to you. It doesn't matter what you do, as long as it is satisfying to your being and it fulfils you.

LOUISE L. HAY, British motivator and author. *The Power is Within You* (Airlift Books, London; Applause Books, New York; Specialist Publications, Concord, New South Wales, 1991).

6 Becoming creative requires the capacity to wish, to want, and to will. Wishing, wanting, and willing do not necessarily lead to being creative. Yet without these qualities, creativity does not mature.

MURIEL JAMES. *Breaking Free* (Addison Wesley, Reading, Massachusetts, 1981).

7 I look in my closet, and if I need it, I design it.

DONNA KARAN, American fashion designer. *Fortune*, Autumn/Winter, 1993.

8 If new ideas are the lifeblood of any thriving organisation – and, trust me, they are – managers must learn to revere, not merely tolerate, the people who come up with those ideas. Sounds obvious, doesn't it? But it's incredible how often people forget this. I've seen lots of organisations where managers and salespeople actually resent their creative people.

MARK H. McCORMACK, American sports marketing consultant, founder and CEO of International Management Group, and author. *McCormack on Managing* (Century, London, 1985).

9 [My father] wasn't a family man – he was a creator and he paid the penalty of all those who create. He devoted up to twenty hours a day to his business until he had built it.

KERRY PACKER, Australian media proprietor. Quoted in Terry Lane, *As the Twig is Bent* (Dove, Victoria, 1979).

10 Being an actor has given me the chance to be creative, something which is denied people in many other lines of business. And this, as most of us know, provides both stimulation and a wonderful kind of emotional satisfaction.

MICKEY ROONEY, American actor. *The Hollywood Reporter*, 24 November 1958.

11 Yesterday seniority signified status. Today creativity drives status.

> DENIS WAITLEY, American personal development counsellor, lecturer and author. *Empires of the Mind: Lessons to Lead and Succeed in a Knowledge-Based World* (William Morrow, New York; Nicholas Brealey, London, 1995). Reprinted by permission of Nicholas Brealey Publishing Limited, London, Tel. (0171) 430-0224, Fax (0171) 404-8311.

12 [A] characteristic, often verified in writers and composers, is an amazing speed of action at times of creative production. It may take a long time to get started, but, once in swing, production goes forward rapidly. Another noteworthy trait of the great genius is the quantity of his production: almost every really great painter, or composer, or writer, or discoverer, or inventor, has produced a surprising number of works. Such industry points to the presence of a strong drive.

> ROBERT S. WOODWORTH (1869–1962), American psychologist, Professor of Psychology at Columbia University, and author. *Dynamic Psychology* (Columbia University Press, New York, 1918; republished Arno Press, New York, 1973).

criticism 18

See also: determination 23; persistence & perseverance 71; praise 75

1 Those who can't do it themselves teach it, or become critics.

> ANON.

2 A most violent attack is preparing for me in the next number of the *Edinburgh Review*, this I have from the authority of a friend who has seen the proof and the manuscript of the Critique; you know the System of the Edinburgh Gentlemen is universal attack, they praise none . . . They defeat their object by universal

abuse ... It is nothing to be abused, when Southey, Moore, Lauderdale, Strangford, and Payne Night share the same fate.

LORD BYRON (George Gordon Byron; 1788–1824), British poet. Letter to the Reverend John Becher, 26 February 1808.

3 If I had listened to the critics I'd have died drunk in the gutter.

ANTON CHEKHOV (1860–1904), Russian author. Attrib.

4 The more vicious the criticism the more I always feel the critic must be a little bit jealous.

JACKIE COLLINS, British author. *OK! Magazine*, December 1994.

5 I am inclined to be rather too impressed by adverse notices and less impressed by good ones. If I am praised too much I think the critics are overdoing it and I cannot be as good as they say. If I am savagely attacked, I think I cannot be quite as bad as all that. But I am inclined to think that one learns more from bad notices than from good ones.

JOHN GIELGUD, British actor. With John Miller, *An Actor and His Time* (Sidgwick & Jackson, London, 1979; Applause Books, New York, 1979).

6 Although criticism should never be made in anger and certainly never in public, it is always best applied as soon as possible after the mistake has occurred. If there is a long delay, the individual tends to cocoon a mistake in a protective carapace which places a lot of the responsibility everywhere except on themselves.

JOHN HARVEY-JONES, British business consultant, broadcaster, author and former Chairman of ICI Industries. *All Together Now* (William Heinemann, London, 1994). Reprinted by permission of The Peters Fraser and Dunlop Group Limited on behalf of John Harvey-Jones.

7 If I were to read, much less answer, all the attacks made on me, this shop might as well be closed for any other business. I do the very best I know how – the very best I can; and I mean to

keep doing so until the end. If the end brings me out all right, what is said against me won't amount to anything. If the end brings me out wrong, ten angels swearing I was right would make no difference.

ABRAHAM LINCOLN (1809–65), American statesman, and 16th President of the United States of America 1861–65. Attrib.

8 Flattery and criticism go down the same drain.

GEORGIA O'KEEFFE (1887–1986), American artist. Attrib.

9 If it hadn't been for a critic in Philadelphia, I might not be in Hollywood now. Maybe I might not even be an actor. Seven years ago, after I had played in several road show companies, Guthrie McClintic offered me a role in *Morning Star*, which would try out in Philadelphia before opening on Broadway. It was my first real chance and I was tense and eager.

The morning after our first performance, I riffled nervously through the newspaper, searching for the review . . . As nearly as I remember, the reviewer extolled me in these words: 'Mr Peck looks more like a wax dummy in a tailor shop than an actor headed for success on Broadway.' Well, I wasn't exactly in a state of exuberance. Never before and never since have I felt so low. I could have slithered right under that proverbial snake's belly. I wasn't even conscious of eating breakfast. I wasn't mad, nor did I feel like writing the review off as the personal dislike of one person for another individual's performance. I suspected strongly that maybe I had been too tense and too eager . . .

My wife, Greta, and I talked matters over and we decided that if we took the review to heart and worked industriously, maybe I might look better to the New York critics by the time we arrived there. That would be a mere week hence. She sweated it out with me, helping me until far into the night, and somehow or other, that one week's prodigious effort did show up because the Broadway critics thought well of my performance.

I don't remember the name of the Philadelphia reviewer or of the newspaper because, in my anxiety at the time, I was only concerned with his critique, but he may easily have saved my career for me. If it hadn't been for him, I might never have known what was specifically wrong with my performance or, for that matter, that anything was wrong with it.

GREGORY PECK, American actor. *The Hollywood Reporter*, 11 October 1948.

10 The critic's first duty is to admit, with absolute respect, the right of every man to his own style.

GEORGE BERNARD SHAW (1856–1950), Irish playwright and critic, Nobel laureate 1925. In a letter to journalist R. E. Golding Bright, 19 November 1894.

11 Every critic knows it is more entertaining to attack than to approve; reviewers make their names by being the pugnacious Butcher of Broadway, the Fearless Voice of outspoken criticism – not by reporting pleasure, by being delighted.

ALAN WHICKER, British television documentary maker and author. *Whicker's New World* (Weidenfeld & Nicolson, London, 1985).

19 customers

See also: communication & communicating 11; consumers 14; human nature 39; marketing 58; negotiation 64; people 70; selling 93; service 94

1 It is more profitable to generate additional business from existing customers than to be always going out after new customers.

ANON.

2 One thing I always try to encourage our store owners and managers to do is to *think like a customer*. Now that may sound

very easy, especially when you're talking about McDonald's, because most people have been a customer on many, many occasions. But it takes some skill and concentration to actually think like a customer and objectively measure the experience you are being delivered instore. Imagine the gains to be had in businesses all over this country if every person who came in contact with a customer thought like a customer every day. The possibilities are enormous.

CHARLIE BELL, Australian business leader and CEO of McDonald's Australia. In a foreword to Stephen Dando-Collins, *The Customer Care Revolution* (Pitman, Melbourne, 1996).

3 If there's one constant about customers, it's that they will change – in taste, in attitude and in demands. So we will continue to learn. Continue to think like a customer and find new ways to give them the best possible experience.

CHARLIE BELL, Australian business leader and CEO of McDonald's Australia. In a foreword to Stephen Dando-Collins, *The Customer Care Revolution* (Pitman, Melbourne, 1996).

4 It's important to get the voice of customers, to capture their words, in order to really understand what they want.

JENNIFER BROTMAN, American market researcher, senior executive of Forum Corp. *Fortune*, Autumn/Winter, 1993. © 1993 Time Inc. All rights reserved.

5 Only the customer, and the customer alone, will pay our costs and provide our profits. So, we have to conduct all business planning from the customer's point of view.

JAN CARLZON, Swedish business leader, former CEO of Scandinavian Airlines System, speaker and author. *Moments of Truth* (Ballinger, Cambridge, Massachusetts, 1987; revised edition Harper & Row, New York, 1989). Copyright © 1987 by Ballinger Publishing Company. Reprinted by permission of HarperCollins Publishers, Inc.

6 Any business organisation seeking to establish a customer orientation and create a good impression ... must flatten the pyramid – that is, eliminate the hierarchical tiers of responsibility in order to respond directly and quickly to customers' needs.

> JAN CARLZON, Swedish business leader, former CEO of Scandinavian Airlines System, speaker and author. *Moments of Truth* (Ballinger, Cambridge, Massachusetts; 1987; revised edition Harper & Row, New York, 1989). Copyright © 1987 by Ballinger Publishing Company. Reprinted by permission of HarperCollins Publishers, Inc.

7 Like a house of cards, customer satisfaction can be difficult to build, but very easy to destroy. That's because there is a customer care chain. The nature of the chain varies industry by industry, organisation by organisation. But even though the chain that applies to one will not apply to another, it only takes one weak link for any chain to be broken, for customer care failure to occur.

> STEPHEN DANDO-COLLINS, Australian author and editor. *The Customer Care Revolution* (Pitman, Melbourne, 1996).

8 In Japan, the word customer translates into 'honoured guest in one's home.' Surely, that is how we want all tourists to feel.

> CATHERINE DEVRYE, Australian lecturer, motivator, author and 1993–94 Australian Executive Woman of the Year. 'She'll Be Right Approach Not Good Enough', *AussieHost News*, February 1997.

9 The absolute fundamental aim is to make money out of satisfying customers.

> JOHN EGAN, British industrialist, Chairman of Jaguar automotive manufacturing company. Attrib.

10 Americans have become very purposeful shoppers. They are reengineering just as corporate America is doing ... 'Precision

shopping' . . . We think it will be here for a long time, if not forever.

11 We cannot conceive how to serve the customer unless we make him something that, as far as we can provide, will last forever . . . We want the man who buys one of our products never to have to buy another.

HENRY FORD (1863–1947), American industrialist. Attrib. (1925).

12 Smart customers look for added value. They already under-stand the technical performance of the product. The choice of supplier will depend on less tangible considerations.

JACQUES HOROVITZ, French business consultant and author. *Winning Ways*, originally *Qualité de Service* (InterEditions, Paris, 1987; republished Productivity Press, Cambridge, Massachusetts, 1990).

13 Dealing with customers takes knowledge, time, and patience – after all, if salespeople don't have that, they should look for another line of work.

14 Customer power brings global markets home – even for local companies doing business only in the area. To survive, local businesses must become more cosmopolitan. Cosmopolitan is a matter of mind-set as much as markets. Businesses must enlarge the geographic scope of their sources of ideas, stan-dards, processes, raw materials, parts, and people in order to find and serve increasingly cosmopolitan customers. They

must be linked to networks that help them look beyond their home region or nation for resources to add value at home.

ROSABETH MOSS KANTER, American academic and author, professor at Harvard Business School. *World Class* (Simon & Schuster, New York, 1995).

15 In this business environment, *satisfy the customer* is a sacred cow. Even most car dealers are doing that. Sales managers and store managers everywhere are imploring their people to put the customer first. But they're all playing catch-up. In the new world of commerce, *satisfying* is only the beginning ... So don't satisfy customers; everyone does that. Surprise them. Give them something they don't expect.

ROBERT KRIEGEL, American business consultant, speaker and author, and DAVID BRANDT, American clinical psychologist, organisational consultant, executive coach and author. *Sacred Cows Make the Best Burgers* (Warner Books, New York, 1996).

16 Don't ever make the mistake of thinking of buildings, computers, consultants, or even employees as your company's greatest assets. Every company's greatest assets are its customers, because without customers there is no company. It's that simple.

MICHAEL LEBOEUF, American business consultant, speaker and author, Professor of Management at the University of New Orleans. *How to Win Customers and Keep Them for Life* (Putnam, New York, 1987). Reprinted by permission of The Putnam Publishing Group. Copyright © 1988 by Michael LeBoeuf, Ph.D.

17 Not only is it important to develop great advertising to reach new customers, but it's equally important to reach existing customers and employees. They need to be reassured they're dealing with a winner.

GEORGE LOIS, American advertising creative executive and author. Bob Lamons, 'Research Won't Yield The Big Idea', *Marketing News* (American

Marketing Association), 18 November 1996, page 18. Reprinted with permission.

18 In my experience, the perfect customer is a friend who is a decision-maker who not only likes what I'm proposing but will help me conquer any pockets of resistance within his or her company. The not-so-perfect customer is someone who says yes, lets me work my way through his company, and then gets talked out of it by subordinates. The least perfect customer, of course, is the one who doesn't agree with me in the first place.

> MARK H. McCORMACK, American sports marketing consultant, founder and CEO of International Management Group, and author. *McCormack on Selling* (Century, London, 1995).

19 When you boil it all down, your customers and clients use three criteria to measure you:
    1. Communication
    2. Service
    3. Added value
    How well you handle these three items is a reliable indicator of how long you'll keep your clients.

> MARK H. McCORMACK, American sports marketing consultant, founder and CEO of International Management Group, and author. *McCormack on Selling* (Century, London, 1995).

20 Being customer driven is much like motherhood and apple pie; it's hard to argue against. However, many firms – indeed, most firms – are not really customer driven, if their actions offer any indication. Too many firms take their customers for granted and make only superficial efforts to satisfy them. For a firm to become truly customer driven, a major shift in corporate philosophy must exist. Such a change in orientation usually results from a gradual, evolutionary process.

It appears there are at least three stages through which a firm must pass to become truly customer driven: 1. bliss, 2. awareness, and 3. commitment. A firm finds itself in one of these evolutionary stages of development based on performance, not on desire. Having a CEO say 'we're customer oriented' is meaningless unless the statement is backed up by real programmes.

EARL NAUMANN, American academic and Professor of Marketing and Finance at Boise State University, Boise, Idaho, and PATRICK W. SHANNON, American academic and Professor of Computer Information Systems and Production Management at Boise State University, Boise, Idaho. 'What is Customer-Driven Marketing?', *Business Horizons,* November–December 1992. © Copyright 1992 by the Foundation for the School of Business at Indiana University. Used with permission.

21 Committed firms realise that achieving customer satisfaction cannot result from just doing the traditional things better. Good product quality warranties, and customer surveys can help, but they are inadequate without something more. The 'something' is changing the customer from a target to a partner.

EARL NAUMANN, American academic and Professor of Marketing and Finance at Boise State University, Boise, Idaho, and PATRICK W. SHANNON, American academic and Professor of Computer Information Systems and Production Management at Boise State University, Boise, Idaho. 'What is Customer-Driven Marketing?', *Business Horizons,* November–December 1992. © Copyright 1992 by the Foundation for the School of Business at Indiana University. Used with permission.

22 Customer satisfaction is so important at Applied Materials, Santa Clara, California, that employees are reminded every payday. 'Your payroll dollars are provided by Applied Materials customers' appears on the front of every cheque.

CHAD RUBEL, American journalist. *Marketing News* (American Marketing Association), 25 March 1996, page 20. Reprinted with permission.

23 Today's workers understand the principle that the only true job security comes from satisfied customers.

> NOEL M. TICHY, American academic and author, and STRATFORD SHERMAN, American journalist and author. *Control Your Destiny or Someone Else Will* (Doubleday, New York, 1993). Copyright © 1993 by Noel M. Tichy and Stratford Sherman. Used by permission of Doubleday, a division of Bantam Doubleday Dell Publishing Group, Inc.

24 Satisfied, loyal repeat customers are the heart of Wal-Mart's spectacular profit margins, and those customers are loyal to us because our associates treat them better than salespeople in other stores do.

> SAM WALTON, American retailing pioneer, and founder and CEO of Wal-Mart. *Sam Walton in His Own Words* (Doubleday, New York, 1992).

25 In too many companies, the customer has become a bloody nuisance whose unpredictable behaviour damages carefully made strategic plans, whose activities mess up computer operations, and who stubbornly insists that purchased products should work.

> LEWIS H. YOUNG, American journalist and editor, Editor-In-Chief of *Business Week*. In a speech ('Views on Management') made to Ward Howell International, Links Club, New York, 2 December 1980.

d

'The key is not to make quick decisions,
but to make timely decisions.'
COLIN POWELL

decisions 20:20

decisions 20

See also: challenge 8; goals & goal-setting 36; leadership 51; mistakes 61

1 Business decisions based purely on instinct may be risky. The next time you have a gut feeling about something, make sure it isn't just indigestion.

ANON.

2 Decisions are like New Year's resolutions – making them is easy; sticking to them is the hard part.

ANON.

3 If in doubt, leave it out.

ANON.

4 Making a decision is like choosing a route through the wilderness – you hope that it's going to take you where you want to go, but you can never be entirely certain.

ANON.

5 All of us have those random moments in our lives that shape us for better or for worse for the rest of the time we inhabit our bodies before we go on to whatever else is beyond this. Most of the time, endurance is not an option. One day we find ourselves faced with a disturbing moment or series of moments and must decide what plan to take to get the hell away from it. Sometimes lots of these moments must transpire before we realise that no one else has the key. And as contemptible as what we get away from seems at the time, often we can look

back at that space, that second, and know that living through it made us stronger.

BRETT BUTLER, American comedienne, actress and author. *Knee Deep in Paradise* (Hyperion, New York, 1996; Transworld, Sydney, 1996). Reproduced by permission of the publisher.

6   In this job there are times when you have to stick with a decision and try to get the best deal you can get. It's not that I enjoy the fight – I just like to achieve a good deal for people, for my team.

JAN CHAPMAN, Australian film producer. *Sydney Morning Herald*, 7 September 1996.

7   I have learned, and I am still learning, my craft, but I don't think I would have got as far as this had I not done a brave thing, in fact the only consciously brave thing I've done in my life. It concerns my second novel. This book took a year to write in longhand, and the publisher accepted it, but in his letter to me he said these words: 'It isn't as good as your first, but we'll do the best we can with it for you.' The best they could with it for me! I sat down and did some hard thinking. I was forty-two years of age, I had arrived where I was under my own steam, I knew no-one in the literary world – still don't; the only help I'd ever had had been from my husband. This sentence of the publishers had a touch of condescension about it; they were going to do the best they could for something of an inferior quality which I had landed them with. Well, was I going to let it go through? In blood I wrote to them, saying, 'Send it back.' And again I cried my eyes out. But from then on I determined that each book I wrote – and I was going to write dozens, God sparing me – must in some way be an improvement on the one before.

CATHERINE COOKSON, British author. 'Touching the Heart of Your Reader', in A. S. Burack (ed.), *The Writer's Handbook* (The Writer, Boston, 1978).

8 In the course of the examination of ideas, decisions will often emerge. It becomes increasingly obvious that an idea does not offer sufficient benefits to take it further. Consensus opinions can gradually emerge; this is how the Japanese make decisions.

EDWARD DE BONO, Maltese-born British scholar, teacher, lecturer and author. *Serious Creativity* (HarperCollins, London, 1992). Reprinted by permission of HarperCollins Publishers Limited.

9 You have to take both decisions and risks: if you are slow to make your mind up, you may lose an opportunity through failing to react in time; and you run the risk, if you pick the wrong opportunity, of setting back your whole career. In almost all my career decisions I have been extraordinarily fortunate . . . Every one of these decisions involved risks, whether of personal injury or of failure to measure up to the task in hand.

PETER DE LA BILLIERE, British soldier, general and commander-in-chief of British Forces, Operation Desert Storm, 1991. *Looking for Trouble* (HarperCollins, London, 1994).

10 Most business decisions are already far beyond the capability of single minds and single individuals. Business decision-making is increasingly a collective operation in which the ability to play as a team member, to listen, to build on the ideas of others and to make two and two equal five rather than three and a half is the key to success.

JOHN HARVEY-JONES, British business consultant, broadcaster, author and former Chairman of ICI Industries. *All Together Now* (William Heinemann, London, 1994). Reprinted by permission of The Peters Fraser and Dunlop Group Limited on behalf of John Harvey-Jones.

11 [Swedish] managers feel the need to obtain and analyse fully all relevant information. There is no pressure to show an assertive management style by driving decisions to an early

conclusion. This does mean that decisions take longer to be made [in Sweden], as more people take part in the negotiations and more information is analysed; but the resulting commitment and lack of conflict are highly valued.

DAVID J. HICKSON, British academic, editor, author and Professor of International Management and Organisation at the University of Bradford Management Centre, and DEREK S. PUGH, British academic, author and Professor of International Management at the Open University Business School. *Worldwide Management: The Impact of Social Culture on Organisations Around the Globe* (Penguin, London, 1995). Copyright © David J. Hickson and Derek S. Pugh, 1995.

12 When it comes time to make decisions, you shouldn't get too old over them. Sure, they won't all be perfect. In fact, some of them will be duds. Learn from them, but don't stop trying.

LEE IACOCCA, American automotive industry leader, former CEO of Chrysler Motors, and director of several other auto manufacturing companies, and author. *Talking Straight* (Bantam, New York, 1988). Copyright © 1988 by Lee Iacocca. Used by permission of Bantam Books, a division of Bantam Doubleday Dell Publishing Group Inc.

13 You have to have a strange and monstrous ego to think that you never make bad decisions.

KEN IVERSON, American industrialist, Chairman of Nucor Steel Corp. Quoted in Mark H. McCormack, *McCormack on Managing* (Century, London, 1995).

14 Saturated with experience of a particular class of materials, an expert intuitively feels whether a newly-reported fact is probable or not, whether a proposed hypothesis is worthless or the reverse. He instinctively knows that, in a novel case, this and not that will be the promising course of action. The well-known story of the old judge advising the new one never to give reasons for his decisions, 'The decisions will probably be right, the reasons will surely be wrong,' illustrates this.

WILLIAM JAMES (1842–1910), American philosopher, psychologist and teacher. *The Principles of Psychology* (Henry Holt, New York, 1890).

15 The last decisions are the ones that are the loneliest. The ones that only [a] leader can make. The ones that there's no book on, no precedent.

ALEX KROLL, American advertising executive and CEO of Young & Rubicam advertising agency, New York. Quoted in Edward de Bono, *Tactics: The Art and Science of Success* (Collins, London, 1985). Reprinted by permission of HarperCollins Publishers Limited.

16 Be often wrong but never in doubt.

KEITH B. MATHER, American academic and Vice Chancellor for Research & Advanced Study, University of Alaska. Quoted in Stephen Dando-Collins, *2000 AD* (Pan, Sydney, 1986).

17 Nothing is more difficult, and therefore more precious, than to be able to decide.

NAPOLEON I (Napoleon Bonaparte; 1769–1821), French soldier and statesman, and Emperor of France 1804–14/15. *Maxims* (1804–1815).

18 I'm a big believer in instinct. If in doubt, don't do it. Always tell the truth. Make the hard decisions first. Just make a decision! But I think the biggest one is, take responsibility for what you do. I have a ruling here: if anything goes wrong, tell me first.

MARIA O'CONNOR, Irish-born Australian businesswoman and CEO of Ticketmaster BASS. *Qantas Club*, October 1996.

19 A business leader has to combine creative thinking with judicial thinking in arriving at decisions. To get surer answers than his own one-man judgement could arrive at, he thinks up ways to pull in the experience of others; he thinks up ways to get *composite* judgement through conference groups, or

through surveys; he thinks up ways to put the problem to actual test.

ALEX F. OSBORN (1888–1966), American academic and author. *Applied Imagination: Principles & Procedures of Creative Thinking* (Charles Scribner's Sons, New York, 1953).

20 When I am faced with a decision – picking somebody for a post, or choosing a course of action – I dredge up every scrap of knowledge I can. I call in people. I phone them. I read whatever I can get my hands on. I use my intellect to inform my instinct. Then I use my instinct to test all this data. 'Hey, instinct, does this sound right? Does it smell right, feel right, fit right?' However, we do not have the luxury of collecting information indefinitely. At some point, before we can have every possible fact in hand, we have to decide. The key is not to make quick decisions, but to make timely decisions.

COLIN POWELL, American military leader, general of the US Army (retired) and former Chairman of US Joint Chiefs of Staff. With Joseph E. Persico, *My American Journey* (Random House, New York, 1995). (Published in the UK and Commonwealth as *A Soldier's Way*, Hutchinson, London, 1995). Copyright © 1995 by Colin L. Powell. Reprinted by permission of Random House Inc.

21 Selling techniques enable you to advance yourself and your ideas, to disarm your opposition, and to resolve or reduce conflict. In a group decision-making situation, they can be invaluable to you in persuading the group to give you the results you want.

THOMAS L. QUICK, American consultant and author. *Power Plays*, (Franklin Watts, Danbury, Connecticut, 1985).

22 I have tried to address every question in the Department of Justice with one overriding issue – What is the right thing to do? Not what is the popular thing to do, but what is the right thing to do according to the evidence and the law?

JANET RENO, American civil servant and US Attorney General in the Clinton Administration. *Vanity Fair*, April 1994.

23 If making decisions is so simple and powerful, then why don't more people follow Nike's advice and 'Just Do It'? I think one of the simplest reasons is that most of us don't recognise what it even means to make a real decision. We don't realise the force of change that a congruent, committed decision creates. Part of the problem is that for so long most of us have used the term 'decision' so loosely that it's come to describe something like a wish list. Instead of making decisions, we keep stating preferences. Making a true decision, unlike saying, 'I'd like to quit smoking,' is cutting off any other possibility. In fact, the word 'decision' comes from the Latin roots *de*, which means 'from,' and *caedere*, which means 'to cut.' Making a true decision means committing to achieving a result, and then cutting yourself off from any other possibility.

ANTHONY ROBBINS, American personal improvement counsellor, lecturer and author. *Awaken the Giant Within* (Fireside/Simon & Schuster, New York and London, 1991). Reprinted with permission of Simon & Schuster. Copyright © 1991 by Anthony Robbins.

24 It is in your moments of decision that your destiny is shaped.

ANTHONY ROBBINS, American personal improvement counsellor, lecturer and author. *Awaken the Giant Within* (Fireside/Simon & Schuster, New York and London, 1991). Reprinted with permission of Simon & Schuster. Copyright © 1991 by Anthony Robbins.

25 • Every decision involves some risk.
• Time does not always improve a situation . . .
• Fundamental errors are inescapable when the unqualified are allowed to exercise judgement and make decisions.
• Quick decisions are not always the best decisions. On the other hand, unhurried decisions are not always the best decisions.

WESS ROBERTS, American author. *Leadership Secrets of Attila the Hun* (Bantam, London, 1989).

26 Another of our biggest fears that keeps us [women] from moving ahead with our lives is our difficulty in making decisions. The irony, of course, is that by not choosing our own path, we *are* choosing which path we follow.

ANITA RODDICK, British businesswoman, co-founder and Chief Executive of The Body Shop International. In a foreword to Eileen Gillibrand & Jenny Mosley, *She Who Dares Wins* (Thorsons, London, 1995).

27 I don't have much advice to give you about decision-making, except this: Whatever you do, don't camp at the fork in the road. Decide. It's far better to make a wrong decision that to not make one at all.

JIM ROHN, American business philosopher, lecturer and author. *Seven Strategies for Wealth and Happiness* (Brolga, Melbourne, 1994).

28 As children we drew certain conclusions from limited evidence. As adults we have access to much more evidence, and we are free to choose to draw other conclusions. Understanding and accepting this fact means taking responsibility for yourself, which can be very difficult. It means recognising that you are always engaged in making decisions. Even when you say 'I'll let someone else decide,' you have made the decision to let someone else decide.

DOROTHY ROWE, Australian-born British-based psychologist, lecturer, researcher, author, and former head of North Lincolnshire Department of Clinical Psychology, UK. *Time on Our Side* (HarperCollins, London, 1993). Reprinted by permission of HarperCollins Publishers Limited.

29 After the key decisions were made, I felt quite calm – even in the most difficult and tense moments. The reason: I was starting to take control of those things that were controllable. I've

often heard top athletes say that the actual event of competition is a calming experience that seems to unravel almost in slow motion. It's the few moments before the action that are the most difficult to deal with. I think this is true in a business crisis as well.

JOHN SCULLEY, American business executive, CEO of Apple Computers, and author. *Odyssey: From Pepsi to Apple* (Collins, London, 1987). Reprinted by permission of HarperCollins Publishers Limited.

30 I try to create an environment in which others make decisions. Success means not making them myself.

RICARDO SEMLER, Brazilian industrialist, CEO of Semco, Brazil, and author. *Maverick!* (Century, London, 1993). Copyright © 1993 by Tableturn Inc. Reproduced by permission of the author c/o Rogers, Coleridge & White Ltd, 20 Powis Mews, London W11 1JN.

31 Even the best strategies seldom take into account more than a few of the consequences that flow from them. In real life, the decision-maker must continually adjust to those consequences, and, in doing so, deviate from the clear course laid out in advance.

ALVIN TOFFLER, American scholar, lecturer and author. *The Adaptive Corporation* (Gower, Aldershot, Hampshire, 1985).

32 Today's selective corporate recruiters want students who have more than just a degree, who will think and make corporate decisions in changing and complex market environments. It is imperative that we expose students to the major marketing challenges of the late 1990s and beyond. Students must be prepared to deal with business implications in globalisation, micromarketing and segmentation, relationship marketing, marketing services and ideas, understanding the value proposition, and entrepreneurial marketing.

ART WEINSTEIN, American academic, Associate Professor of Marketing at

Nova Southeastern University, Fort Lauderdale, Florida. *Marketing News* (American Marketing Association), 12 August 1996, page 12. Reprinted with permission.

21 **defeat**

See also: challenge 8; determination 23; failure 30; obstacles 66; persistence & perseverance 71; success 98; winners & winning 106

1 The road to victory is paved with defeats.

ANON.

2 Defeat is a school in which truth always grows strong.

HENRY WARD BEECHER (1813–87), American clergyman, editor and author. *Proverbs from Plymouth Pulpit* (1887).

3 Few great leaders encountered defeats so consistently before enjoying ultimate victory as did this individual. A frequently reported listing of these failures includes the following:

- Failed in business in 1831
- Ran for the legislature and lost in 1832
- Failed once again in business in 1834
- Sweetheart died in 1835
- Had a nervous breakdown in 1836
- Lost a second political race in 1838
- Defeated for Congress in 1843
- Defeated for Congress in 1846
- Defeated for Congress in 1848
- Defeated for US Senate in 1855
- Defeated for Vice President in 1856
- Defeated for US Senate in 1858

The man was Abraham Lincoln, elected sixteenth president of the United States 1860.

LOUISE E. BOONE, American author. *Quotable Business* (Random House, New York, 1989).

4 You can accept defeat; or you can look it in the eye, until defeat blinks, and walks away.

NIKE CORPORATION. Television commercial (1996).

5 If you are thinking thoughts of defeat, I urge you to rid yourself of such thoughts, for as you think defeat you tend to get it. Adopt the 'I don't believe in defeat' attitude.

NORMAN VINCENT PEALE, American theologian and author. *The Power of Positive Thinking* (Simon & Schuster, New York, 1953; The World's Work, UK, 1953).

details 22

See also: accuracy 1; planning 72

1 It is a common error to suppose that little things can be passed by, and that the greater things are more important, and should receive all attention.

JAMES ALLEN, American theologian and author. *The Mastery of Destiny* (Putnam, New York, 1909).

2 The majority of those who fail and come to grief do so through neglecting the apparently insignificant details.

JAMES ALLEN, American theologian and author. *The Mastery of Destiny* (Putnam, New York, 1909).

3 There is no such thing as a minor detail. All details are major.

ANON.

4 You can't know enough about your customers and suppliers. Little things mean everything.

HARVEY MACKAY, American business executive, CEO of Mackay Envelope Company, motivator and author. In a speech made at the DCI Field & Sales Force Automation Conference, Boston, October 1996. 'Sale Pro Emphasises the Personal Touch', *Marketing News* (American Marketing Association), 4 November 1996, page 8. Reprinted with permission.

5 Our life is frittered away by detail . . . Simplify, simplify.

H. D. THOREAU (1817–62), American poet, naturalist and essayist. *Where I Lived, and What I Lived for.*

23 determination

See also: challenge 8; defeat 21; failure 30; persistence & perseverance 71; success 98

1 Most folks are about as happy as they make up their minds to be.

ABRAHAM LINCOLN (1809–65), American statesman, and 16th President of the United States of America 1861–65. Attrib.

2 To succeed, you have to believe in something with such a passion that it becomes a reality.

ANITA RODDICK, British businesswoman, co-founder and Chief Executive of The Body Shop International. *Body and Soul* (Hutchinson, London, 1991).

3 I knew what I wanted. You never listen to people who say no. The only one who can defeat you is yourself.

SIDNEY SHELDON, American author, screenwriter and playwright. *OK! Magazine*, August 1995.

4 I want to make this movie so much I'd stab *myself* in the back.

JOEL SILVER, American film producer. Comment made about the feature film *Die Hard*. Attrib.

5 My dad has always said to me: You are in the game of life. You
   can either get off the boat or you can hang on in there. It
   doesn't matter whether you win or lose. The important thing is
   to stay on board.

> EMMA STEELE, British television presenter. Comments made in reference to
> her father, singer, actor and dancer Tommy Steele. *Hello!*, 23 September 1995.

discretion 24

See also: decisions 20; judgement 48

1 Judgement is not upon all occasions required, but discretion
   always is.

> LORD CHESTERFIELD (Philip Dormer Stanhope, 4th Earl of Chesterfield;
> 1694–1773), British statesman. Letter to his godson, 1766.

2 He who treads softly goes far.

> CHINESE PROVERB.

3 Act so in the valley that you need not fear those who stand on
   the hill.

> DANISH PROVERB.

4 Discretion is the better part of valour.

> ENGLISH PROVERB.

5 Look before you leap.

> ENGLISH PROVERB.

6 Do not try to fly before you have wings.

> FRENCH PROVERB.

7 A dram of discretion is worth a pound of wisdom.

> GERMAN PROVERB.

25 do it now

See also: getting started 35

1 Procrastination is a total barrier to the acquisition of purposeful action. Nothing should be put off until another time, not even for a few minutes. That which ought to be done now should be done now. This seems a little thing, but it is of far-reaching importance. It leads to strength, success, and peace.

> JAMES ALLEN, American theologian and author. *The Mastery of Destiny* (Putnam, New York, 1909).

2 Let us do something, while we have the chance! It is not every day that we are needed.

> SAMUEL BECKETT (1906–89), Irish playwright, author, critic and Nobel laureate. *Waiting for Godot*, play (1954).

3 When you did make a deal with him, he wanted to dictate the terms with you right there in your office. He had no patience with lawyers. He was a master of the first law of agenting: Close the deal, don't tap dance.

> DAVID BROWN, American film producer. Comment made about Hollywood agent Irving 'Swifty' Lazar, *Vanity Fair*, April 1994.

4 Life isn't a rehearsal. This is it and the day you are born is opening night. When I am an old man, I want to regret the things I did instead of the things I didn't do.

> MICHAEL CAINE, British actor. Quoted in Sarah Sheppard, 'Citizen Caine', *Weekend Australian*, 7 December 1996. © The Weekend Australian.

5 Defer not till tomorrow to be wise, tomorrow's sun to thee may never rise.

> WILLIAM CONGREVE (1670–1729), British dramatist. *Letter to Cobham*.

6 Cosby stumbles along, doing as well as he can and doing it in the here and now. The past is a ghost, the future a dream, and all we ever *have* is now.

> BILL COSBY, American comic, actor, and film and television producer and director. *Time Flies* (Dolphin Doubleday, New York, 1987).

7 Once you've agreed a resolution to a customer complaint, once you have undertaken to pursue a course of action on the customer's behalf, DO IT NOW! Not tomorrow. Not next week . . . If you want to satisfy and recover the customer, DO IT NOW!

> STEPHEN DANDO-COLLINS, Australian author and editor. *The Customer Care Revolution* (Pitman, Melbourne, 1996).

8 If you want the world to change, don't complain about it. Do something. Rather than using up your present moments with all kinds of immobilising anxiety over what you are putting off, take charge of this nasty erroneous zone and live now! Be a doer, not a wisher, hoper or critic.

> WAYNE W. DYER, American psychiatrist and author. *Your Erroneous Zones* (Michael Joseph, London, 1977).

9 The wise do at once what the fool does later.

> BALTASAR GRACIAN (1601–58), Spanish Jesuit priest and author. *The Art of Worldly Wisdom* (1647).

10 He started to sing
As he tackled the thing
That couldn't be done,
And he did it.

> EDGAR A. GUEST (1881–1959), British-born American poet and author. *A Heap o' Livin'* (1916).

11 Gather ye rosebuds while ye may,
Old Time is still a-flying,

And this same flower that smiles today
Tomorrow will be dying.

> ROBERT HERRICK (c. 1591–1674), British poet and cleric. *To the Virgins, to make much of Time* (c. 1648).

12 I suffer from procrastination occasionally. Sometimes I fly half the night to get to my next seminar, and then the next morning I don't want to learn the program I must learn. But I live by three words: DO IT NOW. Try them for 21 days and you'll start a whole new power pattern that will open up new vistas of opportunity for your future.

> TOM HOPKINS, American sales trainer, motivator and author. *How to Master the Art of Selling* (Champion Press, Scottsdale, Arizona, 1982; republished HarperCollins, London, 1994).

13 Seize today, and put as little trust as you can in tomorrow.

> HORACE (Quintus Horatius Flaccus; 65–8 BC), Roman poet and satirist. *Odes* (c. 23–15 BC).

14 Do it, I say! Whatever you want to do, do it *now*! There are only so many tomorrows.

> MICHAEL LANDON (1936–91), American actor, producer and director. Attrib.

15 In our business, the windows of opportunity open and close with dazzling rapidity . . . You'd think everyone would appreciate that. Yet I constantly have to remind people to seize the moment.

> MARK H. McCORMACK, American sports marketing consultant, founder and CEO of International Management Group, and author. *McCormack on Managing* (Century, London, 1995).

16 I don't take tomorrow for granted, because it simply may not be there.

> MARY TYLER MOORE, American actress. *Saturday Evening Post*, November–December 1995.

17 Put off until tomorrow only what you are willing to die having left undone.

>PABLO PICASSO (1881–1973), Spanish artist. Attrib.

18 One of these days is none of these days.

>ENGLISH PROVERB.

19 Tomorrow is the day on which lazy people have the most to do.

>NORWEGIAN PROVERB.

20 These days, if something begins to go wrong, I don't turn my back on it and hope it will go away. I pull it up short. 'Let's face this unpleasant situation now, before it gets any worse.'

>LANA TURNER (1920–95), American actress and author. Lana Turner & Hollis Alpert, *Lana, the Lady, the Legend, the Truth* (E. P. Dutton, New York, 1982). Copyright © 1982 by Eltee Productions and Hollis Alpert. Used by permission of Dutton Signet, a division of Penguin Books USA Inc.

21 My object was always to do the business of the day in the day.

>DUKE OF WELLINGTON (Arthur Wellesley; 1769–1852), British soldier, commander of British armies during the Napoleonic wars, statesman, and Prime Minister 1828–30. Attrib.

22 In a longish life as a professional writer, I have heard a thousand masterpieces talked out over bars, restaurant tables and love seats. I have never seen one of them in print. Books must be written, not talked.

>MORRIS L. WEST, Australian author. 'How to Write a Novel', in A. S. Burack (ed.), *The Writer's Handbook* (The Writer, Boston, 1978).

23 Procrastination is the thief of time.

>EDWARD YOUNG (1683–1765), British poet and playwright. *Night Thoughts* (1742–46).

'Teachers of elementary economics or money and banking begin with definitions of genuine subtlety. These are then carefully transcribed, painfully memorised and mercifully forgotten.'
JOHN KENNETH GALBRAITH'

economics & economists 26:3

economics & economists 26

See also: money 62; profits 81; statistics 96

1 Economists are people who, when they take a cab, sit looking
out the rear window – because in their jobs they are so used to
looking at where we have been, rather than looking ahead to
where we are going.

ANON.

2 Economists have successfully predicted eight of the last four
national economic downturns.

ANON.

3 Television interviewers with a reputation for penetrating
thought regularly begin interviews with economists with the
question: 'Now tell me, just what is money anyway?' The
answers invariably are incoherent. Teachers of elementary economics or money and banking begin with definitions of genuine
subtlety. These are then carefully transcribed, painfully memorised and mercifully forgotten.

JOHN KENNETH GALBRAITH, Canadian-born American economist,
Emeritus Professor of Economics at Harvard University, former senior White
House adviser, diplomat and author. *Money: Whence it Came, Where it Went*
(Penguin, New York; André Deutsch, London, 1975). Copyright © John
Kenneth Galbraith, 1975, 1995.

4 In a way, my whole experience with the computer industry has
been a series of economics lessons. I saw firsthand the effects
of positive spirals and inflexible business models. I watched the
way industry standards evolved. I witnessed the importance of

compatibility in technology, of feedback, and of constant innovation. And I think we may be about to witness the realisation of
Adam Smith's ideal market, at last.

BILL GATES, American information technology pioneer, founder and CEO
of Microsoft Corporation, and author. *The Road Ahead* (Viking Penguin, New
York, 1995). Copyright © 1995 by William H. Gates III. Used by permission
of Viking Penguin, a division of Penguin Books USA Inc.

5 The famous 80–20 rule, set out by a 19th century Italian economist, is basic to better management. Pareto [Vilfredo Pareto,
1848–1923] observed that in any series, a small proportion
accounted for a large share of the outcome; hence the law's
description: 'the significant few and the insignificant many.'
Translating that into business terms, 80 per cent of a firm's
profits will come from 20 per cent of its products; and 80 per
cent of its sales from 20 per cent of its customers.

Analysing a business in this light shows the management where
to concentrate its efforts – and, very possibly, which customers to
drop and which product lines to cast into outer darkness. But the
usefulness of Pareto's Law doesn't stop there. It also tells you that
80 per cent of the value of your stock will be accounted for by 20
per cent of the items held: that 80 per cent of the costs of an
assembly will be accounted for by 20 per cent of the components
– and, again, this analysis is an essential guide to action.

Concentrate on tight control of the significant 20 per cent
and you will achieve vastly greater savings than from effort
wasted on the insignificant 80 per cent.

ROBERT HELLER, British academic and author. *The Pocket Manager*
(Hodder & Stoughton, London, 1985). Reproduced by permission of A. P.
Watt Ltd on behalf of Heller Arts Limited.

6 Economic growth without social progress lets the great majority of the people remain in poverty, while a privileged few reap
the benefits of rising abundance.

JOHN F. KENNEDY (1917–63), American statesman, and 35th President of the United States of America 1960–63. In a message to Congress on the Inter-American Fund for Social Progress, 14 March 1961.

7 Practical men, who believe themselves to be quite exempt from any intellectual influences, are usually the slaves of some defunct economist.

JOHN MAYNARD KEYNES (1883–1946), British economist, financier, journalist and author. Attrib.

8 We need a new economic order for the 21st century. This new economic order must be geared to the real needs of people and the Earth. It must be both enabling and conserving. It must restore to the word 'wealth' its original meaning of wellbeing. It must harmonise economy with ecology, in accordance with the proper meanings of these words – as the management and the science of our earthly home. It must accept that the era of 'the wealth of nations' is past, and treat the 21st century economy as a multi-level one-world economy.

JAMES ROBERTSON, British economist and author. *Future Wealth* (Cassell, London, 1989). Reproduced by permission of Mansell Publishing (a Cassell imprint), London. All rights reserved.

9 If all economists were laid end to end, they would not reach a conclusion.

GEORGE BERNARD SHAW (1856–1950), Irish playwright and critic, Nobel laureate 1925. Attrib.

10 If we are to expose what is unproved and in general try to demystify the language of economists, we must to some extent fight them on their own technical ground, where they seem to hold sway completely. Occupying the high technical ground with a boldness and confidence that to me is not justified, economists have been able to cow the public, press,

policy makers and politicians in ways not usually open to academics and technical people. Paradoxically, this happens even while economists are not held in especially high repute.

LESTER C. THUROW, American sociologist, professor at Massachusetts Institute of Technology and author. *Dangerous Currents* (Random House, New York, 1983). Copyright © 1983 by Lester C. Thurow Inc. Reprinted by permission of Random House Inc.

27 efficiency

See also: progress 82; punctuality 85; quality 87

1 A clean desk is a sign of a sick mind.

ANON.

2 A desk is a wastebasket with drawers.

ANON.

3 Don't make the mistake of confusing activity with progress.

ANON.

4 The only person who got everything done by Friday was Robinson Crusoe.

ANON.

5 There is always a best way of doing everything, even if it be to boil an egg.

RALPH WALDO EMERSON (1803–82), American philosopher, poet and essayist. 'Behaviour', *The Conduct of Life* (1860).

6 The Second Law [of thermodynamics] is one piece of technical bad news from science that has established itself firmly in the nonscientific culture. Everything tends towards disorder ... Perfect efficiency is impossible. The universe is a one-way street.

JAMES GLEICK, American academic and author. *Chaos* (Penguin, New York, 1987). Copyright © 1987 by James Gleick. Reprinted by permission of William Morris Agency, Inc, on behalf of the author.

7 It is easy to lose ourselves in efficiency, to treat that efficiency as an end in itself and not a means to other ends.

CHARLES HANDY, British academic, business consultant and author. *The Age of Paradox* (Harvard Business School Press, Cambridge, Massachusetts, 1994).

8 A new broom is good for three days.

ITALIAN PROVERB.

9 To do two things at once is to do neither.

PUBLILIUS SYRUS (1st century BC), Syrian-born Roman mime writer. *Moral Sayings.*

employees 28

See also: human nature 39; people 70; teams & teamwork 100

1 Keeping employees involved in the success of the company and abreast of company developments is also an important part of customer service because they will understand the benefits of their hard work. Employees who are informed and involved in the total picture will be happier and more enthusiastic and this will show in the way they treat their customers.

CHARLIE BELL, Australian business leader and CEO of McDonald's Australia. In a foreword to Stephen Dando-Collins, *The Customer Care Revolution* (Pitman, Melbourne, 1996).

2 Winning companies . . . realise they are only as strong as the intelligence, judgement and character of their employees.

GEORGE BUSH, American statesman, and 41st President of the United

States of America 1989–93. In a speech made at the Malcolm Baldridge National Quality Awards, Washington DC, 1990.

3 In order to become a customer-oriented company, extensive changes will be required on the part of frontline employees.

JAN CARLZON, Swedish business leader, former CEO of Scandinavian Airlines System, speaker and author. *Moments of Truth* (Ballinger, Cambridge, Massachusetts, 1987; revised edition HarperCollins, New York, 1989). Copyright © 1987 by Ballinger Publishing Company. Reprinted by permission of HarperCollins Publishers, Inc.

4 Too many companies, especially large ones, are driven more and more narrowly by the need to ensure that investors get good quarterly returns and to justify executives' high salaries. Too often, this means that they view most employees as costs, not investments, and that they expend less and less concern on job training, employee profit sharing, family-friendly policies, shared decision making, or even fair pay rises that share with workers – not to mention their families and communities – gains from productivity and profit.

HILLARY RODHAM CLINTON, American lawyer, and First Lady of the United States of America 1993– . *It Takes a Village* (Simon & Schuster, New York, 1996).

5 Start with good people, lay out the rules, communicate with your employees, motivate them, and reward them if they perform.

LEE IACOCCA, American automotive industry leader, former CEO of Chrysler Motors, and director of several other auto manufacturing companies, and author. *Talking Straight* (Bantam, New York, 1988). Copyright © 1988 by Lee Iacocca. Used by permission of Bantam Books, a division of Bantam Doubleday Dell Publishing Group Inc.

6 I feel that you have to be with your employees through all their difficulties, that you have to be interested in them personally.

They may be disappointed in their country. Even their family might not be working out the way they wish it would. But I want them to know that Southwest will always be there for them.

HERB KELLEHER, American airline executive and CEO of Southwest Airlines. *Fortune*, 2 May 1994. © 1994 Time Inc. All rights reserved.

7 The workforce today is screaming for flexibility. If you can help employees meet their outside responsibilities, you're going to have a more productive, more turned on, and more energised workforce. Flexibility is a business tool.

ROBERT LAMBERT, American retailing executive and Executive Vice President of Carter Hawley Stores. *Wall Street Journal*, 13 January 1994. Reprinted by permission of the Wall Street Journal. © 1994 Dow Jones & Company Inc. All Rights Reserved Worldwide.

8 For us, the core of management is the art of mobilising and pulling together the intellectual resources of all employees in the service of the firm. We have measured the scope of the technological and economic challenges – we know that the intelligence of a handful of technocrats, however brilliant, is no longer enough to take them up with a real chance of success. Only by drawing on the combined brain power of all its employees can a firm face up to the turbulence and constraints of today's environment.

KONOSUKE MATSUSHITA, Japanese industrialist and executive adviser to Matsushita Electric Industrial Co, Japan. Quoted in Stephen R. Covey, A. Roger Merrill & Rebecca R. Merrill, *First Things First* (Fireside, New York, 1995).

9 It's a rare employee who can envision his firm's need for economy. A company president who is personally open-handed complained to me: 'During the course of the year I have hundreds of requests from our people for this or that expenditure, but hardly anyone ever comes to me with a suggestion as

to how we could save money.' Just think how favourably one of his young men would make himself stand out by thinking up some money-saving ideas!

ALEX F. OSBORN (1888–1966), American academic and author. *Applied Imagination: Principles & Procedures of Creative Thinking* (Charles Scribner's Sons, New York, 1953).

10 Today's workforce . . . increasingly responds to *sell* rather than tell. Employees want to be considered seriously, to be persuaded and negotiated with. Managers who deal with their employees in this mode usually get greater productivity and loyalty from employees.

THOMAS L. QUICK, American consultant and author. *Power Plays* (Franklin Watts, Danbury, Connecticut, 1985).

11 More and more workers are dissatisfied with being handed table scraps while irresponsible senior executives raid the payroll pantry with impunity. Yet avaricious leaders escape accountability and deny their followers proportional raises and bonuses. As a result, the gap between accomplishment and reward has broadened for many conscientious and capable workers. Those excluded from career and financial opportunities look outside the work world for other kinds of satisfaction.

WESS ROBERTS, American author. *Victory Secrets of Attila the Hun*, (Bantam, London, 1993).

12 When I took over Semco from my father twelve years ago, it was a traditional company in every respect, with a pyramidal structure and a rule for every contingency. But today, our factory workers sometimes set their own production quotas and even come in on their own time to meet them, without prodding from management or overtime pay. They help redesign the products they make and formulate the marketing plans. Their bosses, for their part, can run our business units with extraordinary

freedom, determining business strategy without interference from the top brass. They even set their own salaries, with no strings. Then again, everyone will know what they are, since all financial information at Semco is openly discussed. Indeed, our workers have unlimited access to our books – and we only keep one set. To show we are serious about this, Semco, with the labour unions that represent our workers, developed a course to teach everyone, even messengers and cleaning people, to read balance sheets and cash-flow statements.

For truly big decisions, such as buying another company, everyone at Semco gets a vote. A few years ago, when we wanted to relocate a factory, we closed down for a day and everyone piled into buses to inspect three possible new sites. Then the workers decided.

RICARDO SEMLER, Brazilian industrialist, CEO of Semco, Brazil, and author. *Maverick!* (Century, London, 1993). Copyright © 1993 by Tableturn Inc. Reproduced by permission of the author c/o Rogers, Coleridge & White Ltd, 20 Powis Mews, London W11 1JN.

expectations 29
See also: change 9; defeat 21; failure 30;
goals & goal-setting 36; limitations 53; success 98;
winners & winning 106

1 Expect nothing, and you can never be disappointed. You might even be pleasantly surprised from time to time.

ANON.

2 For people who live on expectations, to face up to their realisation is something of an ordeal.

ELIZABETH BOWEN (1899–1973), Anglo-Irish author. *The Death of the Heart* (1938; republished Jonathan Cape, London, 1967).

3 Nothing is so good as it seems beforehand.

> GEORGE ELIOT (pen name of Mary Ann Cross nee Evans; 1819–80), British novelist. *Silas Marner* (1861).

4 Prospect is often better than possession.

> THOMAS FULLER M.D. (1654–1734), British physician and author. *Gnomologia* (1732).

5 The best part of our lives we pass in counting on what is to come.

> WILLIAM HAZLITT (1778–1830), British critic, poet and essayist. 'On Novelty and Familiarity', *The Plain Speaker* (1826).

6 I've got enough of that Fagan Irish in me to believe that if the curtains are washed, company never comes. If you expect nothing but trouble, maybe a few happy days will turn up. If you expect happy days, look out.

> BILLIE HOLIDAY (aka Lady Day; 1915–59), American blues singer. *Lady Sings the Blues* (Doubleday, New York, 1956).

7 Blessed is he who expects nothing, for he shall never be disappointed.

> ALEXANDER POPE (1688–1744), British satirist and poet. In a letter to John Gay, 6 October 1727.

8 I am a perfectionist, and that brings self-imposed pressures, expectations – and those expectations are landmines.

> CRAIG WARREN, Australian professional golfer. *Sydney Morning Herald*, 30 November 1996.

'Any style of success must also include
a style of failure.'
EDWARD DE BONO

failure 30:10

30 failure

See also: defeat 21; limitations 53; losing 55; obstacles 66; opportunity 68; success 98

1 Australia embraces failure. We celebrate it constantly. Our entire mythology is based on unhappy endings. Look at Gallipoli, Simpson and his donkey, Phar Lap, Les Darcy, Burke and Wills and Gough Whitlam. Australia has, for centuries, conditioned itself to the fizzer, the flop, the dying cadence, the also-ran, the retreat, the defeat. Where other nations, particularly the Americans, go for success, victory, triumphalism, we are more comfortable with coming last.

> PHILLIP ADAMS, Australian broadcaster, columnist and author. *Weekend Australian,* 31 August 1996. © The Weekend Australian.

2 Inventors are original and prolific but not necessarily good business people. Their failure rate is extraordinarily high – 92 per cent. Only one in 1000 inventors gets a product to market. Only one in 5000 dies rich.

> EMMA ALBERICI, Australian television producer, journalist and author. *The Small Business Book* (Penguin, Victoria, 1995).

3 Failures are steps in the ladder of success.

> JAMES ALLEN, American theologian and author. *The Mastery of Destiny* (Putnam, New York, 1909).

4 A setback is when everyone writes to commiserate with you. Failure is when everyone writes you off.

> ANON.

5 Failure is never fatal. Success is never final.

ANON.

6 You have to think of it as an adventure, rather than think, 'If this fails, I fail, and my whole life is a failure.' You have to understand what you're about and also what you want.

LYSETTE ANTHONY, British actress. *Tatler*, November 1991.

7 It's [i.e. New York is] a fantastic place to be at the top of your game. To be young. To be in the thick of it. It is not a place to get older. It is not a place to fail. It is not a place to be off your form.

TINA BROWN, British-born American-based magazine editor, Editor of *The New Yorker*. *The Guardian*, 23 October 1996. The Guardian ©.

8 Failure plays a surprisingly prominent part in many business success stories. Henry Ford, it is said, only developed the Model T because the tractors he built were failures. Edison's 'ticker tape' machine worked, but his failure to secure the patents 'forced' him to look for new areas for work – like developing electric lighting. It is surprisingly hard to find successful managers who got it right first time. The willingness to get up after getting knocked down and to learn from failure is perhaps the single most enduring feature of greatness in managers.

TOM CANNON, British academic, visiting professor, business consultant, broadcaster and author. *How to Get Ahead in Business* (Virgin, London, 1993).

9 The proactive approach to a mistake is to acknowledge it instantly, correct and learn from it. This literally turns a failure into a success.

STEPHEN R. COVEY, American educator, leadership consultant, author and former Professor of Business Management at Brigham Young University. *The 7 Habits of Highly Effective People* (Simon & Schuster, New York, 1989).

10 Any style of success must also include a style of failure. Failure takes different people different ways. It can utterly destroy or build a person's confidence; it can activate a spiral of depression or be a stimulus.

> EDWARD DE BONO, Maltese-born British scholar, teacher, lecturer and author. *Tactics: The Art and Science of Success* (Collins, London, 1985). Reprinted by permission of HarperCollins Publishers Limited.

11 What determines whether failure stops a person or not is how the failure is held . . . I recognise I am the cause . . . When I can hold my failures, it makes me bigger than the failure.

> WERNER ERHARD, American spiritualist and founder of EST. Quoted in Edward de Bono, *Tactics: The Art and Science of Success* (Collins, London, 1985). Reprinted by permission of HarperCollins Publishers Limited.

12 When I was nineteen I caught a look at the future, based my career on what I saw, and I turned out to have been right. But the Bill Gates of nineteen was in a very different position from the one I'm in now. In those days, not only did I have all the self-assurance of a smart teenager, but also nobody was watching me, and if I failed – so what? Today, I am much more in the position of the computer giants of the seventies, but I hope I've learned some lessons from them.

> BILL GATES, American information technology pioneer, founder and CEO of Microsoft Corporation, and author. *The Road Ahead* (Viking Penguin, New York, 1995). Copyright © 1995 by William H. Gates III. Used by permission of Viking Penguin, a division of Penguin Books USA Inc.

13 If you want to earn your living in the theatre you are bound to be in some failures during your career. All the great people – Edith Evans, Laurence Olivier, Peggy Ashcroft – have had their failures at one time or another. It is very interesting, looking back, to see why certain things went wrong. When Beaumont [Hugh 'Binkie' Beaumont, British impresario] was alive I used

sometimes to stay with him at the weekends to try to discuss some production in which he was concerned which had failed, but his other friends would say: 'Not to be mentioned in this house. It's dynamite.' It seems to me that when a play is a failure it is fascinating, once the disappointment has worn off, to examine where you went wrong. A play is always a great experiment. The director, the cast, the way that rehearsals proceed, the rows with the designer, the different ways the play goes through a try-out – all these things contribute. It is very important, when it is all over, to look back and see where the mistakes were, because you work just as hard in a failure as in a success.

JOHN GIELGUD, British actor. With John Miller, *An Actor and His Time* (Sidgwick & Jackson, London, 1979; Applause Books, New York, 1979).

14 The moment you let avoiding failure become your motivator, you're down the path of inactivity. You can stumble only if you're moving.

ROBERTO GOIZUETA (1932–97), Cuban-born American industrialist and CEO of Coca-Cola. *Fortune*, 1 May 1995. © 1995 Time Inc. All rights reserved.

15 If having a knighthood and a coat of arms is supposed to change your attitude towards life then I failed. I always was and always will be the same Jim Hardy.

JAMES HARDY, Australian businessman, Olympian and world champion yachtsman, and author. *An Adventurous Life* (Margaret Gee, Melbourne, 1993; republished Penguin, Victoria, 1995).

16 Half the failures in life arise from pulling in one's horse as he is leaping.

JULIUS CHARLES HARE (1795–1855) and AUGUSTUS WILLIAM HARE (1792–1834), brothers, British clergymen and authors. *Guesses at Truth* (1827).

17 Failure is not an option.

> ED HARRIS, American actor. Line spoken in the role of Gene Krantz, NASA flight director at Mission Control, Houston, in the film *Apollo 13* (Universal Studios, 1995).

18 People who are just in it for money – they usually fail.

> ROBERT HOLMES À COURT, Australian business tycoon. Quoted in Edward de Bono, *Tactics: The Art and Science of Success* (Collins, London, 1985).

19 It's often the fear of failure that makes us bottle up our wants. But failure isn't the worst possible result. Not trying is. If you try you can succeed; if you won't try you have already failed.

> TOM HOPKINS, American sales trainer, motivator and author. *How to Master the Art of Selling* (Champion Press, Scottsdale, Arizona, 1982; republished HarperCollins, London, 1994).

20 There is no failure except in no longer trying.

> ELBERT HUBBARD (1856–1915), American businessman, printer and writer. *The Note Book* (1927).

21 Someone once said that in the great undertakings there is glory even in failure.

> LEE IACOCCA, American automotive industry leader, former CEO of Chrysler Motors, and director of several other auto manufacturing companies, and author. *Iacocca: An Autobiography* (Bantam, New York, 1984; Sidgwick & Jackson, London, 1984). Copyright © 1984 by Lee Iacocca. Used by permission of Bantam Books, a division of Bantam Doubleday Dell Publishing Group Inc.

22 If you haven't had a failure in this business, you haven't been around long enough.

> SANDRA LEVY, Australian film and television producer. *Good Weekend Magazine*, 23 November 1996.

23 If there were but a single thing parents could do to help a child who has entrepreneurial tendencies develop into a successful entrepreneur, it would be to let the youngster know it is all right to fail and that a person's worth is not measured by the results of an inning, or quarter, but rather by the score that can be calculated at the end of the game of life.

> ARTHUR LIPPER III, American businessman. In a foreword to Russel R. Taylor, *Exceptional Entrepreneurial Women* (Praeger, New York, 1988).

24 I think the reason marriage is less forgiving than living together is that married people are formally recognised as a team. It's close to a business partnership. When a business fails, there's a social judgement.

> NORMAN MAILER, American novelist and essayist. *Vanity Fair*, November 1991.

25 Fear of failure is at least as common as the desire for success. In fact, if properly harnessed, it can be the energy that drives the wheel.

> MARK H. McCORMACK, American sports marketing consultant, founder and CEO of International Management Group, and author. *What They Don't Tell You at Harvard Business School* (Collins, London, 1984). Reprinted by permission of HarperCollins Publishers Limited.

26 The two most dangerous factors in an actor's life are success and failure. Failure is dangerous because it makes you insecure and unbalanced. But success is just as bad because you can be trapped by it very quickly.

> HELEN MIRREN, British actress. *Hello!*, 25 February 1995.

27 TOLERATE FAILURE. Top innovators constantly explore ideas that ultimately lead nowhere. Thomas Edison may hold the US record for patents at 1093, but many of these are in fact worthless contraptions. You will win some and lose some.

> NOKIA CORPORATION. From magazine advertisement, 1996.

28 Why do eight out of ten new consumer products fail? Sometimes because they are *too* new. The first cold cereals were rejected by consumers. More often new products fail because they are not new *enough*. They do not offer any perceptible point of difference – like better quality, better flavour, better value, more convenience or better solutions to problems.

DAVID OGILVY, British-born American advertising expert, founder of Ogilvy & Mather international advertising group, New York, and author. *Ogilvy on Advertising* (Pan, London, 1983).

29 Most photographers of my age started taking photographs because they failed at something else. I failed as an architect. Photography only became an acceptable job a few decades ago and I fear that now it's all too serious. For me photography is a way of recording things because I can't draw.

LORD SNOWDON (Anthony Armstrong-Jones), British photographer. *Snowdon: Sittings 1979–1983* (Weidenfeld & Nicolson, London, 1983).

30 My dad once said to me, if you can't fail, you can't do anything, and it was brilliant advice. That made me see that it's important not to be afraid.

EMMA THOMPSON, British actress and screenwriter. *OK! Magazine*, May 1993.

31 Success can deaden an organisation's responses. The executives who presided over the near-collapse of some of the world's greatest corporations all were leaders of proven ability. Their failures stemmed from reliance on ideas and practices that worked splendidly in earlier times. The times changed and they didn't.

NOEL M. TICHY, American academic and author, and STRATFORD SHERMAN, American journalist and author. *Control Your Destiny or Someone Else Will* (Doubleday, New York, 1993). Copyright © 1993 by Noel M. Tichy and Stratford Sherman. Used by permission of Doubleday, a division of Bantam Doubleday Dell Publishing Group, Inc.

32 Often the assumption is that failed businesses are run by crooks. Sometimes they are, but they are also run by people who tried hard but had bad luck or made too many mistakes.

> SARA WILLIAMS, British financial journalist and author, and BOB SIMS, British accountant and author. *Lloyds Bank Small Business Guide* (Penguin, London, 1987; adapted as *The Australian Small Business Guide*, Penguin, Victoria, 1993).

33 Failure is not a crime. Failure to learn from failure is.

> WALTER WRISTON, American finance industry leader, Chairman of Citicorp. In a speech made in Washington DC, 18 September 1981.

focus 31

See also: determination 23; purpose 86; success 98

1 The best focus is always the narrowest one. And the game becomes far easier and the pressure far less if each player concentrates on the ball he is about to face.

> MICHAEL ATHERTON, British sportsman and captain of the England (MCC) cricket team. 'I Won't Walk Out on England', *Weekly Telegraph*, 8 January 1997.

2 Devoting a little of yourself to everything means committing a great deal of yourself to nothing. This leaves you unable to concentrate on those very few projects that have the highest pay-off per investment of your time and energy. Why scatter your efforts by using the shotgun approach when you can concentrate them and be a big gun?

> JACK COLLIS, Australian business lecturer and author, and MICHAEL LEBOEUF, American business consultant, speaker and author, Professor of Management at the University of New Orleans. *Work Smarter Not Harder* (Goal Setting Seminars, 1988; republished HarperBusiness, Sydney, 1995.)

3 Being best in the neighbourhood isn't good enough any more. Companies must look good against the best in the world just to survive in the neighbourhood. Inward-focused organisations must become outward focused, and isolated ones must become network linked. Small and local businesses must join the world class.

ROSABETH MOSS KANTER, American academic and author, professor at Harvard Business School. *World Class* (Simon & Schuster, New York, 1995).

4 A company can become incredibly successful if it can find a way to own a word in the mind of the prospect. Not a complicated word. Not an invented one. The simple words are the best, words taken right out of the dictionary. This is the law of focus. You burn your way into the mind by narrowing the focus to a single word or concept. It's the ultimate marketing sacrifice.

AL RIES and JACK TROUT, American marketing consultants and business authors. *The 22 Immutable Laws of Marketing* (HarperCollins, New York, 1993). Copyright © 1993 by Al Ries and Jack Trout. Reprinted by permission of HarperCollins Publishers, Inc.

5 One of the keys to thinking big is total focus.

DONALD TRUMP, American entrepreneur, developer and author. *Trump: The Art of the Deal* (Century Hutchinson, London, 1988).

32 follow through

See also: do it now 25

1 He loses thanks who promises and delays.
ENGLISH PROVERB.

2 He that promises too much means nothing.
ENGLISH PROVERB.

3 You can create excitement, you can do wonderful promotion and get all kinds of press, and you can throw in a little hyperbole. But if you don't deliver the goods, people will eventually catch on.

> DONALD TRUMP, American entrepreneur, developer and author. *Trump: The Art of the Deal* (Century Hutchinson, London, 1988).

future, the 33

See also: change 9; communication & communicating 11; computers 13; information 44; technology 101

1 There are sources of business profits waiting for us in the future that are only yet in the minds of their creators.

> ANON.

2 To most people, the future is like heaven – sounds great, but they're not ready for it yet.

> ANON.

3 If you want to be one of the first into a new territory you cannot wait for large amounts of evidence. Poring over numbers can't help you see what is ahead.

> JOEL BARKER, American futurist and author. *Success*, April 1992.

4 Let me ask whether cyberspace may also replace some of our transportation needs of the future.

> ULRICH BEZ, German automotive engineer, Vice President of engineering and product development at Daewoo Corporation, Korea, and formerly senior designer with BMW and Porsche. *The Bulletin*, 24 September 1996.

5 What you are now comes from what you have been, and what you will be is what you do now.

THE BUDDHA (Siddhartha Gautama; c. 563 BC – c. 483 BC), Indian teacher and religious leader, and the founder of Buddhism.

6 The day is not far off when unemotional machines may decide that humans are a nuisance and that the world could run more efficiently without them.

> ROLAND BURNS, British academic, Professor of Control Engineering and Director/Joint Head of the Plymouth Teaching Company Centre, Plymouth University, England. *Weekly Telegraph*, 18 September, 1996.

7 There's nothing so hard to find tomorrow as yesterday's paper.

> BEN CHIFLEY (1885–1951), Australian statesman, and Prime Minister 1945–49. Attrib.

8 The empires of the future will be the empires of the mind.

> WINSTON CHURCHILL (1874–1965), British statesman, Prime Minister 1940–45 and 1951–55, artist, historian, author and Nobel laureate. Attrib.

9 In projecting our ideas into the future, much of the technology that exists now is going to be around for the next hundred years. But about every ten years there will come along something completely unexpected, like the transistor and its successors, which will bring in a new dimension.

> ARTHUR C. CLARKE, British author. Quoted in Neil McAleer, *Odyssey: The Authorised Biography of Arthur C. Clarke* (Victor Gollancz, London, 1992).

10 To deal with the future we have to deal with 'possibilities.' Analysis will only tell us 'what is.'

> EDWARD DE BONO, Maltese-born British scholar, teacher, lecturer and author. *Parallel Thinking: From Socratic to de Bono Thinking* (Viking, London, 1994). Copyright © McQuaig Group Inc, 1994.

11 Humanity now faces the greatest crisis in its history. Our planet's very habitability is threatened by overpopulation and

high rates of population growth, excessive consumption, and the frequent use of environmentally malign technologies. If we are to maintain our civilisation, the number of people will have to be gradually lowered by controlling births until it is within the long-term carrying capacity of the planet. Simultaneously, wasteful consumption must be curbed and more suitable technologies deployed. All these steps will require social discussion and political action.

PAUL R. EHRLICH, American academic, Bing Professor of Population Studies at Stanford University, and author. In a preface to Cassandra Pybus & Richard Flanagan (eds), *The Rest of the World is Watching* (Pan Macmillan, Sydney, 1990).

12 I never think of the future. It comes soon enough.

ALBERT EINSTEIN (1879–1955), German–Swiss–American physicist. Attrib.

13 Neither a wise man nor a brave man lies down on the tracks of history to wait for the train of the future to run over him.

DWIGHT D. EISENHOWER (1890–1969), American general and statesman, and 34th President of the United States of America 1953–61. In a campaign speech, October 1952.

14 He that fears not the future may enjoy the present.

THOMAS FULLER M.D. (1654–1734), British physician and author. *Gnomologia* (1732).

15 There will be a day, not far distant, when you will be able to conduct business, study, explore the world and its cultures, call up any great entertainment, make friends, attend neighbourhood markets, and show pictures to distant relatives – without leaving your desk or armchair. You won't leave your network connection behind at the office or in the classroom. It will be more than an object you carry or an appliance you purchase. It will be your passport into a new, mediated way of life.

16 Organisations will become both smaller and bigger at the same time; they will be flatter, more flexible, and more dispersed; similarly our working lives will have to be flatter and more flexible. Life will be unreasonable in the sense that it won't go on as it used to; we shall have to make things happen for us rather than wait for them to happen.

CHARLES HANDY, British academic, business consultant and author. *The Age of Paradox* (Harvard Business School Press, Cambridge, Massachusetts, 1994).

17 The new shape of work will centre around small organisations, most of them in the service sector, with a small core of key people and a collection of stringers or portfolio workers in the space around the core.

CHARLES HANDY, British academic, business consultant and author. *The Age of Paradox* (Harvard Business School Press, Cambridge, Massachusetts, 1994).

18 All things considered, it looks as though Utopia were far closer to us than anyone, only fifteen years ago [in 1931], could have imagined. Then, I projected it six hundred years into the future. Today it seems quite possible that the horror may be upon us within a single century. That is, if we refrain from blowing ourselves to smithereens in the interval. Indeed, unless we choose to decentralise and to use applied science, not as the end to which human beings are to be made the means, but as the means to producing a race of free individuals, we have only two alternatives to choose from: either a number of national, militarised totalitarianisms, having as their root the terror of the atomic bomb and as their consequence the destruction of

civilisation – or, if the warfare is limited, the perpetuation of militarism – or else one supra-national totalitarianism, called into existence by the social chaos resulting from rapid techno-logical progress in general and the atom revolution in particu-lar, and developing, under the need for efficiency and stability, into the welfare-tyranny of Utopia. You pays your money and you takes your choice.

ALDOUS HUXLEY (1894–1963), British author and critic. In a 1946 fore-word to his novel *Brave New World* (Chatto & Windus, London, 1932).

19 Yesterday is not ours to recover, but tomorrow is ours to win or to lose.

LYNDON B. JOHNSON (1908–73), American statesman, and 36th Presi-dent of the United States of America 1963–69. In an address to the nation, 28 November 1963.

20 We should all be concerned about the future because we will have to spend the rest of our lives there.

CHARLES F. KETTERING (1876–1958), American engineer and inventor. Attrib.

21 The international system of the twenty-first century will be marked by a seeming contradiction: on the one hand, frag-mentation; on the other, growing globalisation. On the level of the relations among states, the new order will be more like the European state system of the eighteenth and nineteenth cen-turies than the rigid patterns of the Cold War. It will contain at least six major powers – the United States, Europe, China, Japan, Russia, and probably India – as well as a multiplicity of medium-sized and smaller countries. At the same time, international relations have become truly global for the first time. Communications are instantaneous; the world economy operates on all continents simultaneously. A whole set of issues has surfaced that can only be dealt with on a worldwide

basis, such as nuclear proliferation, the environment, the population explosion, and economic interdependence.

HENRY KISSINGER, German-born American lecturer, consultant and author, former US Secretary of State and senior White House adviser. *Diplomacy* (Touchstone, New York, 1994).

22 Information overload: a phrase we're going to hear more often as the revolution in information technology bites. Rushing gleefully into our information-laden future – a future in which we will be increasingly willing to replace direct experience of the world with mediated data about the world – we may find that an obsessive fascination with information has some unpleasant consequences.

HUGH MACKAY, Australian market researcher, columnist, and author. 'Status Seekers Drown in a Sea of Information', *Weekend Australian*, 16 November 1996. © The Weekend Australian.

23 Arthur [Arthur C. Clarke, author of *2001: A Space Odyssey*] has often stated his genuine hope and intention of seeing the year 2001 . . . the first year of the new millennium – the year he helped make famous. It is not, by the way, the year 2000 because our calendar began with 1 January 1 AD and there is no year zero. The twentieth century, in other words, will run through the year 2000, and the centennial (and millennial) celebrations should not really begin until midnight, 31 December 2000, although it will be impossible to restrain people from celebrating a year earlier. Arthur will be eighty-three years old when New Year's Day 2001 comes to pass.

NEIL McALEER, American author. *Odyssey: The Authorised Biography of Arthur C. Clarke* (Victor Gollancz, London, 1992).

24 Some people see the future as something that will eventually roll along to them, just like a train pulling into a station. They wait hopefully for this train to bring them what they wish

for . . . But the future is not like this. Just as our present is the result of our past, so our future will be the result of our present. Every minute of every day we are weaving threads that will make the cloth of the future.

ANNE SPENCER PARRY (1932–85), Australian psychotherapist, publisher and author, and MARJORIE PIZER, Australian psychotherapist, publisher, poet and author. *Below the Surface* (Pinchgut Press, Sydney, 1982; republished Angus & Robertson, Sydney, 1994). Reprinted by permission of HarperCollins Publishers.

25 I believe the future is only the past again, entered through another gate.

ARTHUR WING PINERO (1885–1934), British playwright. *The Second Mrs Tanqueray* (1893).

26 Too many marketers assume that the future will hold back and wait until they're ready for it. It won't.

FAITH POPCORN, American business consultant, co-founder and CEO of BrainReserve, and author. *The Popcorn Report* (Doubleday, New York, 1991). Copyright 1991 by Faith Popcorn. Used by permission of Doubleday, a division of Bantam Doubleday Dell Publishing Group, Inc.

27 It's absurd to say to people in their 50s that they are unemployable after they lose their job. If only people looked to the future and not into the rear-view mirror. Butter churns and sewing machines have gone. The home toolshed and workshop exist for therapy rather than economic use. All jobs have come from outsourcing things originally done at home. The same principle has created jobs since Adam Smith. The growth of services over the next 40 years will be a continuum of the industrial age.

PHIL RUTHVEN, Australian business and social forecaster, and CEO of IBIS Business Information Services. Quoted in Deborah Hope, 'The Helping Class Revolution', *Weekend Australian*, 28 September 1996. © The Weekend Australian.

28 The future ain't what it used to be.

> CASEY STENGEL, American humorist. Attrib.

29 Time and space – time to be alone, and space to move about –
these may well become the great scarcities of tomorrow.

> EDWIN WAY TEALE, American educator, editor and writer. *Autumn Across America* (1956).

30 The future is not 'knowable' in the sense of exact prediction.
Life is filled with surrealistic surprise. Even the seemingly
'hardest' models and data are frequently based on 'soft'
assumptions, especially where these concern human affairs.

> ALVIN TOFFLER, American scholar, lecturer and author. *Powershift* (Bantam, New York, 1990).

31 America is where the future usually happens first. If we are
suffering from the crash of our old institutions, we are also
pioneering a new civilisation. That means living with high
uncertainty. It means expecting disequilibria and upset. And
it means no-one has the full and final truth about where we
are going – or even where we should go. We need to feel our
way, leaving no group behind, as we create the future in our
midst.

> ALVIN TOFFLER and HEIDI TOFFLER, American scholars, lecturers and authors. *Creating a New Civilisation* (Turner, Atlanta, 1995).

32 For the moment, all that interests me, with a greedy, inquisitive
fever, is the future.

> PETER USTINOV, British actor, producer, playwright, university chancellor and author. *Dear Me* (William Heinemann, London, 1977).

33 I do not believe I go too far when I say that in the future we will
have trains of projectiles in which people will be able to travel
comfortably from the Earth to the Moon.

JULES VERNE (1828–1905), French author. *From the Earth to the Moon* (1865).

34 Heaven knows what seeming nonsense may not tomorrow be demonstrated truth.

A. N. WHITEHEAD (1861–1947), British mathematician, philosopher, Professor of Philosophy at Harvard University and author. *Science and the Modern World* (1925).

35 It is the business of the future to be dangerous.

A. N. WHITEHEAD (1861–1947), British mathematician, philosopher, Professor of Philosophy at Harvard University and author. *Adventures of Ideas* (Harvard University Press, Cambridge, Massachusetts, 1933; reprinted Penguin, New York, 1942).

36 There will continue to be a constant crop of creative talents [in Hollywood]. There will always be new vision. Great courage. And, most of all, there will be an unending stream of dynamic people to dream new dreams. Occasionally, there may still be a secondhand rose. A two-time tulip. But, more often, there will be the scent and mystery of fresh gardenias and violets – the stuff of which romance and dreams will perpetually be made.

TICHI WILKERSON and MARCIA BORIE, American journalists, media proprietors and authors. *Hollywood Legends* (Tale Weaver, Los Angeles, 1988).

'Goals begin behaviours.
Consequences maintain behaviours.'
KENNETH BLANCHARD and SPENCER JOHNSON

goals & goal-setting 36:1

See also: ideas 40; innovation 45; inspiration 46;
intelligence 47; knowledge 49; originality 69; talent 99

1 It sometimes takes genius to recognise genius.

> ANON.

2 Patience is a necessary ingredient of genius.

> BENJAMIN DISRAELI (1804–81), British statesman, novelist, and Prime
> Minister 1868 and 1874–80. *Contarini Fleming* (1832).

3 Inventors and men of genius have almost always been regarded
as fools at the beginning – and very often at the end – of their
careers.

> FYODOR DOSTOEVSKY (1821–81), Russian novelist. *The Idiot* (1868).

4 Genius is one per cent inspiration and ninety-nine per cent perspiration.

> THOMAS ALVA EDISON (1847–1931), American scientist and inventor.
> In a newspaper interview, 1903.

5 Genius always finds itself a century too early.

> RALPH WALDO EMERSON (1803–82), American philosopher, poet and
> essayist. *Journals* (1840).

6 Towering genius disdains a beaten path. It seeks regions hith-
erto unexplored.

> ABRAHAM LINCOLN (1809–65), American statesman, and 16th
> President of the United States of America 1861–65. In a speech made at
> Springfield, Illinois, 27 January 1838.

7 Genius does not run in the blood.

> ALISTAIR McALPINE (Lord McAlpine of West Green), British business leader, political figure and author. *The Servant* (Faber & Faber, London, 1992).

8 Any society's most precious assets are its geniuses, the creators, inventors, explainers of what life is really like and what it could be. They do not grow on every rose bush.

> JAMES McCLELLAND, Australian columnist, author, former lawyer, judge and federal government minister. *Stirring the Possum* (Viking, Victoria, 1988).

9 When a true genius appears in the world, you may know him by this sign, that the dunces are all in confederacy against him.

> JONATHAN SWIFT (1667–1745), British author. *Thoughts on Various Subjects* (1711).

10 I have nothing to declare except my genius.

> OSCAR WILDE (1854–1900), Irish playwright, poet, author and wit. His response to being asked if he had anything to declare at the New York Customs House on landing in the USA in 1882. Attrib.

35 getting started

See also: do it now 25; priorities 77

1 A foundation must first be laid . . . It must receive the greatest care, and be made stronger than any other part.

> JAMES ALLEN, American theologian and author. *The Mastery of Destiny* (Putnam, New York, 1909).

2 First in little things, then in greater, then in greater still.

> JAMES ALLEN, American theologian and author. *The Mastery of Destiny* (Putnam, New York, 1909).

3 Start as you mean to go on.
    ANON.

4 'Begin at the beginning,' the King said, gravely, 'and go till you
   come to the end; then stop.'
       LEWIS CARROLL (real name Charles Dodgson; 1832–98), English math-
       ematician, photographer and author. *Alice's Adventures in Wonderland* (1865).

5 When you're in a desert, the first thing you do is find a road.
       JAMES CARVILLE, American political consultant and author, and
       Campaign Manager for Bill Clinton's 1992 US presidential campaign. Attrib.
       (1996).

6 Using the resources and qualities they have already developed
   in order to cope with being women in today's world, it is possible for women to create a stronger vision of what they want
   and then take that daring leap. 'Daring' leaps are not random,
   arbitrary, ad hoc gestures. Prior to the 'grand gesture' there
   must be a series of small, well planned, organised steps.
       EILEEN GILLIBRAND and JENNY MOSLEY, British counsellors, trainers
       and authors. *She Who Dares Wins* (Thorsons, London, 1995).

7 Once begun,
   A task is easy; half the work is done.
       HORACE (Quintus Horatius Flaccus; c. 65–8 BC), Roman poet and satirist.
       Epistles (c. 20–8 BC).

8 First organise the near at hand, then organise the far removed.
   First organise the inner, then organise the outer. First organise the
   basic, then organise the derivative. First organise the strong,
   then organise the weak. First organise the great, then organise
   the small. First organise yourself, then organise others.
       ZHUGE LIANG (2nd century AD), Chinese general of the Han dynasty.
       Mastering the Art of War: The Way of the General.

9 A journey of a thousand miles must begin with a single step.
CHINESE PROVERB.

10 It is better to begin in the evening than not at all.
ENGLISH PROVERB.

11 What the fool does at the end, the wise man does at the beginning.
ENGLISH PROVERB.

12 You can't write poetry on a computer. So I go buy a 250-page notebook and three black felt pens and three red felt pens, and I say, 'These are the pens I'm going to write "Pulp Fiction" with.'
QUENTIN TARANTINO, American screenwriter and film director. *Vanity Fair*, July 1994.

13 If you believe in something, get on and do it. That doesn't mean you should take blind risks. But having looked at it, and decided it's a good idea, don't then listen to everyone else saying it's a rotten idea. If you listen to all the difficulties, you never really start.
ROWLAND WHITEHEAD, British baronet, Chairman of the Institute of Translation and Interpreting, and founder and member of various charitable institutions. *Country Life*, 28 November 1996.

36 **goals & goal-setting**

See also: decisions 20; leadership 51; strategy 97; training 103

1 Goals begin behaviours. Consequences maintain behaviours.
KENNETH BLANCHARD, American educator, management consultant, trainer and author, and SPENCER JOHNSON, American publisher, lecturer, communications consultant and author. *The One Minute Manager* (Collins, London, 1983). Reprinted by permission of HarperCollins Publishers.

2 Take a minute. Look at your goals. Look at your performance. See if your behaviour matches your goals.

> KENNETH BLANCHARD, American educator, management consultant, trainer and author, and SPENCER JOHNSON, American publisher, lecturer, communications consultant and author. *The One Minute Manager* (Collins, London, 1983). Reprinted by permission of HarperCollins Publishers.

3 If you reach for the stars, you might not quite get one, but you won't end up with a handful of mud, either.

> LEO BURNETT (1891–1971), American advertising expert and founder of Leo Burnett advertising agency, Chicago. Personal and corporate motto.

4 Goal setting is obviously a powerful process. It's based on the same principle of focus that allows us to concentrate rays of diffused sunlight into a force powerful enough to start a fire. It's the manifestation of creative imagination and independent will. It's the practicality of 'eating our elephants one bite at a time,' of translating vision into achievable, actionable doing. It's a common denominator of successful individuals and organisations.

> STEPHEN R. COVEY, American educator, leadership consultant, author and former Professor of Business Management at Brigham Young University; A. ROGER MERRILL, American management and leadership consultant, and author; and REBECCA R. MERRILL, American author. *First Things First* (Fireside/Simon & Schuster, New York, 1994).

5 The person who makes a success of living is the one who sees his goal steadily and aims for it unswervingly.

> CECIL B. DE MILLE (1881–1959), American film producer and director. *Sunshine and Shadow* (1955).

6 Understanding your wants and needs, and identifying some of the things you've got going for you is an essential first stage in your career development. Sadly, this is as far as many people

get because their wishes and objectives remain too daunting, too obscure or too ambitious. The clarification of goals and identification of steps to achieve them is likely to be one of the most important tasks of your career management.

EILEEN GILLIBRAND and JENNY MOSLEY, British counsellors, trainers and authors. *She Who Dares Wins* (Thorsons, London, 1995).

7 It is not enough to take steps which may some day lead to a goal; each step must be itself a goal and a step likewise.

GOETHE (Johann Wolfgang von Goethe; 1749–1832), German poet, playwright and novelist. Quoted in Johann Peter Eckermann, *Conversations with Goethe* (18 September, 1823).

8 Ultimately the businesses that win are those where all the people have the same aim and give freely in their commitment to it.

JOHN HARVEY-JONES, British business consultant, broadcaster, author and former Chairman of ICI Industries. *All Together Now* (William Heinemann, London, 1994). Reprinted by permission of The Peters Fraser and Dunlop Group Limited on behalf of John Harvey-Jones.

9 You can't rise unless you set goals that make you stretch.

TOM HOPKINS, American sales trainer, motivator and author. *How to Master the Art of Selling* (Champion Press, Scottsdale, Arizona, 1982; republished HarperCollins, London, 1994).

10 Not every end is the goal. The end of a melody is not its goal, and yet if a melody has not reached its end, it has not reached its goal.

FRIEDRICH NIETZSCHE (1844–1900), German philosopher and author. *The Wanderer and His Shadow* (1880).

11 Everyone has dreams. But it is what you do with these dreams that is important. Dreams, once you make the decision to act on them, can become reality ... Find a goal, dream about it, it

will inspire you to unleash power and accomplish a direction of positive thinking. Give yourself the freedom to explore the possibility of life without limits. Goals are dreams with deadlines, a means to an end but not the ultimate purpose of life.

GLYNIS NUNN, Australian track and field athlete and Olympic gold medallist. *Good Weekend*, 1 June 1996.

12 Tough, visible goals, aimed at serving the customer and measured so as to engender unit versus unit competition, spur the process onward.

TOM PETERS, American academic, consultant, lecturer and author. In a foreword to Jan Carlzon, *Moments of Truth* (Ballinger, Cambridge, Massachusetts, 1987; revised edition Harper & Row, New York, 1989). Copyright © 1987 by Ballinger Publishing Company. Reprinted by permission of HarperCollins Publishers, Inc.

13 There are two things to aim at in life; first, to get what you want; and after that, to enjoy it.

LOGAN PEARSALL SMITH (1865–1946), American-born British scholar and author. *Afterthoughts* (1931).

14 Instead of constructing permanent edifices, today's adaptive executives may have to *de-construct* their companies to maximise manoeuvrability. They must be experts not in bureaucracy, but in the coordination of ad-hocracy. They must adjust swiftly to immediate pressures – yet think in terms of long-range goals.

ALVIN TOFFLER, American scholar, lecturer and author. *The Adaptive Corporation* (Gower, Aldershot, Hampshire, 1985).

15 Winners in life are people who have developed strong Positive Self-motivation. They have the ability to move in the direction of goals they have set, or roles they want to play, and will tolerate little distraction.

DENIS WAITLEY, American personal development counsellor, lecturer and author. *The Psychology of Winning* (Nightingale-Conant, Chicago, 1979; republished Berkley, New York, 1984).

16 Winners are goal and role oriented. They set and get what they want – consistently. They are self-directed on the road to fulfilment. Fulfilment or success has been defined as the progressive realisation of goals that are worthy of the individual. The 'human' system is goal-seeking by design and, using a very basic analogy, may be compared to a homing torpedo system or an automatic pilot. Set your target and this self-activated system, constantly monitoring feedback signals from the target area and adjusting the course setting in its own navigational guidance computer, makes every correction necessary to stay on target and score a hit.

DENIS WAITLEY, American personal development counsellor, lecturer and author. *The Psychology of Winning* (Nightingale-Conant, Chicago, 1979; republished Berkley, New York, 1984).

'Great wines are the result of judicious blending
and accidents. So are great men and fools.'

PETER USTINOV

human nature 39:15

37 hiring & firing

See also: employees 28; people 70

1 What a terrific waste it is to be fired because of your attitude, rather than because of any lack of talent or ability. Because attitude problems, unlike a lack of talent, can be fixed.

> MARK GOULSTON, American psychiatrist and consultant. *Fortune,* 30 September 1996. © 1996 Time Inc. All rights reserved.

2 When appointing new people it is essential to recognise that, while no appointment should be for ever, one which lasts less than three years should really be considered a failure. Every time a new person is appointed to a team, the nature of the team suffers such a degree of change that it is important to have some idea of what the change may be and to ensure that it will be helpful to the business aims, rather than harmful. Since the whole of business is about change, no appointment should ever seem to be a straight replacement for the man who has gone before. It is an opportunity to create a new input and to make a shift in how the team works, as well as in a larger business sense.

> JOHN HARVEY-JONES, British business consultant, broadcaster, author, and former Chairman of ICI Industries. *All Together Now* (William Heinemann, London, 1994). Reprinted by permission of The Peters Fraser and Dunlop Group Limited on behalf of John Harvey-Jones.

3 It is very hard to employ anybody at all competent if you have a reputation for murdering them, which indicates that the Servant must consider very carefully the Prince whom he has helped to power.

ALISTAIR McALPINE (Lord McAlpine of West Green), British business leader, political figure, and author. *The Servant* (Faber & Faber, London, 1992).

4 A lot of us, when we're evaluating job candidates, tend to be so impressed by braininess, by what's inside a person's head, that we seriously undervalue the passion that person brings to an enterprise. You can rent a brain, but you can't rent a heart. The candidate has to throw that in for free.

MARK H. McCORMACK, American sports marketing consultant, founder and CEO of International Management Group, and author. *McCormack on Managing* (Century, London, 1995).

5 Hire the person who can do the job – and accept that the person who can do the job isn't necessarily the person you want to be best friends with.

MARK H. McCORMACK, American sports marketing consultant, founder and CEO of International Management Group, and author. *What They Didn't Teach Me at Yale Law School* (Collins, New York, 1988; originally published as *The Terrible Truth About Lawyers*, Collins, New York, 1987). Reprinted by permission of HarperCollins Publishers Limited.

6 Never hire your friends. I have made this mistake three times, and had to fire all three. They are no longer my friends.

Never hire your client's children. If you have to fire them, you may lose a client. This is another mistake I have made.

Never hire your own children, or the children of your partners. However able they may be, ambitious people won't stay in outfits which practise nepotism. This is one mistake I did not make; my son is in the real estate business, secure in the knowledge that he owes nothing of his success to his father.

Think twice before hiring people who have been successful in other fields. I have hired a magazine editor, a lawyer and an economist. None of them developed an interest in advertising.

And never hire your clients. The qualities which make some-one a good client are not the qualities required for success in the agency business. I have made this mistake twice.

DAVID OGILVY, British-born American advertising expert, founder of Ogilvy & Mather international advertising group, New York, and author. *Ogilvy on Advertising* (Pan, London, 1983).

7 Job hunting should call for strenuous idea hunting. And yet a famous employer reports: 'In my experience, not one applicant in 500 uses any imagination in applying for a position. Anyone who suggested ideas of possible use to his prospective employer would stand out and be almost sure to get preference – even though his suggestions were unusable.' For 15 years, Sidney Edlund, former head of Lifesavers Incorporated, has made it his hobby to teach people how to go after new jobs. His basic principles are these:
1. Offer a service instead of asking for a position.
2. Appeal to the self-interest of your prospective employer.
3. Be specific as to the job you want, and as to your qualifica-tions.
4. Be different, and still be sincere.
All these principles call for thinking ahead, or thinking cre-atively, or both.

ALEX F. OSBORN (1888–1966), American academic and author. *Applied Imagination: Principles & Procedures of Creative Thinking* (Charles Scribner's Sons, New York, 1953).

38 honesty & integrity
See also: business ethics 7

1 An organisation that rewards its employees with real job satis-faction and a genuine sense of self-worth is more honest to itself and its staff.

JAN CARLZON, Swedish business leader. former CEO of Scandinavian Airlines System, speaker and author. *Moments of Truth* (Ballinger, Cambridge, Massachusetts, 1987; revised edition HarperCollins, New York, 1989). Copyright © 1987 by Ballinger Publishing Company. Reprinted by permission of HarperCollins Publishers, Inc.

2 Would that the simple maxim, that honesty is the best policy, might be laid to heart; that a sense of the true aim of life might elevate the tone of politics and trade till public and private honour became identical.

> MARGARET FULLER (Marquesa Ossoli; 1810–50), American poet, educator, editor and essayist. *Summer on the Lakes* (1844).

3 He that resolves to deal with none but honest men must leave off dealing.

> THOMAS FULLER M.D. (1654–1734), British physician and author. *Gnomologia* (1732).

4 It is always the best policy to speak the truth, unless of course you are an exceptionally good liar.

> JEROME K. JEROME (1859–1927), British playwright and author. *The Idler*, February 1892.

5 Honesty is praised, then left to freeze.

> JUVENAL (Decimus Junius Juvenalis; c. AD 60 – c. AD 140), Roman satirist. *Satires* (c. AD 100).

6 In every survey we conducted, honesty was selected more often than any other leadership characteristic; it consistently emerged as the single most important ingredient in the leader–constituent relationship. It's clear that if we're to willingly follow someone – whether it be into battle or into the boardroom, into the classroom or into the back room, into the front office or to the front lines – we first want to assure ourselves that the

person is worthy of our trust. We want to know that the person is being truthful, ethical, and principled. We want to be fully confident of the integrity of our leaders, whatever the context. That nearly 90 per cent of constituents want their leaders to be honest above all else is a message that all leaders must take to heart.

JAMES M. KOUZES and BARRY Z. POSNER, American educators, management and training consultants, and authors. *The Leadership Challenge* (Jossey-Bass, San Francisco, 1995).

7 Everything she writes is a lie, including 'and' and 'the'.

MARY McCARTHY (1912–89), American author and critic. Comment made about her rival, Lillian Hellman. Attrib.

8 Politicians describing the economy, lawyers and judges describing a crime, every one of us re-inventing our pasts, are myth-makers to a greater or lesser degree. Fiction is what comes naturally to us.

JOHN MORTIMER, British lawyer, screenplay writer, playwright and author. *Murderers and Other Friends* (Viking, London, 1994). Reprinted by permission of the Peters Fraser & Dunlop Group Ltd.

9 The surest way to remain poor is to be an honest man.

NAPOLEON I (Napoleon Bonaparte; 1769–1821), French soldier, statesman, and Emperor of France 1804–14/15. *Maxims* (1804–15).

10 You only lie to two people in your life: your girlfriend and the police. Everybody else you tell the truth to.

JACK NICHOLSON, American actor. *Vanity Fair*, April 1994.

11 Honesty is the best policy.

ENGLISH PROVERB.

12 Plain dealing is praised more than practised.

ENGLISH PROVERB.

13 I don't mind what the opposition say of me, so long as they don't tell the truth.

MARK TWAIN (real name Samuel Clemens; 1835–1910), American journalist, editor and author. In a speech made at Hartford, Connecticut, 26 October 1880.

human nature 39

See also: civilisation 10; people 70

1 People will pay for what they want, but not for what they need; for what looks good to them, but not what is good for them.

ANON.

2 The creative man with an insight into human nature, with the artistry to touch and move people, will succeed. Without them he will fail.

BILL BERNBACH (1911–82), American advertising expert and co-founder of Doyle Dane Bernbach Advertising. Attrib.

3 A person's name is to that person the sweetest and most important sound in the language.

DALE CARNEGIE (1888–1955), American trainer, motivator and author. *How to Win Friends & Influence People* (Simon & Schuster, New York, 1937; revised edition, 1981).

4 Human nature is the same everywhere; the modes are only different.

LORD CHESTERFIELD (Philip Dormer Stanhope, 4th Earl of Chesterfield; 1694–1773), British statesman. Letter to his godson, 1773.

5 The deepest urge in human nature is the desire to be important.

> JOHN DEWEY (1859–1952), American philosopher, educator and author.
> *Human Nature & Conduct* (1922).

6 My whole life, I've heard about stars doing insane things and
I've been, like, wondering, 'What is their problem?' But I obviously have that in me, too. I've felt myself having these
Hollywood feelings, these infantile rages, mostly because I can
get away with it. So now I've had to catch myself in the act and
take some distance from my own so-called stardom and realise
that being an asshole celebrity schmuck is not a dignified
expression of the finer instincts of human nature.

> DAVID DUCHOVNY, American actor. *Good Weekend Magazine*, 20 July
> 1996.

7 Human nature may be an infinitely variant thing. But it has con-
stants. One is that, given a choice, people keep what is the best
for themselves, i.e., for those whom they love the most.

> JOHN KENNETH GALBRAITH, Canadian-born American economist,
> Emeritus Professor of Economics at Harvard University, former senior White
> House adviser, diplomat and author. *Money: Whence it Came, Where it Went*
> (Penguin, New York, André Deutsch, London, 1975). Copyright © John
> Kenneth Galbraith, 1975, 1995.

8 He who abandons his claim to be unique is even less bearable
when he claims to be representative.

> CLIVE JAMES, Australian-born British broadcaster and author. *Falling
> Towards England* (Jonathan Cape, London, 1985).

9 To wait until reminiscence is justified by achievement might
mean to wait for ever. I am also well aware that all attempts to
put oneself in a bad light are doomed to be frustrated. The ego
arranges the bad light to its own satisfaction.

CLIVE JAMES, Australian-born British broadcaster and author. *Unreliable Memoirs* (Jonathan Cape, London, 1980).

10 There are one hundred and ninety-three living species of monkeys and apes. One hundred and ninety-two of them are covered with hair. The exception is a naked ape self-named *Homo sapiens*. This unusual and highly successful species spends a great deal of time examining his higher motives and ignoring his fundamental ones. He is proud that he has the biggest brain of all primates, but attempts to conceal the fact that he also has the biggest penis, preferring to accord this honour falsely to the mighty gorilla. He is an intensely vocal, acutely exploratory, over-crowded ape.

DESMOND MORRIS, British anthropologist and author. *The Naked Ape* (Jonathan Cape, London, 1967).

11 Sheer egoism. Desire to seem clever, to be talked about, to be remembered after death, to get your own back on grown-ups who snubbed you in childhood, etc., etc. . . . Writers share this characteristic with scientists, artists, politicians, lawyers, soldiers, successful businessmen – in short, with the whole top crust of humanity. The great mass of human beings are not acutely selfish. After the age of about thirty, they abandon individual ambition – in many cases, they almost abandon the sense of being individuals at all – and live chiefly for others, or are simply smothered under drudgery. But there is also the minority of gifted, wilful people who are determined to live their own lives to the end.

GEORGE ORWELL (real name Eric Blair; 1903–50) British journalist and author. 'Why I Write', *Gangrel*, No. 4, Summer, 1946. Reprinted in *The Collected Essays, Journalism and Letters of George Orwell, Volume 1: An Age Like This* (Secker & Warburg, London, 1968). Published in the USA in *Such, Such Were the Joys* (Harcourt Brace, Orlando, Florida). © Copyright Mark Hamilton. as literary executor of the estate of the late Sonia Brownell Orwell and Martin

12 It is usually the case with most men that their nature is so constituted that they pity those who fare badly and envy those who fare well.

> BARUCH SPINOZA (1632–77), Dutch philosopher. *Ethics* (1677).

13 Computers will do many wonderful things. But they will still be incapable of *experiencing*, the essence of human nature. 'Computer freaks,' as now, will not understand the significance of this important difference between humans and computers.

> KEITH TAYLOR, Australian academic and professor at the National University of Singapore. Quoted in Stephen Dando-Collins, *2000 AD* (Pan, Sydney, 1986).

14 Any occupation with thousands of practitioners is like an ocean. As you chart the major currents that flow within it, you shouldn't forget that subcurrents and eddies are always present and moving in contrary directions, and a great body of water is always more varied and less settled than the chartmaker's abstractions.

> LESTER C. THUROW, American sociologist, professor at Massachusetts Institute of Technology and author. *Dangerous Currents* (Random House, New York, 1983). Copyright © 1983 by Lester C. Thurow Inc. Reprinted by permission of Random House Inc.

15 Great wines are the result of judicious blending and accidents. So are great men and fools.

> PETER USTINOV, British actor, producer, playwright, university chancellor and author. *My Russia* (Macmillan, London, 1983).

'We are drowning in information
and starved for knowledge.'

JOHN NAISBITT and PATRICIA ABURDENE

information 44:8

40 ideas

See also: change 9; imagination 42; innovation 45;
inspiration 46; originality 69

1 Nothing is more dangerous than an idea, when it is the only
idea we have.

> ALAIN (real name Emile Chartier; 1868–1951), French philosopher, teacher
> and essayist. *Libres-propos* (1908–14).

2 No one person has a mortgage on good ideas. We can all be
ideas people.

> ANON.

3 Nothing is more compelling than an idea whose time has come.

> ANON.

4 Nothing is more futile yet so magnificent as an idea before its
time.

> ANON.

5 Defeat is a fact and victory can be a fact. If the idea is good, it
will survive defeat, it may even survive the victory.

> STEPHEN VINCENT BENÉT (1898–1943), American poet and short-
> story writer. *John Brown's Body* (1928).

6 A new idea is delicate. It can be killed by a sneer or a yawn; it
can be stabbed to death by a quip and worried to death by a
frown on the right man's brow.

> CHARLES BROWER, American advertising executive. *Advertising Age*,
> 10 August 1959.

7 I once suggested to the Russians that they should set up an Academy of Change with the specific purpose of seeing what would happen if bureaucrats were pointed, formally, in this direction. I would also suggest a minister or a secretary of state for ideas, as some way of focusing attention on this need.

> EDWARD DE BONO, Maltese-born British scholar, teacher, lecturer and author. *I Am Right – You Are Wrong* (Viking, London, 1990). Copyright © Mica Management Resources Inc, 1990.

8 The traditional habits of thinking are very effective at developing ideas but not very good at restructuring them. Lateral thinking is designed to supplement traditional thinking, and especially to introduce the discontinuity that is necessary for restructuring ideas. The basic process of lateral thinking is the escape from old ideas and the provocation of new ones.

> EDWARD DE BONO, Maltese-born British scholar, teacher, lecturer, author, and creator of the title and concept of 'lateral thinking'. *Lateral Thinking for Management* (McGraw-Hill, London, 1971).

9 Old ideas give way slowly; for they are more than abstract logical forms and categories. They are habits, predispositions, deeply ingrained attitudes of aversion and preference.

> JOHN DEWEY (1859–1952), American philosopher, educator and author. *The Influence of Darwinism on Philosophy* (1909).

10 If at first an idea isn't totally absurd, there's no hope for it.

> ALBERT EINSTEIN (1879–1955), German–Swiss–American physicist. Attrib.

11 I maintain that ideas are events.

> GUSTAVE FLAUBERT (1821–80), French novelist. In a letter to Louise Colet, 15 January 1853.

12 The speed of modern communications and the force of international competition require the quickest possible adoption of new ideas if companies are to survive.

> JOHN HARVEY-JONES, British business consultant, broadcaster, author and former Chairman of ICI Industries. *All Together Now* (William Heinemann, London, 1994). Reprinted by permission of The Peters Fraser and Dunlop Group Limited on behalf of John Harvey-Jones.

13 A man may die, nations may rise and fall, but an idea lives on. Ideas have endurance without death.

> JOHN F. KENNEDY (1917–63), American statesman, and 35th President of the United States of America 1961–63. In a speech made in Greenville, North Carolina, 8 February 1963.

14 The ideas of economists and political philosophers, both when they are right and when they are wrong, are more powerful than is commonly understood.

> JOHN MAYNARD KEYNES (1883–1946), British economist, financier, journalist and author. Attrib.

15 The thinker dies, but his thoughts are beyond the reach of destruction. Men are mortal; but ideas are immortal.

> WALTER LIPPMANN (1889–1974), American editor, columnist and author. *A Preface to Morals* (1929).

16 Just as our eyes need light in order to see, our minds need ideas in order to conceive.

> NICOLAS MALEBRANCHE (1638–1715), French theologian and philosopher. *Recherche de la vérité* (1674).

17 If you are possessed by an idea, you find it expressed everywhere, you even smell it.

> THOMAS MANN (1875–1955), German essayist and novelist. *Death in Venice* (1903).

18 The Idea is the philosophy on which the Prince will base all of his actions. The Idea starts with the Prince, and while men and women may say that they advise the Prince, they will really be attracted by the Idea. The Idea is the instrument of the Prince.

> ALISTAIR McALPINE (Lord McAlpine of West Green), British business leader, political figure and author. *The Servant* (Faber & Faber, London, 1992).

19 A young man must let his ideas grow, not be continually rooting them up to see how they are getting on.

> WILLIAM McFEE (1881–1966), British-born American novelist and essayist. 'The Idea', *Harbours of Memory* (1921).

20 The ideal top executive is both a creative pace-setter and a creative coach. He cultivates the creativity of those around him and makes it bloom. Above all else, he must feel a real regard for the power of ideas.

> ALEX F. OSBORN (1888–1966), American academic and author. *Applied Imagination: Principles & Procedures of Creative Thinking* (Charles Scribner's Sons, New York, 1953).

21 A powerful idea communicates some of its power to the man who contradicts it.

> MARCEL PROUST (1871–1922), French novelist. *Within a Budding Grove* (1918).

22 In the study of ideas, it is necessary to remember that insistence on hard-headed clarity issues from sentimental feeling, as if it were a mist, cloaking the perplexities of fact. Insistence on clarity at all costs is based on sheer superstition as to the mode in which human intelligence functions. Our reasonings grasp at straws for premises and float on gossamers for deductions.

A. N. WHITEHEAD (1861–1947), British mathematician, philosopher, Professor of Philosophy at Harvard University and author. *Adventures of Ideas* (Harvard University Press, Cambridge, Massachusetts, 1933; reprinted Penguin, New York, 1942).

41 image

See also: advertising 3; marketing 58; presentation 76; publicity 84

1 Fashions may go out of style, but style will never go out of fashion.

ANON.

2 Workers are rarely dressed down for being dressed up.

ANON.

3 Paint makes the image, but painting makes the picture.

CHARLES BLACKMAN, Australian artist. *Qantas Club*, February 1997.

4 Grooming is very important to me. You present to the world the way you feel about yourself. If you go around looking like a slob, you probably have a slobby attitude. If someone is reasonably well-presented you can usually assume that person is a reasonably well-informed and well-intentioned person.

JOAN COLLINS, British actress, producer and author. *Hello!*, 23 September 1995.

5 Our culture impedes the clear definition of any faithful self-image – indeed, of any clear image whatever. We do not break images; there are few iconoclasts among us. Instead, we blur and soften them.

EDGAR Z. FRIEDENBERG, American sociologist and author. *The Vanishing Adolescent* (1959).

6 Life is the art of being well deceived; and in order that the deception may succeed it must be habitual and uninterrupted.

WILLIAM HAZLITT (1778–1830), British critic, poet and essayist. 'On Pedantry', *The Round Table* (1817).

7 Image and identity, like advertising . . ., influence both customers and employees. Employees who work in attractive physical surroundings and wear uniforms they like perform their jobs better, with higher productivity and a higher degree of customer care.

LINDA M. LASH, British training and development counsellor and author. *The Complete Guide to Customer Service* (John Wiley & Sons, New York, 1989). Copyright © 1989 Linda M. Lash. Reprinted by permission of John Wiley & Sons Inc.

8 Glamour is a youth's form of blindness that lets in light, incoherent colour, but nothing defined. Like the rainbow, it is a once uplifting vision that moves away the closer you come to it.

ARTHUR MILLER, American playwright, screenwriter and author. *Timebends* (Methuen, London, 1987).

9 I wasn't good at celebrity. Other people like Madonna, Demi Moore and Roseanne Barr are great celebrities. They know what to wear to a premiere and how to present themselves. They're aware of the absurdity of celebrity and they play with it.

MEG RYAN, American actress. *Sydney Morning Herald*, 7 September 1996.

10 Fashions fade; style is eternal.

YVES ST LAURENT, French couturier. Attrib.

11 In matters of grave importance, style, not sincerity, is the vital thing.

OSCAR WILDE (1854–1900), Irish playwright, poet, author and wit. *The Importance of Being Earnest*, play (1895).

42 imagination

See also: creativity 17; genius 34; ideas 40; innovation 45; inspiration 46; originality 69

1 The imagination of the English affluent classes is fixed less on sex than on homes.

CLIVE ASLET, British journalist and editor of *Country Life* magazine. *Weekly Telegraph*, 23 October 1996.

2 Computers will be so dominant that minds will be stunted and will lose much of their agility and power of imagination.

RUDOLPH BRASCH, Australian rabbi, lecturer, broadcaster and author. Quoted in Stephen Dando-Collins, *2000 AD* (Pan, Sydney, 1986).

3 You create your own universe as you go along. The stronger your imagination, the more variegated your universe. When you leave off dreaming, the universe ceases to exist.

WINSTON CHURCHILL (1874–1965), British statesman, Prime Minister 1940–45 and 1951–55, artist, historian, author and Nobel laureate. *My Early Life* (Macmillan, London, 1930).

4 Imagination, not invention, is the supreme master of art as of life.

JOSEPH CONRAD, (original name Teodor Jósef Konrad Korzeniowski; 1857–1924), Polish-born British author. *A Personal Record* (1912).

5 The problems of the world cannot possibly be solved by sceptics or cynics whose horizons are limited by the obvious realities. We need men who can dream of things that never were.

JOHN F. KENNEDY (1917–63), American statesman, and 35th President of the United States of America 1961–63. In a speech made in Dublin, Ireland, 28 June 1963.

6 Imagination grows by exercise and contrary to common belief is more powerful in the mature than in the young.

W. SOMERSET MAUGHAM (1874–1965), British playwright and novelist. *The Summing Up* (1938).

7 Being a man of supreme imagination, the Servant will meet a better class of woman in his dreams, and these women come when the mind calls and go at his command, silently, telling nothing.

ALISTAIR McALPINE (Lord McAlpine of West Green), British business leader, political figure and author. *The Servant* (Faber & Faber, London, 1992).

8 Imagination is the cornerstone of human endeavour; it is, without doubt, responsible for man's survival as an animal, and it has caused him, as a human being, to conquer the world. It may well lead him to subdue the universe.

ALEX F. OSBORN (1888–1966), American academic and author. *Applied Imagination: Principles & Procedures of Creative Thinking* (Charles Scribner's Sons, New York, 1953).

9 Whether you are looking for a job, or trying to get ahead in a business, imagination is the key to achievement.

ALEX F. OSBORN (1888–1966), American academic and author. *Applied Imagination: Principles & Procedures of Creative Thinking* (Charles Scribner's Sons, New York, 1953).

10 You can't depend on your judgement when your imagination is out of focus.

MARK TWAIN (real name Samuel Clemens; 1835–1910), American journalist, editor and author. *Notebook* (1935).

43 incentive/s & rewards

See also: goals & goal-setting 36; leadership 51; motivation 63

1 Of course, competent people are paid well for their contributions, but receiving well-defined responsibility and the trust and active interest of others is a much more personally satisfying reward.

> JAN CARLZON, Swedish business leader, former CEO of Scandinavian Airlines System, speaker and author. *Moments of Truth* (Ballinger, Cambridge, Massachusetts, 1987; revised edition Harper & Row, New York, 1989). Copyright © 1987 by Ballinger Publishing Company. Reprinted by permission of HarperCollins Publishers, Inc.

2 The richest reward of all is being proud of your work.

> JAN CARLZON, Swedish business leader, former CEO of Scandinavian Airlines System, speaker and author. *Moments of Truth* (Ballinger, Cambridge, Massachusetts, 1987; revised edition Harper & Row, New York, 1989). Copyright © 1987 by Ballinger Publishing Company. Reprinted by permission of HarperCollins Publishers, Inc.

3 High profile and universally recognised rewards create internally-driven competition which becomes the engine for improved performance.

> STEPHEN DANDO-COLLINS, Australian author and editor. *The Customer Care Revolution* (Pitman, Melbourne, 1996).

4 The evidence is quite consistent, if you reward the good and ignore or forgive the bad, the good will occur more frequently and the bad will gradually disappear.

> CHARLES HANDY, British academic, business consultant and author. *The Age of Unreason* (Business Books, London, 1989).

5 A boss who not only told me exactly what I need to do but who gave me the feeling that if I did it I would benefit in some way – a raise, a promotion, an extra week of vacation – could easily manage me.

MARK H. McCORMACK, American sports marketing consultant, founder and CEO of International Management Group, and author. *McCormack on Managing* (Century, London, 1995).

6 In Britain, Europe and America, there is a 'political class' which believes in slow, steady growth, no inflation and high interest rates. But if we're going to have a society that gives hope to young people, then we've got to have one that's got many more incentives to work and more opportunities.

RUPERT MURDOCH, Australian-born American media proprietor and CEO of News Corporation, 20th Century Fox, Fox TV, BSkyB TV and Star TV. In a speech quoted in B. A. Santamaria, 'Who Rules Australia Anyway?', *Weekend Australian*, 30 December 1995. © The Weekend Australian.

7 Men can be stimulated by hope or driven by fear, but the hope and the fear must be vivid and immediate if they are to be effective without producing weariness.

BERTRAND RUSSELL (3rd Earl Russell; 1872–1970), British philosopher, mathematician, social reformer and writer. 'Technique and Human Nature', *Authority and the Individual* (1949).

information 44

See also: communication & communicating 11; computers 13; decisions 20; future, the 33; knowledge 49; learning 52; technology 101

1 Information is currency.
ANON.

2 Information's pretty thin stuff, unless mixed with experience.
CLARENCE DAY (1874–1935), American essayist and author. 'The Three Tigers', *The Crow's Nest* (1921).

3 When I need some information, my first thought is still of a book – and the library. When I have an inquiry, I still turn first to the telephone. The latter has served with improvement but no basic change for rather more than a century; books have survived far longer. They will endure the information revolution; they will not be lost on that superhighway. The problem will still be finding the relevant and sorting out the true from the false. Our problem . . . is not a shortage of information or in its transfer. It is in deciding what is useful and what is right.

JOHN KENNETH GALBRAITH, Canadian-born American economist, Emeritus Professor of Economics at Harvard University, former senior White House adviser, diplomat and author. 'The Outlines of an Emerging World', *1996 Britannica Book of the Year* (Encyclopaedia Britannica, Chicago, 1996). © 1996 Encyclopaedia Britannica Inc.

4 You'll know the information highway has become part of your life when you begin to resent it if information is not available via the network.

BILL GATES, American information technology pioneer, founder and CEO of Microsoft Corporation, and author. *The Road Ahead* (Viking Penguin, New York, 1995). Copyright © 1995 by William H. Gates III. Used by permission of Viking Penguin, a division of Penguin Books USA Inc.

5 It has already set a process in motion that will eventually change our thinking about computers, our thinking about information, and even our thinking about thinking. In terms of our relationship with information, Macintosh changed everything.

STEVEN LEVY, American journalist and author. *Insanely Great: The Life and Times of Macintosh, the Computer that Changed Everything* (Viking, New York and London, 1994; revised edition Penguin, 1995). Copyright © Steven Levy, 1994, 1995.

6 Information is not the pathway to enlightenment, happiness or wisdom. Information is only data, after all, and it is possible

to have too much of it. In fact, information can get in the way of wisdom unless we leave ourselves sufficient time and energy to reflect on it, make sense of it, and integrate it into our lives.

HUGH MACKAY, Australian market researcher, columnist and author. 'Status Seekers Drown in a Sea of Information', *Weekend Australian*, 16 November 1996. © The Weekend Australian.

7 Instead of being liberated by the intellectual freedom of information, we are becoming mired in a deepening morass of fractured images, soundbytes, experiences, and information we can't and don't access.

RUDY MAGNANI and PETER BENKENDORF, American marketing consultants and principals of Magnani & Associates, Chicago. 'Info Glut, or Marketing in The Blur Age', *Marketing News* (American Marketing Association), 20 January 1997, page 4. Reprinted with permission.

8 We are drowning in information and starved for knowledge.

JOHN NAISBITT and PATRICIA ABURDENE, American social forecasters, academics and authors. *Megatrends* (William Morrow, New York, 1980).

9 Consumers want information and they want it fast.

FAITH POPCORN, American business consultant, co-founder and CEO of BrainReserve, and author. *The Popcorn Report* (Doubleday, New York, 1991). Copyright 1991 by Faith Popcorn. Used by permission of Doubleday, a division of Bantam Doubleday Dell Publishing Group, Inc.

10 To live effectively is to live with adequate information.

NORBERT WIENER (1894–1964), American mathematician and educator. *The Human Use of Human Beings* (1954).

45 innovation

See also: creativity 17; genius 34; ideas 40; imagination 42; inspiration 46; originality 69; talent 99

1 From a Darwinian perspective, innovation is a source of potential diversity analogous to genetic variation. In one version of this analogy, the variation occurs within a population of firms when one of them adopts a new management practice or a new technology. The innovating firm then competes with established firms in a competitive struggle for survival. The industry constitutes an environmental niche in which the struggle goes on. Imitation constitutes a social mechanism by which the characteristics of the successful innovation are transmitted to rival firms. In the long run only the fittest firms in the industry – those using best practice techniques – earn a normal rate of profit and so survive.

MARK CASSON, British academic, author and Professor of Economics at the University of Reading. In an introduction to *Entrepreneurship* (Edward Elgar, Aldershot, Hampshire, 1990).

2 Consumers have expectations. Innovators produce exciting solutions, sometimes so far ahead of expectations that minds are collectively blown – for a few moments. For no sooner has the solution arrived than consumer expectations move ahead. So innovators address these new expectations, and, with luck, exceed them. The consumer looks at it and says, 'That's nice. But wouldn't it be nicer if it did *this*, as well?' They're never satisfied. Neither should you be. Keep generating great ideas. Keep one step ahead of your marketplace.

TIMOTHY R. V. FOSTER, British video producer and presenter, consultant and author. *Positive Thinking: 101 Ways to Generate Great Ideas* (Kogan Page, UK, 1991; Wrightbooks, Victoria, 1992).

3 Successful firms pay more attention to the market than do failures. Successful innovators innovate in response to market needs, involve potential users in the development of the innovation, and understand user needs better.

> CHRISTOPHER FREEMAN, British economist at the University of Sussex, London. 'Success and Failure in Industrial Innovation: Report of Project SAPPO' (Science Policy Research Unit, University of Sussex, London), February 1972.

4 Things don't turn up in this world until somebody turns them up.

> JAMES A. GARFIELD (1831–81), American statesman, and 20th President of the United States of America 1881. Attrib.

5 I think the tendency for successful companies to fail to innovate is just that: a tendency. If you're too focused on your current business, it's hard to change and concentrate on innovating.

> BILL GATES, American information technology pioneer, founder and CEO of Microsoft Corporation, and author. *The Road Ahead* (Viking Penguin, New York, 1995). Copyright © 1995 by William H. Gates III. Used by permission of Viking Penguin, a division of Penguin Books USA Inc.

6 One doesn't discover new lands without consenting to lose sight of the shore for a very long time.

> ANDRE GIDE (1869–1951), French novelist, editor, critic, translator and essayist. *The Counterfeiters* (1925).

7 Innovative organisations enter unexplored territories as opposed to playing it safe. If you immediately know how to implement an idea, you're probably not looking at a breakthrough innovation.

> CRIS GOLDSMITH, American marketing executive and managing partner of CreativeRealities, Boston. 'Overcoming Roadblocks to Innovation', *Marketing News* (American Marketing Association), 18 November 1996, page 4. Reprinted by permission.

8 Risk-taking is the essence of innovation.

HERMAN KAHN (1922–83), American physicist, strategist, futurist and author. Attrib.

9 An innovation will usually suggest its own market.

JOHN KAY, British academic at London Business School. *Foundations for Corporate Success* (Oxford University Press, Oxford, 1993). By permission of Oxford University Press.

10 There are few geographical boundaries in innovation. While most innovating firms will begin in their home markets, successful innovation is rarely inhibited by national boundaries.

JOHN KAY, British academic at London Business School. *Foundations for Corporate Success* (Oxford University Press, Oxford, 1993). By permission of Oxford University Press.

11 The leader's primary contribution is in the recognition of good ideas, the support of those ideas, and the willingness to challenge the system in order to get new products, processes, services, and systems adopted. It might be more accurate, then, to say that leaders are early *adopters* of innovation. Leaders know well that experimentation, innovation, and change all involve risk and failure, but they proceed anyway.

JAMES M. KOUZES and BARRY Z. POSNER, American educators, management and training consultants, and authors. *The Leadership Challenge* (Jossey-Bass, San Francisco, 1995).

12 An enemy of innovation could be your own sales organisation, if it has too much power, because very often these organisations discourage innovation. When you make innovative new products, you must re-educate the sales force about them so the salesmen can educate and sell the public.

AKIO MORITA, Japanese industrialist, co-founder and CEO of Sony

Corporation. *Made in Japan: Akio Morita and Sony* (Collins, London, 1987). Reprinted by permission of HarperCollins Publishers Limited.

13 The best leaders are apt to be found among those executives who have a strong component of unorthodoxy in their characters. Instead of resisting innovation, they symbolise it – and companies cannot grow without innovation.

> DAVID OGILVY, British-born American advertising expert, founder of Ogilvy & Mather international advertising group, New York, and author. *Ogilvy on Advertising* (Pan, London, 1983).

14 Innovation is a low-odds business – and luck sure helps.

> TOM PETERS, American academic, consultant, lecturer and author. *Liberation Management* (Alfred A. Knopf, New York, 1992).

15 Innovation, I believe, is the only way that America will regain the initiative in a global dynamic economy. The way to increase our productivity is to make people more creative, resourceful, and innovative in the things they do.

> JOHN SCULLEY, American business executive, CEO of Apple Computers and author. *Odyssey: Pepsi to Apple* (Collins, London, 1987). Reprinted by permission of HarperCollins Publishers Limited.

16 Innovation has a lot to do with your ability to recognise surprising and unusual phenomena.

> HERBERT SIMON, American social scientist and 1978 Nobel laureate for economics. Attrib.

17 First-class quality, competitive pricing, and drastic cost-cutting are still not enough. Once all the surviving contenders in a market can offer value, the battle shifts to speed and innovation. To distinguish themselves, companies must offer something unique. They all are racing to find the new ideas, the new processes, that will enable them to win customers.

46 inspiration

See also: creativity 17; genius 34; ideas 40; imagination 42; innovation 45; motivation 63; originality 69; talent 99

1 The more the perspiration, the more the inspiration.
    ANON.

2 Inspiration is a farce that poets have invented to give themselves importance.
    JEAN-MARIE-LUCIEN-PIERRE ANOUILH (1910–87), French playwright and screenwriter. Attrib.

3 Just as appetite comes by eating, so work brings inspiration, if inspiration is not discernible at the beginning.
    IGOR STRAVINSKY (1882–1971), Russian-born American composer. *An Autobiography* (1936).

47 intelligence

See also: ideas 40; inspiration 46; judgement 48; knowledge 49; learning 52

1 We are the victims of our own intelligence. Or the lack of it.
    ANON.

2 Some highly intelligent people are not very effective. Perhaps their intelligence gives them doubts, fears and anxieties.

Perhaps there is the paralysis of analysis. Yet without effectiveness that intelligence is somewhat wasted. Intelligence may be something with which you were born. But effectiveness is a skill you can develop.

EDWARD DE BONO, Maltese-born British scholar, teacher, lecturer and author. *Handbook for the Positive Revolution* (Viking, London, 1991). Copyright © McQuaig Group Inc, 1991.

3 It is not enough to have a good mind; the main thing is to use it well.

RENÉ DESCARTES (1596–1650), French philosopher and mathematician. *Discourse on Method* (1639).

4 We should take care not to make the intellect our god; it has, of course, powerful muscles, but no personality.

ALBERT EINSTEIN (1879–1955), German–Swiss–American physicist. *Out of My Later Life* (1950).

5 The test of a first-rate intelligence is the ability to hold two opposed ideas in the mind at the same time, and still retain the ability to function.

F. SCOTT FITZGERALD (1896–1940), American novelist and short-story writer. *The Crack-Up* (1945).

6 One of the great errors of all time: association with money, especially large amounts, conveys a dangerously compelling impression of intelligence, at least until the day of final reckoning.

JOHN KENNETH GALBRAITH, Canadian-born American economist, Emeritus Professor of Economics at Harvard University, former senior White House adviser, diplomat and author. *Money: Whence it Came, Where it Went* (Penguin, New York; André Deutsch, London, 1975). Copyright © John Kenneth Galbraith 1975, 1995.

j

'Society cannot thrive on judgement alone.'
EDWARD DE BONO

judgement 48:2

judgement 48

See also: decisions 20; discretion 24; knowledge 49;
learning 52; mistakes 61; responsibility & responsibilities 90

1 I have always had good instincts. They've always been based on logic and responsibility.

> SANDRA BULLOCK, American actress. Comments made on 'Entertainment Tonight', a Paramount Pictures television program, 16 January 1997.

2 Society cannot thrive on judgement alone. Judgement may be enough to resist change but not enough to benefit from change.

> EDWARD DE BONO, Maltese-born British scholar, teacher, lecturer and author. *Parallel Thinking: From Socratic to de Bono Thinking* (Viking, London, 1994). Copyright © McQuaig Group Inc, 1994.

3 Vertical thinking is selection by exclusion. Judgement is the method of exclusion and the negative – 'no', 'not' – is the tool of exclusion.

> EDWARD DE BONO, Maltese-born British scholar, teacher, lecturer and author. *Lateral Thinking* (Ward Lock Education, London, 1970).

4 He hath a good judgement that relieth not wholly on his own.

> THOMAS FULLER M.D. (1654–1734), British physician and author. *Gnomologia* (1732).

5 In ethical, psychological, and aesthetic matters, to give a clear reason for one's judgement is universally recognised as a mark of rare genius.

> WILLIAM JAMES (1842–1910), American philosopher, psychologist and teacher. *The Principles of Psychology* (Henry Holt, New York, 1890).

6 Imagination is vital to precautionary judgement. One of the ablest executives I know recently said to his board of directors: 'We're sailing along fine but we ought to be on the lookout for rocks ahead. I made up a list of 20 things that might wreck us. Here they are.' Later, he enlisted the help of five creative men with business experience and worked out a check list of 179 such hazards.

ALEX F. OSBORN (1888–1966), American academic and author. *Applied Imagination: Principles & Procedures of Creative Thinking* (Charles Scribner's Sons, New York, 1953).

7 Knowledge is the treasure, but judgement the treasurer of a wise man.

WILLIAM PENN (1644–1718), British Quaker and founder of Pennsylvania, USA. *Some Fruits of Solitude* (1693).

8 'Tis with our judgements as our watches, none
Go just alike, yet each believes his own.

ALEXANDER POPE (1688–1744), British satirist and poet. *Essay on Criticism* (1711).

9 It is only shallow people who do not judge by appearances.

OSCAR WILDE (1854–1900), Irish playwright, poet, author and wit. *The Picture of Dorian Gray* (1891).

10 Many things happen as we get older. We acquire more compassion, for example. Suddenly you realise that nothing is black and white but there's a great deal of grey. It becomes impossible to be truly judgemental of people because you realise how little you ever know about what goes on in people's homes and how they really live.

PAULA YATES, British journalist, broadcaster and author. *The Autobiography* (HarperCollins, London, 1995).

'The more we increase our technical capacity,
the more powerless we become.'

CHARLES HANDY

knowledge 49:9

49 knowledge

See also: decisions 20; intelligence 47; judgement 48;
learning 52

1 A little knowledge is dangerous.

ANON.

2 Knowledge is like money – you can never have enough.

ANON.

3 People who think they know it all are especially annoying to
those of us who do.

ANON.

4 Knowledge is power.

FRANCIS BACON (1561–1626), British statesman, philosopher and essayist. 'De Haeresibus', *Meditationes Sacrae* (1597).

5 Many men are stored full of unused knowledge. Like loaded
guns that are never fired off, or military magazines in times of
peace, they are stuffed with useless ammunition.

HENRY WARD BEECHER (1813–87), American clergyman, lecturer and
author. *Proverbs from Plymouth Pulpit* (1887).

6 Knowledge is power. Unfortunate dupes of this saying will keep
on reading, ambitiously, till they have stunned their native initiative, and made their thoughts weak.

CLARENCE DAY (1874–1935), American essayist and author. *This Simian
World* (1920).

7 The older I get, the more intrigued I am about the way things are, and the less I seem to know.

    ROBERT DREWE, Australian novelist. *Australian Magazine*, 28 September 1996.

8 A little knowledge that *acts* is worth infinitely more than much knowledge that is idle.

    KAHLIL GIBRAN (1883–1931), Lebanese–American philosophical essayist, mystic poet, novelist and artist. *A Third Treasury of Kahlil Gibran* (Citadel, Secausus, New Jersey, 1965).

9 Sometimes it seems that the more we know, the more confused we get; that the more we increase our technical capacity, the more powerless we become.

    CHARLES HANDY, British academic, business consultant and author. *The Age of Paradox* (Harvard Business School Press, Cambridge, Massachusetts, 1994).

10 If a little knowledge is dangerous, where is the man who has so much as to be out of danger?

    T. H. HUXLEY (1825–95), British biologist, teacher, writer and grandfather of Aldous Huxley. 'On Elemental Instruction in Physiology' (1877).

11 Integrity without knowledge is weak and useless, and knowledge without integrity is dangerous and dreadful.

    SAMUEL JOHNSON (Doctor Johnson; 1709–84), British poet, essayist, critic, journalist and lexicographer. *Rasselas* (1759).

12 Charles Lamb's classic 1822 essay 'A Dissertation on Roast Pig' [gives] a satirical account of how the art of roasting was discovered in a Chinese village that did not cook its food. A mischievous child accidentally set fire to a house with a pig inside, and the villagers poking around in the embers discovered a new delicacy. This eventually led to a rash of house fires. The moral of the story is: when

you do not understand how the pig gets cooked, you have to burn a whole house down every time you want a roast pork dinner.

ROSABETH MOSS KANTER, American academic and author, professor at Harvard Business School. *The Changemasters* (Simon & Schuster, New York, 1983).

13 The greater our knowledge increases, the greater our ignorance unfolds.

JOHN F. KENNEDY (1917–63), American statesman, and 35th President of the United States of America 1961–63. In a speech made at Rice University, Houston, Texas, 12 September 1962.

14 It is a nuisance that knowledge can only be acquired by hard work.

W. SOMERSET MAUGHAM (1874–1965), British playwright and novelist. Attrib.

15 He who does not know one thing knows another.

KENYAN PROVERB.

16 Knowledge fuelled by emotion equals action.

JIM ROHN, American business philosopher, lecturer and author. *Seven Strategies for Wealth and Happiness* (Brolga, Melbourne, 1994).

17 The desire for knowledge, like the acquisition of riches, increases ever with the acquisition of it.

LAURENCE STERNE (1713–68), British novelist. *Tristram Shandy* (1759–67).

18 If we value the pursuit of knowledge, we must be free to follow wherever that search may lead us. The free mind is no barking dog, to be tethered on a ten-foot chain.

ADLAI STEVENSON (1900–65), American politician, diplomat and US Ambassador to the United Nations 1960–65. In a speech made at the University of Wisconsin, Madison, 8 October 1952.

19 We are creating and using up ideas and images at a faster and faster pace. Knowledge, like people, places, things and organisational forms, is becoming disposable.

> ALVIN TOFFLER, American scholar, lecturer and author. *Future Shock* (The Bodley Head, London, 1970).

20 With knowledge now the key raw material for creating all economic wealth, the new power struggles will reach deep into our minds.

> DENIS WAITLEY, American personal development counsellor, lecturer and author. *Empires of the Mind: Lessons to Lead and Succeed in a Knowledge-Based World* (William Morrow, New York; Nicholas Brealey, London, 1995). Reprinted by permission of Nicholas Brealey Publishing Limited, London, Tel. (0171) 430-0224, Fax (0171) 404-8311.

21 In a sense, knowledge shrinks as wisdom grows: for details are swallowed up in principles. The details of knowledge which are important will be picked up ad hoc in each avocation of life, but the habit of the utilisation of well-understood principles is the final possession of wisdom.

> A. N. WHITEHEAD (1861–1947), British mathematician, philosopher, Professor of Philosophy at Harvard University and author. 'The Rhythmic Claims of Freedom and Discipline', *The Aims of Education and Other Essays* (New American Library, New York).

22 Knowledge is always accompanied with accessories of emotion and purpose.

> A. N. WHITEHEAD (1861–1947), British mathematician, philosopher, Professor of Philosophy at Harvard University and author. *Adventures of Ideas* (Harvard University Press, Cambridge, Massachusetts, 1933; reprinted Penguin, New York, 1942).

'A true leader is one who designs the cathedral
and then shares the vision that inspires others
to build it.'

JAN CARLZON

leadership 51:12

lawyers 50
See also: business ethics 7; honesty & integrity 38

1 A lawyer, it has been said, is a person who gets two people to strip for a fight and then runs off with their clothes.
   ANON.

2 Talk is cheap. Unless you have to hire a lawyer.
   ANON.

3 If there were no bad people there would be no good lawyers.
   CHARLES DICKENS (1812–70), British novelist. *The Old Curiosity Shop* (1840).

4 Give a wise man an honest brief to plead and his eloquence is no remarkable achievement.
   EURIPIDES (480–405 BC), Greek playwright. *The Bacchae* (c. 405 BC).

5 You're an attorney. It's your duty to lie, conceal and distort everything, and slander everybody.
   JEAN GIRAUDOUX (1882–1944), French playwright, novelist and essayist. *The Madwoman of Chaillot* (1945).

6 As a peace-maker, the lawyer has a superior opportunity of being a good man. There will be business enough.
   ABRAHAM LINCOLN (1809–65), American statesman, and 16th President of the United States of America 1861–65. Attrib.

7 I would say that probably the best way to deal with lawyers is not to deal with them.

> MARK H. McCORMACK, American sports marketing consultant, founder and CEO of International Management Group, and author. *What They Didn't Teach Me at Yale Law School* (Collins, New York, 1988; originally published as *The Terrible Truth About Lawyers*, Collins, New York, 1987). Reprinted by permission of HarperCollins Publishers Inc.

8 Lawyers and painters can soon change white to black.
   DANISH PROVERB.

51 **leadership**

See also: decisions 20; goals & goal-setting 36; listening 54; success 98

1 *A Short Course on Leadership*
   The six most important words – 'I admit I made a mistake.'
   The five most important words – 'I am proud of you.'
   The four most important words – 'What is your opinion?'
   The three most important words – 'If you please.'
   The two most important words – 'Thank you.'
   The one most important word – 'We.'
   The least most important word – 'I.'

   JOHN ADAIR, British management trainer and author. *Effective Leadership* (Pan, London, 1983).

2 A boss says 'Go.' A leader says 'Let's go!'
   ANON.

3 Leadership is all about taking. Followers take orders, leaders take chances.
   ANON.

[Alternatively:]

4 Leadership is all about taking. Followers take orders, leaders take charge.

ANON.

5 Life is like a dog-sled team – if you aren't the lead dog, the scenery never changes.

ANON.

6 What's the difference between a leader and a manager? Leaders know the best course of action, while managers only know the best way to follow it.

ANON.

7 He who has never learned to obey cannot be a good commander.

ARISTOTLE (384–322 BC), Greek philosopher. *Politics* (4th century BC).

8 True leadership is all about example. Nothing more clearly determines the culture, and ultimately the success of a business than a leader who understands the powerful influence of their own example.

BOB ASHFORD, Australian tourism industry executive, National Manager of the AussieHost Program of the Inbound Tourism Organisation of Australia. *AussieHost News*, August 1995.

9 Leaders learn by leading, and they learn best by leading in the face of obstacles. As weather shapes mountains, problems shape leaders.

WARREN BENNIS, American academic, professor at the University of Southern California and author. *On Becoming a Leader* (Addison Wesley, Reading, Massachusetts, 1988).

10 Effective managers have a range of management styles that they can use comfortably. They have developed some flexibility in using those styles in different situations. Effective managers

also have a knack for being able to diagnose what their people need from them in order to build their skills and confidence in doing the tasks they are assigned. Finally, effective leaders can communicate with their staff – they are able to reach agreements with them not only about their tasks but also about the amount of direction and support they will need to accomplish these tasks. These three skills – *flexibility*, *diagnosis*, and *contracting* – are three of the most important skills managers can use to motivate better performance on the part of the people with whom they work.

KENNETH BLANCHARD, American educator, management consultant, trainer and author; PATRICIA ZIGARMI, American business consultant and author; and DREA ZIGARMI, American business consultant, researcher and author. *Leadership and the One Minute Manager* (Collins, London, 1986). Reprinted by permission of HarperCollins Publishers Limited.

11 Follow me who can!

PHILIP BROKE (d. 1841), British naval captain. Words used in the War of 1812 when leading HMS *Shannon*'s boarding party in the storming and taking of the USS *Chesapeake*, 1 June 1813. Quoted in Kenneth Poolman, *Guns Off Cape Ann* (Evans Brothers, London, 1961).

12 A true leader is one who designs the cathedral and then shares the vision that inspires others to build it.

JAN CARLZON, Swedish business leader, former CEO of Scandinavian Airlines System, speaker and author. *Moments of Truth* (Ballinger, Cambridge, Massachusetts, 1987; revised edition Harper & Row, New York, 1989). Copyright © 1987 by Ballinger Publishing Company. Reprinted by permission of HarperCollins Publishers, Inc.

13 Once I learned how to be a leader rather than a manager, I was able to open up each company to new, market-oriented possibilities and to the creative energy of its employees.

JAN CARLZON, Swedish business leader, former CEO of Scandinavian Airlines System, speaker and author. *Moments of Truth* (Ballinger, Cambridge, Massachusetts, 1987; revised edition Harper & Row, New York, 1989). Copyright © 1987 by Ballinger Publishing Company. Reprinted by permission of HarperCollins Publishers, Inc.

14 Each one of us, in large or small ways, is a leader. Some have an official title for their roles as leaders, while others may lead their brothers, sisters, or friends on the playground. Leadership is a state of mind – what you do to yourself, not what you do to others.

CHIN-NING CHU, Chinese-born American lecturer, corporate trainer and author, President of Asian Marketing Consultants Inc. *Thick Face, Black Heart* (AMC, Beavertown, Oregon, 1992). Reprinted by permission of Warner Books, Inc. Copyright © 1992 by Chin-Ning Chu. All rights reserved.

15 The prince is like the wind and the people like the grass; it is the nature of grass to bend with the wind.

CONFUCIUS (c. 551 – c. 479 BC), Chinese teacher, philosopher and political theorist. *Analects* (6th century BC).

16 Management is efficiency in climbing the ladder of success; leadership determines whether the ladder is leaning against the right wall.

STEPHEN R. COVEY, American educator, leadership consultant, author and former Professor of Business Management at Brigham Young University. *The 7 Habits of Highly Effective People* (Simon & Schuster, New York, 1989).

17 I, if anyone, am the living embodiment of the 'toothpaste' theory: all along, it has been the competence of the people working for me that has squeezed me out at the top.

PETER DE LA BILLIÈRE, British soldier, general and commander-in-chief of British Forces, Operation Desert Storm, 1991. *Looking for Trouble* (HarperCollins, London, 1994).

18 Management is doing things right; leadership is doing the right things.

> PETER DRUCKER and WARREN BENNIS. American academics and authors. Quoted in Stephen R. Covey, *The 7 Habits of Highly Effective People* (Simon & Schuster, New York, 1989).

19 Controlling men is like handling a piece of string. If you push it, it will go anywhere. If you lead it, you can make it go anywhere you want.

> DWIGHT D. EISENHOWER (1890–1969), American general and statesman, 34th President of the United States of America 1953–61. Attrib.

20 I suppose leadership at one time meant muscles, but today it means getting along with people.

> INDIRA GANDHI (1917–84), Indian stateswoman, and Prime Minister 1966–77 and 1980–84. Attrib.

21 Leaders will be those who empower others ... Empowering leadership means bringing out the energy and capabilities people have and getting them to work together in a way they wouldn't do otherwise.

> BILL GATES, American information technology pioneer, founder and CEO of Microsoft Corporation, and author. *Entrepreneur*, January 1994.

22 *A Leader's Prayer*

Dear Lord, help me to become the kind of leader my management would like to have me be. Give me the mysterious something which will enable me at all times satisfactorily to explain policies, rules, regulations and procedures to my workers even when they have never been explained to me.

Help me to teach and to train the uninterested and dimwitted without ever losing my patience or my temper.

Give me that love for my fellow men which passeth all understanding so that I may lead the recalcitrant, obstinate, no-good worker into the paths of righteousness by my own example, and by soft persuading remonstrance, instead of busting him on the nose.

Instil into my inner-being tranquillity and peace of mind that no longer will I awake from my restless sleep in the middle of the night crying out 'What has the boss got that I haven't got and how did he get it?'

Teach me to smile if it kills me.

Make me a better leader of men by helping develop larger and greater qualities of understanding, tolerance, sympathy, wisdom, perspective, equanimity, mind-reading and second sight.

And when, Dear Lord, Thou has helped me to achieve the high pinnacle my management has prescribed for me and when I shall have become the paragon of all supervisory virtues in this earthly world, Dear Lord, move over. Amen.

CHARLES HANDY, British academic, business consultant and author. *Understanding Organisations* (Penguin, London, 1976; fourth edition 1993). Copyright © Charles Handy, 1976, 1981, 1985, 1993.

23 You don't manage people, you manage things. You lead people.

GRACE HOPPER, American admiral, United States Navy (retired). Quoted in Chin-Ning Chu, *Thick Face, Black Heart* (AMC, Beavertown, Oregon, 1992). Reprinted by permission of Warner Books, Inc. Copyright © 1992 by Chin-Ning Chu. All rights reserved.

24 Sizing up opponents to determine victory, assessing dangers and distances, is the proper course of action for military leaders.

LIU JI (14th century AD), Chinese general. Quoted in Sun Tzu, *The Art of War.*

25 America's survival and progress will depend . . . on its ability to make choices which reflect contemporary reality . . . What no leader must ever do is to suggest that choice has no price, or that no balance needs to be struck.

HENRY KISSINGER, German-born American lecturer, consultant and author, former US Secretary of State and senior White House adviser. *Diplomacy* (Touchstone, New York, 1994).

26 When they were at their personal best, the leaders we studied were able to:
   • Challenge the process
   • Inspire a shared vision
   • Enable others to act
   • Model the way
   • Encourage the heart

JAMES M. KOUZES and BARRY Z. POSNER, American educators, management and training consultants, and authors. *The Leadership Challenge* (Jossey-Bass, San Francisco, 1995).

27 How much in military matters depends on one master mind?

ABRAHAM LINCOLN (1809–65), American statesman, and 16th President of the United States of America 1861–65. Attrib.

28 The most important quality in a leader is that of being acknowledged as such. All leaders whose fitness is questioned are clearly lacking in force.

ANDRÉ MAUROIS (real name Emile Herzog; 1885–1967), French biographer, essayist and author. *The Art of Living*.

29 The most important trait of a good leader is knowing who you are. You have to do all your homework, but then you have to go with your intuition without letting your mind get in the way.

GEORGE McCRACKEN, American computer industry leader, CEO of Silicon Graphics. *Fortune*, 22 August 1994. © 1994 Time Inc. All rights reserved.

30 Great actor–personalities, I have come to think, are like trained bears in that they attract us with their discipline while their

powerful claws threaten us; a great star implies he is his own person and can be mean and even dangerous, like a great leader.

ARTHUR MILLER, American playwright, screenwriter and author. *Timebends* (Methuen, London, 1987).

31 The real leader has no need to lead – he is content to point the way.

HENRY MILLER (1891–1980), American author and artist. *The Wisdom of the Heart* (New Directions, New York, 1941).

32 The leader must have infectious optimism and the determination to persevere in the face of difficulties. He must also radiate confidence, even when he himself is not too certain of the outcome.

BERNARD MONTGOMERY (Viscount Montgomery of Alamein; 1887–1976), British soldier, and field marshal in World War Two. Attrib.

33 Management is not dictatorship. Top management of a company has to have the ability to manage people by leading them.

AKIO MORITA, Japanese industrialist, co-founder and CEO of Sony Corporation. *Made in Japan: Akio Morita and Sony* (Collins, London, 1987). Reprinted by permission of HarperCollins Publishers Limited.

34 Few men of action have been able to make a graceful exit at the appropriate time.

MALCOLM MUGGERIDGE (1903–91), British editor, columnist and author. 'Twilight of Greatness', *The Most of Malcolm Muggeridge* (Collins, London, 1966). Reprinted by permission of HarperCollins Publishers Limited.

35 Leaders recognise that while capital and technology are important resources, people make or break a company. To harness their power, leaders inspire commitment and empower people by sharing authority. Responding to labour shortages with flexibility, they enable their firms to attract, reward, and motivate

the best people. But effective leadership must also monitor the external environment, tracking trends, markets, technological change, and product cycles.

JOHN NAISBITT and PATRICIA ABURDENE, American social forecasters, academics and authors. *Megatrends 2000* (William Morrow, New York, 1990).

36 A leader is a dealer in hope.

NAPOLEON I (Napoleon Bonaparte; 1769–1821), French soldier, statesman, and Emperor of France 1804–14/15. *Maxims* (1804–1815).

37 Vision is the key to understanding leadership, and real leaders have never lost the childlike ability to dream dreams . . . Vision is the blazing campfire around which people will gather. It provides light, energy, warmth and unity.

BILL NEWMAN, Australian broadcaster, speaker and author. *The Ten Laws of Leadership* (BNC, Brisbane, 1993).

38 I have had unique opportunities for observing men who manage great corporations – my clients. Most of them are good *problem-solvers* and *decision-makers*, but few are outstanding *leaders*. Some of them, far from inspiring their lieutenants, display a genius for castrating them . . .

There has been a lot of research into leadership. It is the consensus among the social scientists that success in leadership depends on the circumstances. For example, a man who has been an outstanding leader in an industrial company can be a flop when he goes to Washington as Secretary of Commerce. And the kind of leadership which works well in a new company seldom works well in a mature company.

There appears to be no correlation between leadership and academic achievement. I was relieved to learn this, because I have no college degree. The motivation which makes a man a good student is not the kind of motivation which makes him a good leader . . .

Great leaders almost always exude *self-confidence*. They are never petty. They are never buck-passers. They pick themselves up after defeat . . .

Great leaders are always fanatically committed to their jobs. They do not suffer from the crippling need to be universally loved. They have the guts to make unpopular decisions – including the guts to fire non-performers . . .

Good leaders are *decisive*. They grasp nettles.

I do not believe that fear is a tool used by good leaders. People do their best work in a happy atmosphere . . .

The most effective leader is the one who satisfies the psychological needs of his followers.

DAVID OGILVY, British-born American advertising expert, founder of Ogilvy & Mather international advertising group, New York, and author. *Ogilvy on Advertising* (Pan, London, 1983).

39 In public life or in business, creative thinking is vital to leadership. Although an executive must possess judicial judgement to a marked degree, he cannot be solely a judge – he must also excel in resourcefulness. Then, too, he needs to recognise the value of creativity, and to know how to tap and encourage the creative power of his associates.

ALEX F. OSBORN (1888–1966), American academic and author. *Applied Imagination: Principles & Procedures of Creative Thinking* (Charles Scribner's Sons, New York, 1953).

40 It is not all lofty visions and grand language when you are a leader. I can safely say that no organisational transformation has occurred without changes in key personnel. No organisation that I know of has changed its direction and gone down a new path behind a leader without different people being involved.

KEN PARRY, Australian academic, leadership consultant and author. *Transformational Leadership* (Pitman, Melbourne, 1996).

41 If you want me you can always find me in the lead tank.

> GEORGE S. PATTON (1885–1945), American soldier, US Army general in World War Two. In a speech to the 761st 'Black Panther' Tank Battalion, France, 1944.

42 Leadership, many have said, is different from management. Management is mostly about 'to do' lists – can't live without them! Leadership is about tapping the wellsprings of human motivation – and about fundamental relations with one's fellows.

> TOM PETERS, American academic, consultant, lecturer and author. In a foreword to James M. Kouzes & Barry Z. Posner, *The Leadership Challenge* (Jossey-Bass, San Francisco, 1995).

43 Leadership is the privilege to have the responsibility to direct the actions of others in carrying out the purposes of the organisation, at varying levels of authority and with accountability for both successful and failed endeavours. It does not constitute a model or system. No model or system of leadership behaviours can anticipate the circumstances, conditions and situations in which the leader must influence the actions of others.

> WESS ROBERTS, American author. *Leadership Secrets of Attila the Hun* (Bantam, London, 1989).

44 Before people are hired or promoted to leadership positions [at Semco], they are interviewed and approved by all who will be working for them. And every six months managers are evaluated by those who work under them. The results are posted for all to see. Does this mean workers can fire their bosses? I guess it does, since anyone who consistently gets bad grades usually leaves Semco, one way or another.

> RICARDO SEMLER, Brazilian industrialist, CEO of Semco, Brazil, and author. *Maverick!* (Century, London, 1993). Copyright © 1993 by Tableturn Inc. Reproduced by permission of the author c/o Rogers, Coleridge & White Ltd, 20 Powis Mews, London W11 1JN.

45 Skilled managers in any organisations need to be able leaders who can listen and communicate, who are competitive by nature, resilient and mentally tough. Determined to achieve the apparently impossible, they must also possess clarity of thought and vision.

ALLEN SHEPPARD, British business leader, Chairman and Group Chief Executive of Grand Metropolitan. In a foreword to Jeremy G. Thorn, *Developing Your Career in Management* (Mercury Books, London, 1992).

46 While in the past many managers could succeed by imitating another company's strategy or organisational model, today's leaders are forced to invent, not copy: there are no sure-fire strategies or models to copy. Above all, the adaptive manager today must be capable of radical action – willing to think beyond the thinkable: to reconceptualise products, procedures, programs and purposes before crisis makes drastic change inescapable.

ALVIN TOFFLER, American scholar, lecturer and author. *The Adaptive Corporation* (Gower, Aldershot, Hampshire, 1985).

47 True leadership must be for the benefit of the followers, not the enrichment of the leaders. In combat, officers eat last. Most people in big companies today are administered, not led. They are treated as personnel, not people.

ROBERT TOWNSEND, American business executive, CEO of Avis car rental group, and author. *Further Up the Organisation* (Alfred A. Knopf, New York, 1970; revised edition Michael Joseph, London, 1984).

48 Yesterday leaders commanded and controlled. Today leaders empower and coach.

DENIS WAITLEY, American personal development counsellor, lecturer and author. *Empires of the Mind: Lessons to Lead and Succeed in a Knowledge-Based World* (William Morrow, New York; Nicholas Brealey, London, 1995). Reprinted by permission of Nicholas Brealey Publishing Limited, London, Tel. (0171) 430-0224, Fax (0171) 404-8311.

49 A leader must have the ability to hold their team like a bird. Just right.

> KEVIN WELDON, Australian publisher and author. *Good Enough is Never Good Enough* (Angus & Robertson, Sydney, 1995). Reprinted by permission of HarperCollins Publishers.

52 learning

See also: intelligence 47; knowledge 49; mistakes 61; motivation 63; training 103

1 To maximise your earning power, maximise your learning power.

> ANON.

2 Learning without thought is labour lost; thought without learning is perilous.

> CONFUCIUS (c. 551 – c. 479 BC), Chinese teacher, philosopher and political theorist. *Analects* (6th century BC).

3 Liberty without learning is always in peril, and learning without liberty is always in vain.

> JOHN F. KENNEDY (1917–63), American statesman, and 35th President of the United States of America 1961–63. In a speech made at Vanderbilt University, Nashville, Tennessee, 18 May 1963.

4 You grab a challenge, act on it, then honestly reflect on why your actions worked or didn't. You learn from it and then move on. That continuous process of lifelong learning helps enormously in a rapidly changing economic environment.

> JOHN KOTTER, American academic at Harvard Business School. *Fortune*, 22 August 1994. © 1994 Time Inc. All rights reserved.

5 It would be ridiculous to assert that those who fail over and over again eventually succeed as leaders. Success in any endeavour

isn't a process of simply buying enough lottery tickets. The key that unlocks the door to opportunity is learning ... In other words, leaders are learners. They learn from their failures as well as their successes.

JAMES M. KOUZES and BARRY Z. POSNER, American educators, management and training consultants, and authors. *The Leadership Challenge* (Jossey-Bass, San Francisco, 1995).

6 A little learning is a dangerous thing.

ALEXANDER POPE (1688–1744), British poet and satirist. *An Essay on Criticism* (1711).

7 There are no national frontiers to learning.

JAPANESE PROVERB.

8 Education is an admirable thing, but it is well to remember from time to time that nothing that is worth knowing can be taught.

OSCAR WILDE (1854–1900), Irish playwright, poet, author and wit. 'The Critic as Artist', *Intentions* (1891).

limitations 53

See also: challenge 8; obstacles 66;
problems & problem-solving 78

1 I ... always underestimate the Americans' ability to be shocked. The hysterical moralism of the American psyche cannot be underestimated.

TINA BROWN, British-born American-based magazine editor, Editor of *The New Yorker. The Guardian*, 23 October 1996. The Guardian ©.

2 Men cease to interest us when we find their limitations.

RALPH WALDO EMERSON (1803–82), American philosopher, poet and essayist. 'Circles', *Essays: First Series* (1841).

3 A bird can roost on but one branch. A mouse can drink no more than its fill from a river.

CHINESE PROVERB.

54 **listening**

See also: advice 4; negotiation 64; selling 93

1 The word *listen* contains the same letters as the word *silent*.

ALFRED BRENDEL, Austrian pianist. Attrib.

2 There are meetings that can be dominated by active listeners, just as there are those which can be dominated by active talkers.

EDWARD DE BONO, Maltese-born British scholar, teacher, lecturer and author. *Tactics: The Art and Science of Success* (HarperCollins, London, 1985). Reprinted by permission of HarperCollins Publishers Limited.

3 Good listening can increase your negotiation power by increasing the information you have about the other side's interests or about possible options. Once you understand the other side's feelings and concerns, you can begin to address them, to explore areas of agreement and disagreement, and to develop useful ways to proceed in the future.

ROGER FISHER, American law professor at Harvard Law School, conflict management consultant and author; WILLIAM URY, American negotiation consultant and lecturer, and author; and BRUCE PATTON, American law lecturer, negotiation skills teacher and author. *Getting to Yes* (Houghton Mifflin, New York, 1981 & 1991; Hutchinson, London, 1982; revised edition Business Books, London, 1991). Copyright © 1981, 1991 by Roger Fisher and William Ury. Reprinted by permission of Houghton Mifflin Company. All rights reserved.

4 Some of the smart people we're hiring now are a lot younger than I am ... They're extraordinarily talented and will contribute

new visions. If Microsoft can combine these visions with listening carefully to customers, we have a chance to continue to lead the way.

BILL GATES, American information technology pioneer, founder and CEO of Microsoft Corporation, and author. *The Road Ahead* (Viking Penguin, New York, 1995). Copyright © 1995 by William H. Gates III. Used by permission of Viking Penguin, a division of Penguin Books USA Inc.

5 The ability to listen, really hear what someone is saying, has far greater business implications, of course, than simply gaining insight into people. In selling, for instance, there is probably no greater asset.

MARK H. McCORMACK, American sports marketing consultant, founder and CEO of International Management Group, and author. *What They Don't Teach You at Harvard Business School* (Collins, London, 1984). Reprinted by permission of HarperCollins Publishers Limited.

6 If the idea is on-trend for the future, the consumer won't know yet whether she'll want it or not. Be cautious about taking her rejection too seriously. Instead, listen for 'creative builds' on the idea, or listen to how she associates the new idea with other things in her life right now: a great source of future usage clues . . . Being able to hear what the consumer is saying is the foundation of our trends. And, if the truth be known, it's the foundation of the future.

FAITH POPCORN, American business consultant, co-founder and CEO of BrainReserve, and author. *The Popcorn Report* (Doubleday, New York, 1991). Copyright 1991 by Faith Popcorn. Used by permission of Doubleday, a division of Bantam Doubleday Dell Publishing Group, Inc.

7 From listening comes wisdom, and from speaking repentance.
ITALIAN PROVERB.

8 **Give every man thine ear, but few thy voice.**

WILLIAM SHAKESPEARE (1564–1616), British poet and playwright. *Hamlet* (1600).

9 **It takes two to speak the truth – one to speak, and another to hear.**

H. D. THOREAU (1817–62), American poet, naturalist and essayist. 'Wednesday', *A Week on the Concord and Merrimack Rivers* (1849).

10 **I do my negotiating on the basis of listening to what the man is saying, what the whole thing's about.**

GORDON WHITE, British-born American-based businessman, Chairman of Hanson Industries, New York. Quoted in Alan Whicker, *Whicker's New World* (Weidenfeld & Nicolson, London, 1985).

11 **The reason why we have two ears and only one mouth is that we may listen the more and talk the less.**

ZENO OF CITIUM (c. 335 BC–c. 263 BC), Greek philosopher and founder of the Stoic school of philosophy. Quoted in Diogenes Laertius, *Lives and Opinions of Eminent Philosophers* (3rd century AD).

55 losing

See also: challenge 8; change 9; defeat 21; failure 30; mistakes 61; persistence & perseverance 71

1 **There are no prizes for losing.**

ANON.

2 **Loss is nothing else but change, and change is Nature's delight.**

MARCUS AURELIUS (AD 121–180), Roman emperor and philosopher. *Meditations* (2nd century AD).

3 **Juggling a number of commercial balls in several different places has the added advantage that if one important business**

contact should fall hopelessly by the wayside, there will always be another somewhere else. For this reason, top Hong Kong businessmen started cultivating operations in places such as Bangkok, Singapore and Vietnam well before 1997 was an issue.

> CLAUDIA CRAGG, British author. *The New Taipans* (Century, London, 1995).

4 You must lose a fly to catch a trout.

> GEORGE HERBERT (1593–1633), British clergyman and poet. *Jacula Prudentum* (1651).

5 To be second best is to be a loser among equals.

> JEFF KENNETT, Australian state politician, Premier of Victoria 1992– . In a speech made in Sydney, 17 November 1997.

6 Australians love a loser and hate a winner.

> MAX LAKE, Australian surgeon, author, vigneron and founder of Lake's Folly vineyard, Pokolbin, New South Wales. *Tatler*, November 1991.

loyalty 56

See also: incentive/s & rewards 43; leadership 51; motivation 63

1 Loyalty has changed. It's no longer about the employer being a mother ship to a person for their whole life ... People need certainty, control, to know what demands are expected of them, and support in the workplace. If you get those factors happening in the workplace, you're going to engender more loyalty, more commitment.

> SHARON BENT, Australian organisational psychologist at the Sydney University Cumberland Health and Research Centre. *Sydney Morning Herald*, 23 November 1996.

2 It is the tyranny of the market that has destroyed the loyalty of corporations to their communities; customers to their neighbourhood merchants; athletes to their local teams; teams to their cities.

ALAN EHRENHALT, American author. Attrib.

3 ·An ounce of loyalty is worth a pound of cleverness.

ELBERT HUBBARD (1856–1915), American businessman, printer and writer. *The Note Book* (1927).

4 The average business spends six times more to attract new customers than it does to keep old ones. Yet customer loyalty is in most cases worth ten times the price of a single purchase.

MICHAEL LEBOEUF, American business consultant, speaker and author, Professor of Management at the University of New Orleans. *How to Win Customers & Keep Them for Life* (Putnam, New York, 1987). Reprinted by permission of The Putnam Publishing Group. Copyright © 1988 by Michael LeBoeuf, Ph.D.

5 Loyalty plays no part in the world inhabited by Princes and their Servants, and to believe in it leads only to betrayal and deep disappointment.

ALISTAIR McALPINE (Lord McAlpine of West Green), British business leader, political figure and author. *The Servant* (Faber & Faber, London, 1992).

6 The quality or characteristic which I think I have learned from my father and other people who have influenced me, which I think is important, is loyalty. You have to give loyalty in order to receive it. I believe you offer loyalty to everyone, which is not as big a strain as it sounds, because very few people pick it up. It's a two-way street. It's looking after one's friends when its inconvenient or difficult for you to do so. Anyone can look after someone if it's no problem, but it's real loyalty when you have

to choose between something which you wanted or wanted to do, and their need. Then you have to choose to serve their need. I believe that's above everything else. You kid yourself if you think you can buy loyalty. You can't. You earn it through consideration and through being there when other people need you, regardless of what other commitments you have.

KERRY PACKER, Australian media proprietor. Quoted in Terry Lane, *As the Twig is Bent* (Dove, Victoria, 1979).

7 Every great man nowadays has his disciples, and it's usually Judas who writes his biography.

OSCAR WILDE (1854–1900), Irish playwright, poet, author and wit. Attrib.

8 People give you their loyalty when they feel appreciated. One study found that 46 per cent of people who leave their job do so because they don't feel appreciated by management.

ZIG ZIGLAR, American sales trainer and motivator. *Success*, November 1994.

luck 57

See also: achieving 2; opportunity 68; success 98

1 Luck is the residue of diligence.

ANON.

2 Luck is when preparation meets opportunity.

ANON.

3 You make your own luck.

ANON.

4 Everybody needs luck – but luck will get you only so far. Luck, in my experience, presents you with a series of opportunities,

that come past you as if on an endless conveyor belt. As each opportunity passes, you have a short time in which to inspect it and decide whether to grab it or let it go by.

PETER DE LA BILLIERE, British soldier, general and commander-in-chief of British Forces, Operation Desert Storm, 1991. *Looking for Trouble* (HarperCollins, London, 1994).

5 Human beings are going to get stuck in the rat-race they're in if they don't get over this notion of luck.

WERNER ERHARD, American spiritualist and founder of EST. Quoted in Edward de Bono, *Tactics: The Art and Science of Success* (Collins, London, 1985).

6 It is a great piece of skill to know how to guide your luck even while waiting for it.

BALTASAR GRACIAN (1601–58), Spanish Jesuit priest and author. *The Art of Worldly Wisdom* (1647).

7 Luck can be assisted by care.

BALTASAR GRACIAN (1601–58), Spanish Jesuit priest and author. *The Art of Worldly Wisdom* (1647).

8 There is no good or bad luck except wisdom and foolishness.

BALTASAR GRACIAN (1601–58), Spanish Jesuit priest and author. *The Art of Worldly Wisdom* (1647).

9 Leaders venture out. While many people in our studies attributed their success to 'luck' or 'being in the right place at the right time,' none of them sat idly by waiting for fate to smile upon them. Those who lead others to greatness seek and accept challenge.

JAMES M. KOUZES and BARRY Z. POSNER, American educators, management and training consultants, and authors. *The Leadership Challenge* (Jossey-Bass, San Francisco, 1995).

10 The group that is 'naturally lucky' can see the tiniest crack and turn it into a crevice. The group that 'never gets a break' wouldn't see an opportunity if it jumped up and down and then mugged them.

> MARK H. McCORMACK, American sports marketing consultant, founder and CEO of International Management Group, and author. *What They Don't Teach You at Harvard Business School* (Collins, London, 1984). Reprinted by permission of HarperCollins Publishers Limited.

11 Nothing works in life without luck. It's the ultimate thing and the greatest man in the world gets nowhere without it.

> KERRY PACKER, Australian media proprietor. Quoted in Terry Lane, *As the Twig is Bent* (Dove, Victoria, 1979).

12 If you believe that success does owe a lot to luck, and that luck in turn owes a lot to getting in the way of unexpected opportunities, you need not throw up your hands in despair. There *are* strategies you can pursue to get a little nuttiness into your life, and perhaps, then, egg on good luck.

> TOM PETERS, American academic, consultant, lecturer and author. *Liberation Management* (Alfred A. Knopf, New York, 1992).

13 The harder I practise, the luckier I get.

> GARY PLAYER, South African golfer. Quoted in Mark H. McCormack, *What They Don't Teach You at Harvard Business School* (Collins, London, 1984).

14 Diligence is the mother of good luck.

> ENGLISH PROVERB.

15 Ill luck is good for something.

> ENGLISH PROVERB.

16 See a pin and let it lie,
    You'll want a pin before you die.

See a pin and pick it up,
All the day you'll have good luck.
ENGLISH PROVERB.

17 Misfortune lives next door to Stupidity.
RUSSIAN PROVERB.

18 The worse luck now, the better another time.
SCOTTISH PROVERB.

19 Luck never made a man wise.
SENECA (Lucius Annaeus Seneca, The Younger; c. 4 BC – AD 65), Roman
philosopher, playwright, poet, administrator, tutor and later chief minister to
Emperor Nero. *Letters to Lucilius* (c. AD 30).

20 Fortune brings in some boats that are not steered.
WILLIAM SHAKESPEARE (1564–1616), British poet and playwright.
Cymbeline (1609–10).

21 Fortune favours the brave.
TERENCE (Publius Terentius Afer; c. 190–159 BC). Roman playwright.
Phormio (161 BC).

22 Fortune sides with him who dares.
VIRGIL (Publius Vergilius Maro; 70–19 BC), Roman poet. *Aeneid* (30–19 BC).

23 'Tis better to be fortunate than wise.
JOHN WEBSTER (c. 1580 – c. 1625), British playwright. *The White Devil*
(1612).

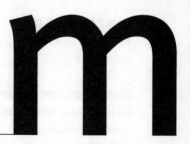

'Consumers are faced with a Hobson's choice; the illusion of choice when there aren't any real alternatives. Hobson was a liveryman 400 years ago who insisted that each client take the horse closest to the door or none.'

HERBERT ROTFELD

marketing 58:6

58 marketing

1 Marketing drives people into McDonald's restaurants and plays an important role in encouraging trial . . . But McDonald's substantial growth is built on repeat business, repeat visits.

> CHARLIE BELL, Australian business leader and CEO of McDonald's Australia. In a foreword to Stephen Dando-Collins, *The Customer Care Revolution* (Pitman, Melbourne, 1996).

2 One of the most attractive features about I-way marketing is that it is so inexpensive, you can afford to make mistakes. A small business might drown in the cost of a few big city newspaper advertisements. On the Internet, the expense of experimentation, test marketing, and general advertising becomes negligible. The single greatest resources required are no longer money, but creativity and the willingness to try something novel. You can give your pioneering instincts full range of expression without risking the family farm in the process.

> LAURENCE A. CANTER and MARTHA S. SIEGEL, American lawyers and authors. *How to Make a Fortune on the Information Superhighway* (HarperCollins, London, 1995). Reprinted by permission of HarperCollins Publishers Limited.

3 You can't lose yourself too much in your world, you've still got to make it 'street' and give it an edge.

> COLLETTE DINNIGAN, South-African-born New Zealand fashion designer. Quoted in Carrie Kablean, 'Hail the supreme knicker queen', *Weekend Australian*, 31 August 1996. © The Weekend Australian.

4 Baby boomers want to feel that they have grown up, not old, and that they retain the childlike sense of wonder and enjoyment of their youth. Wise marketers can reinforce these deep desires to their advantage by wrapping promotional messages in the cosy warmth of some of boomers' most cherished memories.

> SID GOOD and BRUCE GOOD, American marketing consultants and principals of Good Marketing Inc, Cleveland. 'Boomers Need Security Blanket', *Marketing News* (American Marketing Association), 9 September 1996, page 6. Reprinted with permission.

5 The most important aspect of a Web site from a marketing standpoint is to keep it changing. Marketers need to keep the mindset that the Web site is almost like a storefront.

> STEVE JONES, American communications professor and consultant at the University of Tulsa, Oklahoma. *Services Marketing Today* (American Marketing Association), August 1996.

6 When the engineering-over-marketing mentality is pervasive enough, the consumers are faced with a Hobson's choice; the illusion of choice when there aren't any real alternatives. Hobson was a liveryman 400 years ago who insisted that each client take the horse closest to the door or none. As engineers determine product features and marketing gets misplaced, consumers often must do the equivalent.

> HERBERT ROTFELD, American academic, marketing professor at Auburn University, Alabama. 'Added Features Sometimes Detract from the Product', *Marketing News* (American Marketing Association), 4 November 1996, page 11. Reprinted with permission.

7 To the chagrin of early telephone company executives, who looked on their service as a serious, guy-type thing, it was women who took to it. For years phone company executives tried to get women to stop using it for 'idle gossip' and

'frivolous' talk. It was not until the 1920s that AT&T began selling the service as a way to reach out and touch someone.

NICHOLAS VON HOFFMAN, American journalist, playwright and novelist. 'Say Hello to Videoconferencing', *Architectural Digest*, May 1996.

8 The goal of marketers should be to limit the choices and bundle their services or goods to make the lives of their customers easier.

PAUL WEITZEL, American marketing consultant at Bishop Consulting, Barrington, Illinois. *Services Marketing Today* (American Marketing Association), August 1996.

59 **media**

See also: advertising 3; communication & communicating 11; marketing 58; publicity 84; technology 101

1 Some television programs are so much chewing gum for the eyes.

JOHN MASON BROWN (1900–69), American literary critic, lecturer and essayist. In an interview, 28 July 1955.

2 The hand that rules the press, the radio, the screen and the far-spread magazine, rules the country.

LEARNED HAND (1872–1961), American jurist. Memorial address for Justice Brandeis, 21 December 1942.

3 The media, I tell pedants in the government, is like an oil painting. Close up, it looks like nothing on earth. Stand back and you get the drift.

BERNARD INGHAM, British newspaper columnist. In a speech to the British Parliamentary Press Gallery, 7 February 1990. Reprinted in *Daily Express*, 16 September 1996.

4 Each day a few more lies eat into the seed with which we are born, little institutional lies from the print of newspapers, the shock waves of television, and the sentimental cheat of the movie screen.

NORMAN MAILER, American novelist and essayist. 'First Advertisement for Myself', *Advertisements for Myself* (Collins, London, 1959). Reprinted by permission of HarperCollins Publishers Limited.

5 It is easy, in the era of the communications revolution when everything from the most trivial to the most momentous gets an airing in the constantly expanding media outlets, to draw conclusions based on what gets the most coverage. The violent, the sleazy, the meretricious side of life is more exposed to view than ever before. The noble, the selfless, the creative, the beautiful side of humanity is still there, even though it is less frequently on camera than the ugly side.

JAMES McCLELLAND, Australian columnist, author, former lawyer, judge and federal government minister. *Stirring the Possum* (Viking, Victoria, 1988).

meetings 60

See also: communication & communicating 11; decisions 20; do it now 25; efficiency 27; focus 31; follow through 32; getting started 35; goals & goal-setting 36; listening 54; motivation 63; negotiation 64; problems & problem-solving 78; productivity 79; teams & teamwork 100

1 He [George Robertson, British Labour Party shadow spokesman on Scottish affairs] went into the meeting to argue about two questions in one referendum, and emerged committed to three questions in two referendums. One commentator said a committee asked to design a horse had come up with a two-legged, three-humped camel.

AUSIAN CRAMB, British journalist. *Weekly Telegraph*, 11 September 1996. © Telegraph Group Limited, London, 1996.

2 No grand idea was ever born in a conference, but a lot of foolish ideas have died there.

> F. SCOTT FITZGERALD (1896–1940), American novelist and short-story writer. *The Crack-up* (1945).

3 Meetings are indispensable when you don't want to do anything.

> JOHN KENNETH GALBRAITH, Canadian-born American economist, Emeritus Professor of Economics at Harvard University, former senior White House adviser, diplomat and author. *Ambassador's Journal* (Houghton Mifflin, New York, 1969). Copyright © 1969 by John Kenneth Galbraith. Reprinted by permission of Houghton Mifflin Company. All rights reserved.

4 Breakfast, lunch and dinner meetings are an important part of my business day . . . I prefer them to office meetings: they are automatically more intimate, friendly and less formal; they are more revealing about the person; and the other person is more vulnerable and receptive. I take great care to assure that the atmosphere of these meetings is not only relaxed but conducive to business.

> MARK H. McCORMACK, American sports marketing consultant, founder and CEO of International Management Group, and author. *What They Don't Teach You at Harvard Business School* (Collins, London, 1984). Reprinted by permission of HarperCollins Publishers Limited.

5 When in doubt, don't call a meeting.

> MARK H. McCORMACK, American sports marketing consultant, founder and CEO of International Management Group, and author. *McCormack on Managing* (Century, London, 1995).

6 I usually have a good idea of how many people should be in a meeting and when that number is too large to be productive. In a sales meeting, my ideal number is two – the customer and I –

because I can sell best one on one. If the size of the meeting gets unwieldy for me, I won't plough through my agenda . . . If your meeting is too crowded, don't fool yourself into thinking you can tame the crowd. You're better off waiting for another day, when the crowd has vanished and your voice can be more clearly heard.

MARK H.McCORMACK, American sports marketing consultant, founder and CEO of International Management Group, and author. *McCormack on Selling* (Century, London, 1995).

7 According to one survey, the average CEO spends 18 hours a week on 'outside activities.' The next time-waster is internal meetings. The average CEO spends 17 hours a week attending corporate meetings and 6 hours a week preparing for those meetings. Since the typical top executive works 61 hours a week, that leaves only 20 hours for everything else, including managing the operation and going down to the front . . . Cut back on . . . the meetings. Instead of talking things over, walk out and see for yourself. As Gorbachev told Reagan, 'It is better to see once than to hear a hundred times.'

AL RIES and JACK TROUT, American marketing consultants and business authors. *The 22 Immutable Laws of Marketing* (HarperCollins, New York, 1993). Copyright © 1993 by Al Ries and Jack Trout. Reprinted by permission of HarperCollins Publishers, Inc.

mistakes 61

See also: challenge 8; defeat 21; failure 30; learning 52; obstacles 66

1 Everybody makes mistakes. It's what we make of our mistakes that makes us what we are.

ANON.

2 Smart people make mistakes. But dumb people make the same mistakes over and over again.

ANON.

3 To err is human; to forgive is against company policy.

ANON.

4 If there's one thing above all from which I've learnt how to survive in business, it's been from making mistakes – and the more mistakes you make the more you learn.

RICHARD BRANSON, British entrepreneur, founder and CEO of Virgin Group. In 'Entrepreneurship', a paper (1973) reprinted in Tom Canon (ed.), *How to Get Ahead in Business* (Virgin, London, 1993).

5 I made the unforgivable mistake of assuming.

JAN CARLZON, Swedish business leader, former CEO of Scandinavian Airlines System, speaker and author. *Moments of Truth* (Ballinger, Cambridge, Massachusetts, 1987; revised edition Harper & Row, New York, 1989). Copyright © 1987 by Ballinger Publishing Company. Reprinted by permission of HarperCollins Publishers, Inc.

6 Any man can make mistakes, but only an idiot persists in his error.

CICERO (Marcus Tullius Cicero; 106–43 BC), Roman statesman, orator and scholar. *Philippics* (44–43 BC).

7 The man who can own up to his error is greater than he who merely knows how to avoid making it.

CARDINAL DE RETZ (Jean François-Paul de Gondi; 1614–79), French prelate and writer. *Mémoires* (1718).

8 I've not tried to hide the mistakes I've made and I've tried to show other women that they can learn and grow and evolve.

JANE FONDA, American actress and author. Quoted in Wendy Sheather, 'Fonda Being the Perfect Wife', *Sunday Telegraph*, Sydney, 22 December 1996.

9 The greatest mistake you can make in life is to be continually fearing you will make one.

> ELBERT HUBBARD (1856–1915), American businessman, printer and author. *The Note Book* (1927).

10 A fear of having to admit having been wrong or of making a mistake should not be an impediment to taking salvaging, corrective action. If more entrepreneurs and private company investors or 'angels' . . . were to invest using more consideration and therefore more slowly, and exit from declining situations more quickly, they would die richer.

> ARTHUR LIPPER III, American businessman. In a foreword to Russel R. Taylor, *Exceptional Entrepreneurial Women* (Praeger, New York, 1988).

11 To be mistaken is a misfortune to be pitied, but to know the truth and not to conform one's actions to it is a crime which Heaven and Earth condemn.

> GIUSEPPE MAZZINI (1805–72), Italian patriot and writer. *The Duties of Man and Other Essays* (1910).

12 Mistakes sometimes turn into lucky accidents. One day when William H. Mason went to lunch, he forgot to turn off the heat and pressure on an experimental press in which he was trying to create a new form of porous insulation out of exploded wood fibre. He dawdled at lunch, and when he went back to his lab was chagrined to find that heat and pressure were still being applied on his experimental fibre. He assumed that the batch was ruined; but when he released the pressure, there he had a hard dense, smooth board – the first piece of 'hardboard' ever made. That new 'Masonite Presdwood' of his was only one of his creative triumphs, and the only one in which accident played a part.

> ALEX F. OSBORN (1888–1966), American academic and author. *Applied Imagination: Principles & Procedures of Creative Thinking* (Charles Scribner's Sons, New York, 1953).

13 As I keep telling my dog, Perry, it's only human – and dog-like – to make a mistake, but only a mutt will commit the same error twice over.

GREGORY PECK, American actor. *The Hollywood Reporter*, 11 October 1948.

14 The man who makes no mistakes does not usually make anything.

EDWARD JOHN PHELPS (1822–1900), American lawyer and diplomat. In a speech made in London, 24 January 1899.

15 To err is human, to forgive divine.

ALEXANDER POPE (1688–1744), British satirist and poet. *Essay on Criticism* (1711).

16 Wise men learn by other men's mistakes; fools, by their own.

LATIN PROVERB.

17 A life spent making mistakes is not only more honourable but more useful than a life spent doing nothing.

GEORGE BERNARD SHAW (1856–1950), Irish playwright and critic, Nobel laureate 1925. 'Preface on Doctors: The Technical Problem', *The Doctor's Dilemma* (1913).

18 I have made many mistakes, and been guilty of many errors of judgement, sometimes while trying too hard to do what I thought was right.

PETER USTINOV, British actor, producer, playwright, university chancellor and author. *Dear Me* (William Heinemann, London, 1977).

19 Experience is the name everyone gives to their mistakes.

OSCAR WILDE (1854–1900), Irish playwright, poet, author and wit. *Lady Windermere's Fan*, play (1892).

20 Most people die of a sort of creeping common sense, and discover when it is too late that the only things one never regrets are one's mistakes.

> OSCAR WILDE (1854–1900), Irish playwright, poet, author and wit. *The Picture of Dorian Gray* (1891).

21 When I first went into business it was a mystery. I made mistakes, but because I started small I was able to learn from them and survive through them.

> CARLA ZAMPATTI, Australian fashion designer. *Sydney Morning Herald*, 7 December 1996.

money 62

See also: business ethics 7; economics & economists 26; power 73; profits 81; responsibility & responsibilities 90; success 98

1 By the time many men have reached the stage where they have money to burn, their fire has gone out.

> ANON.

2 Make money your God, and it will plague you like the devil.

> ANON.

3 Retirement is the time when you stop saving from your earnings and start earning from your savings.

> ANON.

4 You pays your money and you takes your choice.

> ANON.

5 Money is like muck, not good except it be spread.

> FRANCIS BACON (1561–1626), British statesman, philosopher and essayist. *Of Seditions and Troubles*.

6 He's the eighth dwarf – Greedy.

> ALEC BALDWIN, American actor. Comment made about a senior executive with Disney Studios. Attrib. (1991).

7 Only when the last tree has died and the last river has been poisoned and the last fish been caught will we realise we cannot eat money.

> CREE INDIAN SAYING.

8 If two persons equal in judgement play for a considerable sum, he that loves money the most shall lose; his anxiety for the success of the game confounds him.

> BENJAMIN FRANKLIN (1706–90), American statesman, inventor, scientist, printer and author. *Journals of a Voyage* (1726).

9 Money, like dung, does no good till 'tis spread.

> THOMAS FULLER M.D. (1654–1734), British physician and author. *Gnomologia* (1732).

10 Hollywood is a dirt sandwich. The more bread you have, the less dirt you have to eat.

> MEL GIBSON, Australian actor, film director and producer. *OK! Magazine*, October 1995.

11 It would have been cheaper to lower the Atlantic.

> LEW GRADE (Lord Grade of Elstree), Russian-born British television and film producer, and Chairman of ATV. Comment allegedly made when the continually rising budget for the film *Raise the Titanic!* threatened to sink his production company. Attrib.

12 A bank is a place that will lend you money if you can prove that you don't need it.

> BOB HOPE, American comedian and actor. Attrib.

13 A subsidiary result of the enfeeblement of the middle class has been an enfeeblement of the wealth-creating process so that the whole nation is the poorer.

> PATRICK HUTBER, British journalist, newspaper editor and author. *London Telegraph Sunday Magazine*, 21 November 1976. © Telegraph Group Limited, London, 1976.

14 There are few ways in which a man can be more innocently employed than in getting money.

> SAMUEL JOHNSON (Dr Johnson; 1709–84), English poet, essayist, critic, journalist and lexicographer. In a letter to William Strahan, 27 March 1775.

15 No man but a blockhead ever wrote except for money.

> SAMUEL JOHNSON (Dr Johnson; 1709–84), British poet, essayist, critic, journalist and lexicographer. In a letter to William Strahan, 5 April 1776.

16 Prince Johannes von Thurn und Taxis has never concerned himself greatly about concealing his wealth.

'Why are you wearing that dinner jacket?' demanded a long-haired demonstrator on one occasion as the Prince strolled in handcut suit with red carnation, into a Munich society gathering.

'Because,' replied the Prince with the cherubic and apparently ingenuous smile in which he specialises, 'I am very rich.'

> ROBERT LACEY, British author and broadcaster. *Aristocrats* (Hutchinson & BBC, London, 1983).

17 In the final analysis, the customer is the real boss. Management may allocate the money but the customer determines how much there is.

> MICHAEL LEBOEUF, American business consultant, speaker and author, Professor of Management at the University of New Orleans. *How to Win Customers and Keep Them for Life* (Putnam, New York, 1987). Reprinted by permission of The Putnam Publishing Group. Copyright © 1988 by Michael LeBoeuf, Ph.D.

18 For many, successful entrepreneuring is an exercise in the successful use of leverage. It is a fact of life that most start-up businesses just do not have the funds necessary to achieve their projections.

> ARTHUR LIPPER III, American businessman. In a foreword to Russel R. Taylor, *Exceptional Entrepreneuring Women* (Praeger, New York, 1988).

19 Sometimes there is more money to be made from letting people out of contracts than by holding them to commitments that are disadvantageous to them.

> MARK H. McCORMACK, American sports marketing consultant, founder and CEO of International Management Group, and author. *What They Don't Teach You at Harvard Business School* (Collins, London, 1984). Reprinted by permission of HarperCollins Publishers Limited.

20 Almost anyone can be an author; the business is to collect money and fame from this state of being.

> A. A. MILNE (1882–1956), British author. Attrib.

21 A fool and his money are soon parted.

> ENGLISH PROVERB.

22 If money be not thy servant, it will be thy master.

> ENGLISH PROVERB.

23 Time is money.

> ENGLISH PROVERB.

24 Money is round and rolls away.

> ITALIAN PROVERB.

25 Economy is too late at the bottom of the purse.

> LATIN PROVERB.

26 Never make your physician your heir.
   LATIN PROVERB.

27 When money speaks, the truth keeps silent.
   RUSSIAN PROVERB.

28 I finally know what distinguishes man from the other beasts:
   financial worries.
   JULES RENARD (1864–1910), French playwright and novelist. *Journal*
   (1887–1910).

29 I have been accused of being undignified. That is quite true, I
   am. If you take your dignity to a pawnbroker he won't give you
   much for it.
   JOHN RUSSELL (13th Duke of Bedford), British aristocrat. Attrib. (1971).

30 My life is a bubble; but how much solid cash it costs to keep
   that bubble floating!
   LOGAN PEARSALL SMITH (1865–1946), American-born British scholar
   and author. *Afterthoughts* (1931).

31 There was a time when a fool and his money were soon parted,
   but now it happens to everybody.
   ADLAI STEVENSON (1900–65), American politician, diplomat and US
   Ambassador to the United Nations 1960–65. *The Stevenson Wit* (1966).

32 I been rich. I been poor. Rich is better.
   SOPHIE TUCKER (1884–1966), American singer and entertainer. Attrib.

33 Some men worship rank, some worship heroes, some worship
   power, some worship God, and over these ideals they dispute –
   but they all worship money.
   MARK TWAIN (real name Samuel Clemens; 1835–1910), American journalist, editor and author. *Notebook* (1935).

34 I don't like to ask for money from the state. The state is a lousy shareholder.

> FERDINANDO VENTRIGLIA, Italian banker, Director-General of Banco di Napoli. Attrib. (1983).

35 We don't have power, but we have money. With money, you can get power.

> CHEN WEI, Chinese businesswoman, owner of Beijing computer company. *Washington Post*, 11 April 1993.

36 When I was young, I thought that money was the most important thing in life; now that I am old, I know it is.

> OSCAR WILDE (1854–1900), Irish playwright, poet, author and wit. *The Importance of Being Earnest*, play (1895).

63 **motivation**

See also: incentive/s & rewards 43; learning 52; mistakes 61; money 62; training 103

1 That which brings rewards is done.

> ANON.

2 When the chips are down anyone with any get up and go gets up and goes.

> ANON.

3 All that we do is done with an eye to something else.

> ARISTOTLE (384–322 BC), Greek philosopher. *Nicomachean Ethics* (4th century BC).

4 Only in bad novels do people do things for one reason.

> PETER CAREY, Australian novelist. *Good Weekend*, 2 August 1997.

5 My motivation and aim in life is very simple . . . the privilege of the harlot throughout the ages, which is power without responsibility.

ARTHUR C. CLARKE, British author. Quoted in Neil McAleer, *Odyssey: The Authorised Biography of Arthur C. Clarke* (Victor Gollancz, London, 1992).

6 Too many organisations use their appraisal schemes and their confidential files to record our errors and our small disasters. They use them to chastise us with, hoping to inspire us, or to frighten us to do better. It might work once, but in future we will make sure that we do not venture far enough from the beaten track to make any mistake. Yet no experiment, no test of new ideas, means no learning and no change.

CHARLES HANDY, British academic, business consultant and author. *The Age of Unreason* (Business Books, London, 1989).

7 Each time we tell ourselves we have reached the limit we find we can go the extra mile. The fact that we do not have the tools to measure this gap does not, however, excuse us from making the effort. It is extraordinary that we are prepared to put more effort into improving our accountancy than into motivating our people.

JOHN HARVEY-JONES, British business consultant, broadcaster, author and former Chairman of ICI Industries. *All Together Now* (William Heinemann, London, 1994). Reprinted by permission of The Peters Fraser and Dunlop Group Limited on behalf of John Harvey-Jones.

8 Intrinsic motivation must be present if people are to do their best. And contrary to the hierarchical theory of motivation, we believe that it's possible to excel even when fighting for survival. We believe that what *is* rewarding gets done. We can never pay people enough to care – to care about their products, services, communities, or families, or even the bottom line. True leaders tap into peoples' hearts and minds, not merely their hands and wallets.

JAMES M. KOUZES and BARRY Z. POSNER, American educators, management and training consultants, and authors. *The Leadership Challenge* (Jossey-Bass, San Francisco, 1995).

9 In Japan, business executives and their families unquestioningly accept the priority of business life over the family . . . *Bimbo hima nashi* is an expression commonly used to explain why one works without rest from morning to late at night. It means: 'The poor have no time for rest.' Underlying it is a stark fear of failure, failure in particular to survive, which is stronger by far in motivating economic behaviour than the fear of not winning that Westerners are more accustomed to.

ROBERT M. MARCH, American management consultant, lecturer, seminar leader, author and former university professor. *Honouring the Customer* (John Wiley, New York, & Longman Professional, Melbourne, 1990).

10 I don't want to get any messages saying, 'I'm holding my position.' We're not holding anything! Let the Hun do that. We are advancing constantly and are not interested in holding anything, except the enemy. We're going to hold on to him and kick the hell out of him all the time. Our basic plan of operation is to advance and to keep on advancing regardless of whether we have to go over, under, or through the enemy. We have one motto, '*L'audace, l'audace, toujours l'audace!*' Remember that, gentlemen. From here on out, until we win or die in the attempt, we will always be audacious.

GEORGE S. PATTON (1885–1945), American soldier, US Army general in World War Two. In a speech to his Third Army, England, 1944.

11 Many people have the mistaken idea that personal motivation is an option – like an hors d'oeuvre which can be taken or left alone. But everything an individual does, whether positive or negative, intentional or unintentional, is the

result of motivation. Everyone is self-motivated – a little or a lot – positively or negatively . . . For too long, however, it has been wrongly assumed that motivation is extraneous – that it can be pumped in from the outside through incentives, pep talks, contests, rallies, and sermons. Such activities do provide concepts, encouragement and inspiration for individuals to turn on their creative powers – *but only if they want to.*

DENIS WAITLEY, American personal development counsellor, lecturer and author. *The Psychology of Winning* (Nightingale-Conant, Chicago, 1979; republished Berkley, New York, 1984).

12 Motives do not operate in a vacuum, and the behaviour in which they do operate is affected by the processes of perception, learning and thinking. Theories of motivation ought to be related to theories of learning and perception.

ROBERT S. WOODWORTH (1869–1962), American psychologist, Professor of Psychology at Columbia University and author. *Dynamics of Behaviour* (Columbia University Press, New York, 1918; republished Methuen, London, 1958).

13 Sometimes the most effective motivation is just to say 'thank you.'

ZIG ZIGLAR, American sales trainer and motivator. *Success*, November 1994.

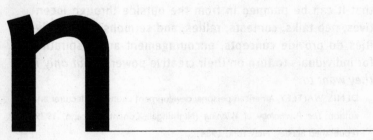

n

'Only man negotiates as an alternative
to the use of brute force.'
MARK H. McCORMACK

negotiation 64:11

negotiation 64

See also: determination 23; listening 54; people 70;
persistence & perseverance 71; selling 93; training 103

1 Secret negotiations are usually neither.

ANON.

2 You don't get what you deserve, you get what you negotiate.

ANON.

3 Effective negotiators *persuade* their counterparts. They understand that it is usually more persuasive to convince the other
side that a given result would be *fair* rather than convince by
stubbornness. Arguing about what they will or won't do creates
a contest in which the other side knows that stubbornness will
be rewarded. That is not an incentive we would like to create for
either side. We would like both parties to be open to new ideas.
We are not saying 'Be fair to be nice,' or even 'Be fair to produce
a fair agreement.' Those are possible by-products. We are sug-
gesting that criteria of fairness are valuable as a sword to persuade others and as a shield to protect ourselves from being
unfairly treated.

ROGER FISHER, American law professor at Harvard Law School, conflict
management consultant and author, and DANNY ERTEL, American dispute
resolution counsellor, columnist and author. *Getting Ready to Negotiate*
(Penguin, New York, 1995). Copyright © 1995 Conflict Management Inc.
Used by permission of Penguin, a division of Penguin Books USA Inc.

4 Failing to deal with others sensitively as human beings prone
to human reactions can be disastrous for a negotiation.

Whatever else you are doing at any point during a negotiation, from preparation to follow-up, it is worth asking yourself, 'Am I paying enough attention to the people problem?'

ROGER FISHER, American law professor, conflict management facilitator and author; WILLIAM URY, American negotiation consultant and lecturer, and author; and BRUCE PATTON, American law lecturer, negotiation skills teacher and author. *Getting to Yes* (Houghton Mifflin, New York, 1981 & 1991; Hutchinson, London, 1982; revised edition Business Books, London, 1991). Copyright © 1981, 1991 by Roger Fisher and William Ury. Reprinted by permission of Houghton Mifflin Company. All rights reserved.

5 To make the most of your potential negotiating power, you should use each source of power in harmony with other sources. Negotiators sometimes look for their strongest source of power and try to use it alone. For example, if a negotiator has a strong BATNA (Best Alternative To a Negotiated Agreement), he or she may confront the other side with it, threatening to walk away unless the last offer is accepted. This is likely to detract from the persuasive power of the negotiator's arguments about why the offer is fair.

ROGER FISHER, American law professor at Harvard Law School, conflict management consultant and author; WILLIAM URY, American negotiation consultant and lecturer, and author; and BRUCE PATTON, American law lecturer, negotiation skills teacher and author. *Getting to Yes* (Houghton Mifflin, New York, 1981 & 1991; Hutchinson, London, 1982; revised edition Business Books, London, 1991). Copyright © 1981, 1991 by Roger Fisher and William Ury. Reprinted by permission of Houghton Mifflin Company. All rights reserved.

6 He that speaks ill of the mare will buy her.

BENJAMIN FRANKLIN (1706–90), American statesman, scientist, inventor, printer and author. *Poor Richard's Almanack* (1732–57).

7 Let us never negotiate out of fear. But let us never fear to negotiate.

JOHN F. KENNEDY (1917–63), American statesman, and 35th President of the United States of America 1961–63. In his inauguration address, 20 January 1961.

8 A friend once introduced me to a college audience where I was invited to speak by saying, 'It's easy to understand the advice Mr. McCormack is about to give you if you realise that he starts with the premise that *everything you know is wrong!*' I'm not sure my friend is 100 per cent correct, but I appreciated the sentiment . . . Every negotiating situation, no matter how much deja vu it inspires, is in some sense new and unfamiliar. Identifying the new elements is what keeps negotiating from ever becoming stale or predictable for me. It demands a response that is unconventional, even if only by a few degrees. In that sense, I guess I am guilty of believing that 'everything you know is wrong.' I remind myself of that every day.

MARK H. McCORMACK, American sports marketing consultant, founder and CEO of International Management Group, and author. *McCormack on Negotiating* (Century, London, 1995).

9 If you have to boil down your negotiating attitude to two things, you can do a lot worse than *question everything* and *think big.*

MARK H. McCORMACK, American sports marketing consultant, founder and CEO of International Management Group, and author. *McCormack on Negotiating* (Century, London, 1995).

10 Negotiating in business is often more complicated than it has to be. We make it so – by insisting that everyone follow certain rules, by believing outdated assumptions, by overthinking the other side's position or adhering too tightly to ours, and most obviously, by putting too much faith in 'conventional wisdom' – whatever that means!

MARK H. McCORMACK, American sports marketing consultant, founder and CEO of International Management Group, and author. *McCormack on Negotiating* (Century, London, 1995).

11 Only man negotiates as an alternative to the use of brute force. To all other creatures brute force *is* the essence of negotiating.
MARK H.McCORMACK, American sports marketing consultant, founder and CEO of International Management Group, and author. *McCormack on Negotiating* (Century, London, 1995).

12 A miser and a liar bargain quickly.
GREEK PROVERB.

13 There are two fools in every market. One asks too little, one asks too much.
RUSSIAN PROVERB.

'There is nothing so revivifying as the bewitching appearance of opportunity.'

LAURENCE OLIVIER

opportunity 68:18

65 observation

See also: customers 19; learning 52; listening 54;
negotiation 64; selling 93; training 103

1 Watch less, observe more.

 ANON.

2 I think I've been lucky to learn by observing the actors I've been
 working with and being directed by some wonderful directors.
 I think a lot of craft and technique is basically common sense.

 GLENN CLOSE, American actress. *The Australian Way*, September 1996.

3 You see, but you do not observe.

 ARTHUR CONAN DOYLE (1859–1930), British physician and author.
 Words spoken by Sherlock Holmes in *The Adventures of Sherlock Holmes:
 A Scandal in Bohemia* (1891).

4 Observation capitalises inspiration.

 ALEX F. OSBORN (1888–1966), American academic and author. *Applied
 Imagination: Principles & Procedures of Creative Thinking* (Charles Scribner's
 Sons, New York, 1953).

5 After the First World War, Du Pont had a huge amount of
 left-over explosives on hand. To salvage this material, chemists
 thought they might make from it a new kind of paint. They conducted thousands of experiments, and came close to the
 answer; but no paint worthy of the Du Pont name came out of
 their research. One of those chemists happened one day to
 visit another Du Pont chemist and on his way out of the latter's
 laboratory noticed a can of stuff which he picked up and

smelled. Excitedly he asked, 'What is *this*?' The other chemist said it was just one of those mistakes. 'I got some of that material you fellows are working on, hoping it might do for something I am trying to make. I put the stuff in an oven, but forgot to take it out when I went home last evening.' The paint chemist dashed back to his lab yelling 'We've got it! We've nearly had it for a long time. We didn't know we had to heat it *all night*.' Thus Duco was discovered. Luck played a part, but that chemist's observation provided the magic.

ALEX F. OSBORN (1888–1966), American academic and author. *Applied Imagination: Principles & Procedures of Creative Thinking* (Charles Scribner's Sons, New York, 1953).

6 Where observation is concerned, chance favours only the prepared mind.

LOUIS PASTEUR (1822–95), French chemist and microbiologist. In a speech made at the inauguration of the Faculty of Science at the University of Lille, 7 December 1854.

7 Watch what successful people do. Why? Because success leaves clues. Watch how the successful man shakes the hand of someone else. Watch how the successful woman asks questions. People who do well *own* the habits of success. They create patterns of winning behaviour just as the struggler creates patterns of losing behaviour. You want to be promoted? Observe your superiors. Want to make as much money as your uncle? Observe how he manages his money and his lifestyle.

JIM ROHN, American business philosopher, lecturer and author. *Seven Strategies for Wealth and Happiness* (Brolga, Melbourne, 1994).

8 A stander-by may sometimes, perhaps, see more of the game than he that plays it.

JONATHAN SWIFT (1667–1745), British author. *A Critical Essay Upon the Faculties of the Mind* (1707).

66 obstacles

See also: failure 30; limitations 53; mistakes 61; persistence & perseverance 71; problems and problem-solving 78

1 Hindrances stimulate the man of purpose ... Mistakes, losses, pains do not subdue him ... For he is ever conscious of the certainty of final achievement.

> JAMES ALLEN, American theologian and author. *The Mastery of Destiny* (Putnam, New York, 1909).

2 Every setback is the starting point for a comeback.

> ANON.

3 It doesn't matter where you come from, it's where you're going that's important.

> ANON.

4 Obstacles are made to be overcome.

> ANON.

5 Obstacles cannot crush me
Every obstacle yields to stern resolve
He who is fixed to a star does not change his mind.

> LEONARDO DA VINCI (1452–1519), Italian artist, scientist and inventor. *Notebooks* (c. 1500).

6 Braving obstacles and hardships is nobler than retreat to tranquillity. The butterfly that hovers around the lamp until it dies is more admirable than the mole that lives in a dark tunnel.

> KAHLIL GIBRAN (1883–1931), Lebanese–American philosophical essayist, mystic poet, novelist and artist. *A Third Treasury of Kahlil Gibran* (Citadel, Secausus, New Jersey, 1965).

7 If you don't experience dark clouds, rain and storms there is no
way of measuring sunshine.

> JAMES HARDY, Australian businessman, Olympian, world champion
> yachtsman and author. *An Adventurous Life* (Margaret Gee, Melbourne,
> 1993; republished Penguin, Victoria, 1995).

8 The man who invented the Singer Sewing machine reached an
impasse when he could not get the thread to run through the
needle consistently. When he was at his wit's end, he dreamed
one night that he was being chased by natives carrying spears.
As they came closer, he noticed that every spear had a hole at
the bottom of the blade, and the next morning he made a needle
with its eye near the point, instead of at the top. His machine was
complete.

> JOE KEETON, British hypnotherapist and author. *The Power of the Mind*
> (Robert Hale, London, 1988).

9 Everyone has setbacks. This is a normal fact of life. And when
you have more than one in a row, as sometimes happens, it can
be very discouraging. If you allow it to be so, it can take the life
out of you. But you should always remember that even so, you
still have a lot of rebound left.

> NORMAN VINCENT PEALE, American theologian and author. *The Plus
> Factor* (Cedar/Heinemann, London, 1987).

10 Problems teach us fortitude and, when the pendulum swings
upwards again, the joy and elation are all the keener.

> MICKEY ROONEY, American actor. *The Hollywood Reporter*, 24 November
> 1958.

11 When you are faced with an impasse you have to crash through
or you've got to crash. And I crashed through in a few impasses
in the past.

> GOUGH WHITLAM, Australian politician, statesman, and Prime Minister

1972–75. In a television interview with David Frost for the Seven Network Australia, August 1972.

67 opinion/s

See also: human nature 39; judgement 48

1 He changes his opinion as frequently as other men change their underwear.

ANON.

2 The other man's word is an opinion; yours is the truth; and your boss's is law.

ANON.

3 How long halt thee between two opinions?

THE BIBLE. 1 Kings.

4 If in the last few years you haven't discarded a major opinion or acquired a new one, check your pulse – you may be dead.

GELETT BURGESS (1866–1951), American humorist and illustrator. Attrib.

5 I have in general no very exalted opinion of the virtue of paper government.

EDMUND BURKE (1729–97), British statesman, orator and writer. In a speech on conciliation with America, 22 March 1775.

6 Opinion is a flitting thing,
But Truth outlasts the Sun.

EMILY DICKINSON (1830–86), American poet. (c. 1879).

7 The best we have depends on the opinion of others.

BALTASAR GRACIAN (1601–58), Spanish Jesuit priest and author. *The Art of Worldly Wisdom* (1647).

8 Error of opinion may be tolerated where reason is left free to combat it.

> THOMAS JEFFERSON (1743–1826), American statesman, and 3rd President of the United States of America 1801–09. In his first inaugural address, 4 March 1801.

9 We credit scarcely any persons with good sense except those who are of our opinion.

> LA ROCHEFOUCAULD (François, Duc de la Rochefoucauld; 1613–80), French aristocrat and writer. *Maxims* (1665).

10 New opinions are always suspected, and usually opposed, without any other reason but because they are not already common.

> JOHN LOCKE (1632–1704), British philosopher. 'The Epistle Dedicatory', *An Essay Concerning Human Understanding* (1690).

11 People will often overestimate the value of their opinions or even if anyone wants to hear them.

> MARK H. McCORMACK, American sports marketing consultant, founder and CEO of International Management Group, and author. *McCormack on Managing* (Century, London, 1995).

12 Intelligence will never hold sway in the judgement of public opinion.

> PIER PAOLO PASOLINI (1925–75), Italian filmmaker, poet and novelist. Attrib.

13 It were not best that we should all think alike; it is difference of opinion that makes horse-races.

> MARK TWAIN (real name Samuel Clemens; 1835–1910), American journalist, editor and author. 'Pudd'nhead Wilson's Calendar', *Pudd'nhead Wilson* (1894).

14 It is only about things that do not interest one that one can give a really unbiased opinion, which is no doubt the reason why an unbiased opinion is always absolutely valueless.

> OSCAR WILDE (1854–1900), Irish playwright, poet, author and wit. 'The Critic as Artist', *Intentions* (1891).

68 opportunity

See also: ambition 5; luck 57; problems & problem-solving 78; success 98

1 Behind every problem there lies an opportunity. All you have to do is identify it.

> ANON.

2 It often comes to you in disguise. This is why so many people do not recognise opportunity when it stares them in the face.

> ANON.

3 Opportunity only knocks once.

> ANON.

4 Two things in life, once lost, can never be regained – virginity, and opportunity.

> ANON.

5 A wise man will make more opportunities than he finds.

> FRANCIS BACON (1561–1626), British statesman, philosopher and essayist. 'Of Ceremonies and Respects', *Essays* (1625).

6 There is an ad running in Asia . . . with a headline which reads: 'This man is the chef, the chauffeur, and the chief executive. In short, an entrepreneur.' The picture below portrays a fairly typical street hawker astride his bicycle food cart, waiting to sell

his noodles to passers-by. 'Businessmen in Asia,' the text continues, 'rarely stand still. If there's an opportunity round the corner they'll take it.' That advertisement sums up the attitude of the taipans [big bosses]. Most have built themselves up from itinerant traders to become highly respected and influential business leaders.

CLAUDIA CRAGG, British author. *The New Taipans* (Century, London, 1995).

7 In lean times, even businessmen who have substantial operations have been known to move back down the hierarchy to set up a small shop that will at least provide a subsistence living. Stanley Ho, of Macau hydrofoil and casino fame, has won and lost fortunes several times over the years. With time and patience, even the most humble of businesses presents an opportunity to expand and regain status.

CLAUDIA CRAGG, British author. *The New Taipans* (Century, London, 1995).

8 I wait for an opportunity and take it. As long as you don't push yourself into things before you're ready, then you'll probably find you can cope with anything.

LIZ DAVENPORT, Australian fashion designer. *Australian Women's Weekly,* October 1996.

9 Next to knowing when to seize an opportunity, the most important thing in life is to know when to forego an advantage.

BENJAMIN DISRAELI (1804–81), British statesman, novelist, and Prime Minister 1868 and 1874–80. Attrib.

10 Employees are like suppliers; they have a responsibility to help their employers either lower costs or increase sales. To the extent that people seize the opportunity to serve their employers, they will create opportunities for themselves. Opportunities abound in all organisations, in all industries.

SAL DIVITA, American academic, marketing professor at George Washington University, Washington DC. 'Why Keep Options Open?', *Marketing News* (American Marketing Association), 4 November 1996, page 13. Reprinted with permission.

11 Opporchunity knocks at ivry man's dure wanst.

FINLEY PETER DUNNE (1867–1936), American journalist and humorist. 'Mr Carnegie's Gift', *Mr Dooley's Opinions*, newspaper essay (1901).

12 In the middle of difficulty lies opportunity.

ALBERT EINSTEIN (1879–1955), German–Swiss–American physicist. Attrib.

13 Education is society's great leveller, and any improvement in education goes a long way toward equalising opportunity.

BILL GATES, American information technology pioneer, founder and CEO of Microsoft Corporation, and author. *The Road Ahead* (Viking Penguin, New York, 1995). Copyright © 1995 by Willam H. Gates III. Used by permission of Viking Penguin, a division of Penguin Books USA Inc.

14 The more attention you give to determining priorities and learning the decision making process, the more likely you are to recognise chances when they occur and have the confidence to take them.

EILEEN GILLIBRAND and JENNY MOSLEY, British counsellors, trainers and authors. *She Who Dares Wins* (Thorsons, London, 1995).

15 He who tries to seize an opportunity after it has passed him by is like one who sees it approach but will not go to meet it.

KAHLIL GIBRAN (1883–1931), Lebanese–American philosophical essayist, mystic poet, novelist and artist. *A Third Treasury of Kahlil Gibran* (Citadel, Secausus, New Jersey, 1965).

16 There is no security on this earth; there is only opportunity.

DOUGLAS MACARTHUR (1880–1964), American soldier, general of the US Army, World War Two and Korea. Quoted in Courtney Weaver, *MacArthur: His Rendezvous with History* (1955).

17 I want to build a society where opportunity is open to everyone, regardless of background, to set their own ambitions, to work for them, and to achieve them.

JOHN MAJOR, British statesman, and Prime Minister 1990–97. 'Trust My Instincts', *Weekly Telegraph*, 8 January 1997.

18 To a mere man, and a career man at that, there is nothing so revivifying as the bewitching appearance of opportunity.

LAURENCE OLIVIER (Lord Olivier; 1907–89), British actor, and stage and screen producer and director. *Confessions of an Actor* (Weidenfeld & Nicolson, London, 1982).

19 While we stop to think, we often miss our opportunity.

PUBLILIUS SYRUS (1st century BC), Syrian-born Roman mime writer. *Moral Sayings.*

20 We are all unequal. No-one, thank heavens, is quite like anyone else . . . We believe that everyone has the right to be unequal. But to us, every human being is equally important. Engineers, miners, manual workers, shop assistants, farmworkers, postmen, housewives – these are the essential foundations of our society, and without them there would be no nation. But there are others with special gifts who should also have their chance, because if the adventurers who strike out in new directions in science, technology, medicine, commerce and industry are hobbled, there can be no advance. The spirit of envy can destroy; it can never build. Everyone must be allowed to develop the abilities he knows he has within him, and she knows she has within her, in the way they choose.

MARGARET THATCHER (Baroness Thatcher), British stateswoman, and

Prime Minister 1979–90. In a speech made at the Conservative Party Conference, Brighton, 10 October 1975, eight months after her election as party leader.

69 originality

See also: genius 34; ideas 40; imagination 42; innovation 45; inspiration 46; talent 99

1 Imitation is the sincerest form of television;

FRED ALLEN (real name John F. Sullivan; 1894–1956), American comedian. Attrib.

2 Nothing is original. Not even this observation.

ANON.

3 Originality can be defined as the art of concealing one's source.

ANON.

4 Originality has no nationality or place of origin.

COCO CHANEL (1883–1971), French couturier. Attrib.

5 In strong contrast to those agreeable twaddlers who spend their lives 'dipping buckets into empty wells, and growing old in drawing *nothing* up,' stands out this Californian author. He is not of the 'pretty' school. His work is not hammered out until an inch of thought becomes a yard of writing.

MARCUS CLARKE (1846–81), Australian journalist, editor, critic and author. In a review of Francis Bret Harte, *The Luck of Roaring Camp, Australian Journal*, March 1871.

6 Creating a new perfume is really like writing a story. We are not concerned so much with what our friends in the industry are doing. I mean they write their story and we write our story as

only we can tell it. Developing a new fragrance is like history itself. It varies. When two people are in love, something happens, a new human is born. It is like this with a new perfume. Everyone works on the concept and the type of person. It also has to be a surprise. We work on code names. When everything is together, then we disclose it to the press and the industry.

JEAN COURTIÈRE, French perfume industry chief and Président Directeur Générale of Parfums Givenchy, Paris. *Millionaire*, October 1989.

7 As all organisations reach a plateau of competence, it is only better concepts that will provide the competitive advantage.

EDWARD DE BONO, Maltese-born British scholar, teacher, lecturer and author. *Serious Creativity* (HarperCollins, London, 1992). Copyright © The McQuaig Group Inc. 1992.

8 There are only two themes in all of literature: someone goes on a journey, and the stranger comes to town.

JOHN W. GARDNER, American foundation executive, public official and author. Attrib.

9 A thought is often original, though you have uttered it a hundred times.

OLIVER WENDELL HOLMES SNR (1809–94), American physician, humorist, poet and author. *The Autocrat of the Breakfast Table* (1858).

10 I can catch ideas anywhere, but I can't always make 'em go in harness. Simple stuff is the best. One day I picked up a pair of pants and found they had a hole in the stern and I wrote, 'You've got to face your troubles when your pants begin to go.' That hit them where they lived, for most of them had to face their troubles in life.

HENRY LAWSON (1867–1922), Australian poet and short-story writer. Quoted in A. B. 'Banjo' Paterson, 'Singers Among Savages', a newspaper article (c. 1920), and reprinted in *A Literary Heritage: Banjo Paterson* (Octopus, Melbourne, 1988).

11 It really gets down to, 'What do we want to be? Do we want to be like everybody else?' ... In the end, we would rather be first in a new place than seventh in a place everyone's rushing to.

BOB LUTZ, American business executive and President of Chrysler Motors, USA. 'Company of the Year – Chrysler', *Forbes*, 13 January 1997. Reprinted by permission of FORBES Magazine. © Forbes Inc 1997.

12 All good things which exist are the fruits of originality.

JOHN STUART MILL (1806–73), British philosopher, economist and author. *On Liberty* (1859).

13 The original genius often shows originality in more than one field ... Some have been productive in two related lines, as painting and sculpture, or even generalship and government, or physics and mathematics. Sometimes a genius productive in one line has produced interesting, though not really important, works in a quite different line – Goethe's theory of colours, Caesar's works on grammar.

ROBERT S. WOODWORTH (1869–1962), American psychologist, Professor of Psychology at Columbia University and author. *Dynamic Psychology* (Columbia University Press, New York, 1918; reprinted Arno Press, New York, 1973).

p

'If you think the game is worth it,
you play the hand you're dealt.'
CHRISTOPHER REEVE

persistence & perseverance 71:17

70 **people**

See also: business ethics 7; civilisation 10; consumers 14; corporate culture 15; customers 19; employees 28; human nature 39

1 Put people before profit, and all will prosper.

ANON.

2 There is practically no area of business where the difference between rhetoric and actuality is greater than in the handling of people.

JOHN HARVEY-JONES, British business consultant, broadcaster, author and former Chairman of ICI Industries. *All Together Now* (William Heinemann, London, 1994). Reprinted by permission of The Peters Fraser and Dunlop Group Limited on behalf of John Harvey-Jones.

3 You can fool all the people some of the time, and some of the people all the time, but you cannot fool all the people all the time.

ABRAHAM LINCOLN (1809–65), American statesman, and 16th President of the United States of America 1861–65. In a speech made in Clinton, Illinois, 8 September 1858.

4 If you want 10 days of happiness, grow grain. If you want 10 years of happiness, grow a tree. If you want 100 years of happiness, grow people.

HARVEY MACKAY, American business executive, CEO of Mackay Envelope Company, motivator and author. In a speech made at the DCI Field & Sales Force Automation Conference, Boston, October 1996. 'Sales Pro Emphasises the Personal Touch', *Marketing News* (American Marketing Association), 4 November 1996, page 8. Reprinted with permission.

5 Remember that any buzzword, no matter how clever or attractive, must eventually run through that unpredictable filter known as people. A management concept is meaningless without a shrewd understanding of people.

> MARK H. McCORMACK, American sports marketing consultant, founder and CEO of International Management Group, and author. *McCormack on Managing* (Century, London, 1995).

6 [We are] our people. Our success depends on them. Knowledge resides in their minds and feet. Too many companies fail to grasp that feet can walk out the door as easily as they walked in.

> ROGER MEADE, American information systems developer and CEO of Scitor Corp. *IndustryWeek*, 18 October 1993. Reprinted with permission. © Copyright Penton Publishing, Inc, Cleveland, Ohio.

7 The good news for internationally-minded companies is that the welcome sign is out for them – all over the world. But the welcome does not mean that they have carte blanche to do what they used to do, maximising their profits at the expense of people.

> MILTON MOSKOWITZ, American journalist and author. *The Global Marketplace* (Macmillan, New York, 1987).

8 The way management treats the associates [salespeople] is exactly how the associates will treat the customers.

> SAM WALTON, American retailing pioneer, founder and CEO of Wal-Mart. *Sam Walton in His Own Words* (Doubleday, New York, 1992).

persistence & perseverance 71

See also: challenge 8; defeat 21; determination 23; obstacles 66; success 98

1 Their [i.e. of the British in Hollywood] resilience ... is admirable, for Hollywood bashes every ego and dashes every dream. As the local saying goes, 'If you want a friend in LA, get a dog.' Only the strong survive.

> JESSICA BERENS, British journalist. *Tatler*, November 1991.

2 Be like a postage stamp – stick to one thing until you get there.

> JOSH BILLINGS (real name Henry Wheeler Shaw; 1818–85), American humorist and columnist. *Everybody's Friend* (1874).

3 I'm certainly not yet at the middle of my sort of commitment curve.

> TINA BROWN, British-born American-based magazine editor, Editor of *The New Yorker*. *The Guardian*, 23 October 1996. The Guardian ©.

4 If you get run off the road, you get right up and start over again.

> MICHAEL J. COLES, American businessman and co-founder of The Great American Chocolate Chip Cookie Co. Shortly after establishing the company, Coles suffered crippling injuries in a road accident. Not only did he recover fully and pilot his company to multi-million-dollar success, he later cycled across the USA in record time. Attrib.

5 Early in my career, one of my manuscripts was returned without a covering letter, but written across the back page in red ink were the words: 'Strongly advise author not to take up writing as a career.' I cried my eyes out and stopped writing for a fortnight. Then I said to myself, 'What do they know?'

> CATHERINE COOKSON, British author. 'Touching the Heart of Your Reader', in A. S. Burack (ed.), *The Writer's Handbook* (The Writer, Boston, 1978).

6 Nothing in the world can take the
place of persistence.
Talent will not; nothing is more common
than unsuccessful men with talent.

Genius will not; unrewarded genius is
almost a proverb.
Education will not; the world is full
of educated derelicts.
Persistence and determination alone
are omnipotent.
The slogan 'press on' has solved and always will solve
the problems of the human race.

CALVIN COOLIDGE (1872–1933), American statesman, and 30th
President of the United States of America 1923–29. Attrib.

7 There are heroic tales of persistence in which a string of failures and rejections ultimately leads to success.

EDWARD DE BONO, Maltese-born British scholar, teacher, lecturer and
author. *Tactics: The Art and Science of Success* (Collins, London, 1985).
Reprinted by permission of HarperCollins Publishers Limited.

8 The strangest thing is, I thought I was elderly, past my peak, in
1944.

JOHN GIELGUD, British actor. Comment made on his 92nd birthday,
1996. Attrib.

9 It's glorious to know that you are only as good as your last picture; that your future, your career and your happiness depend
upon an ability to act when you would sooner die; to smile
when you're fretting about headlines; and to weep when you
feel like laughing.

RITA HAYWORTH (1918–87), American actress. *The Hollywood Reporter*,
8 October 1940.

10 I accepted Andrew Carnegie's commission to organise and pub-
lish the principles of success when I was a law student at
Georgetown University. Other than reimbursement for some
travelling expenses, I got no compensation from Carnegie for

my efforts. My dedication to my task placed strains on my life. I had a family to support, and many of my relatives ridiculed me for my goal. In spite of this opposition, I worked for twenty years, interviewing presidents, inventors, founders of great companies, and famous philanthropists . . .

Believe me, there were times when, between the needling of my relatives and the hardships I endured, it was not easy to maintain a positive mental attitude and persevere. Sometimes, in barren hotel rooms, I almost believed my family was right. The thing that kept me going was my conviction that one day I would not only successfully complete my work but also be proud of myself when it was finished.

Sometimes, when the flames of hope dwindled to a flicker, I had to fan them with everything I possessed to keep them from going out.

NAPOLEON HILL (d. 1970), American motivator and author. The resulting book, *Think and Grow Rich,* became a bestseller and made Hill famous and successful. Matthew Sartwell (ed.), *Napoleon Hill's Keys to Success* (Dutton/ Penguin, New York, 1994). Copyright © 1994 by The Napoleon Hill Foundation. Used by permission of Dutton Signet, a division of Penguin Books USA Inc.

11 After climbing a great hill, one only finds that there are many more hills to climb . . . I dare not linger, for my long walk is not yet ended.

NELSON MANDELA, South African leader, and President of the Republic of South Africa 1994– . *The Long Walk to Freedom* (Little, Brown, London, 1994).

12 Persistence is certainly right up there, among the basic sales commandments, with 'know your product' and 'believe in your product.'

MARK H. McCORMACK, American sports marketing consultant, founder and CEO of International Management Group, and author. *What They Don't Teach You at Harvard Business School* (Collins, London, 1984).

13 I rode in forty races before I rode my first placed horse.

GEORGE MOORE, champion Australian jockey. In a television interview on 'Sports Tonight', Channel 10 Australia, 9 January 1997.

14 Perseverance capitalises inspiration.

ALEX F. OSBORN (1888–1966), American academic and author. *Applied Imagination: Principles & Procedures of Creative Thinking* (Charles Scribner's Sons, New York, 1953).

15 Dream creative dreams.
Set high and worthwhile goals.
Take the first decisive step toward your goal.
And then what?
Then take another step, and another, and another, until the goal is reached, the ambition realised, the mission accomplished. No matter what it takes, *persist*.
No matter how discouraged you may get, *persevere*. No matter how much you want to quit, *hang in there*.

NORMAN VINCENT PEALE, American theologian and author. *The Plus Factor* (Cedar/Heinemann, London, 1987).

16 If you sit by the river long enough, the body of your enemy will float by.

HINDU PROVERB.

17 If you think the game is worth it, you play the hand you're dealt.

CHRISTOPHER REEVE, American actor and director, following a riding accident that left him a quadriplegic. Comment made to Barbara Walters, in a television interview on ABC, USA, 29 September 1995.

18 The succession of defeats lasted unbroken until I was thirty-one. By that time I had written little books and little essays and short stories, and got patted on the back and paid for them – though not enough to live upon. I had quite a reputation. I was

the successful man. I passed my days in toil, the futility of which would sometimes make my cheek to burn – that I should spend a man's energy upon this business, and yet could not earn a livelihood; and still there shone ahead of me an unattained ideal. Although I had attempted the thing with vigour not less than ten or twelve times, I had not yet written a novel. All – all my pretty ones – had gone for a little, and then stopped inexorably, like a schoolboy's watch. I might be compared to a cricketer of many years' standing who should never have made a run . . .

On a chill September morning, by the cheek of a brisk fire, and the rain drumming on the window, I began *The Sea Cook*, for that was the original title . . .

Fifteen days I stuck to it, and turned out fifteen chapters; and then, in the early paragraphs of the sixteenth, ignominiously lost hold. My mouth was empty; there was not a word more of *Treasure Island* in my bosom . . .

I was thirty-one; I was head of a family; I had lost my health; I had never yet paid my way, had never yet made two hundred pounds a year; my father had quite recently bought back and cancelled a book that was judged a failure; was this to be another and last fiasco? I was indeed very close on despair; but I shut my mouth hard, and during the journey to Davos, where I was to pass the winter, had the resolution to think of other things . . .

Arrived at my destination, down I sat one morning to the unfinished tale, and behold! it flowed from me like small talk; and in a second tide of delighted industry, and again at the rate of a chapter a day, I finished *Treasure Island* . . .

Had not the tale flowed from me with singular ease, it must have been laid aside like its predecessors, and found a circuitous and unlamented way to the fire. Purists may suggest it would have been better so. I am not of that mind. The tale seems to have given much pleasure, and it brought – or was the means of bringing – fire and food and wine to a deserving family in which I took an interest. I need scarce say I mean my own.

ROBERT LOUIS STEVENSON (1850–94), British author. In an introduction to a Gordon Classic Library edition of *Treasure Island* (Thomas Nelson, Edinburgh, c. 1887).

19 We [Australians] have a lot of drive and we don't give up. If things go bad for us, it's like water under the bridge. Dust yourself off and start all over again. We have a great fighting spirit. Look at Greg Norman.

RICHARD TYLER, American-based Australian fashion designer. Quoted in Suzy Freeman-Greene, 'Frock Shock! Boy from Sunshine Makes Good!', *Age*, 31 August 1996.

planning 72

See also: decisions 20; goals & goal-setting 36;
success 98; training 103

1 Failing to plan is planning to fail.

ANON.

2 The best-laid schemes o' mice an' men
Gang aft agley.

ROBERT BURNS (1756–96), British poet and songwriter, and the national poet of Scotland. 'To a Mouse' (1785).

3 If you don't want to plan for success and happiness, what right do you have to worry about non-success and unhappiness? If you're not planning where you want to be, what reason or excuse do you have for worrying about being nowhere?

TOM HOPKINS, American sales trainer, motivator and author. *How to Master the Art of Selling* (Champion Press, Scottsdale, Arizona, 1982; republished HarperCollins, London, 1994).

4 Life is what happens when we're making other plans.

> JOHN LENNON (1940–80), British songwriter, recording artist, performer, artist, author and member of The Beatles. Attrib.

5 Plans get you into things but *you* got to work your way out.

> WILL ROGERS (1879–1935), American actor, performer and humorist. *The Autobiography of Will Rogers* (1949).

6 It is a bad plan that admits of no modification.

> PUBLILIUS SYRUS (1st century BC), Syrian-born Roman mime writer. *Moral Sayings.*

7 I plan for the future by focusing exclusively on the present.

> DONALD TRUMP, American entrepreneur, developer and author. *Trump: The Art of the Deal* (Century Hutchinson, London, 1988).

73 **power**

See also: civilisation 10; decisions 20; human nature 39; leadership 51; success 98

1 Power tends to corrupt and absolute power corrupts absolutely.

> LORD ACTON (Sir John Emerich Edward Dalberg-Acton, 1st Baron Acton; 1834–1902), British historian. In a letter to Mandell Creighton, 5 April 1887.

2 The whole notion of power is not something women have grown up with or are accustomed to.

> JENNIE GEORGE, Australian trade union leader and President of the Australian Council of Trade Unions. Quoted in Susan Mitchell, 'Power with Passion', *Weekend Australian*, 30 November 1996. © The Weekend Australian.

3 Deny a strong man his due, and he will take all he can get.

> LUCAN (Marcus Annaeus Lucanus; AD 39–65), Roman poet and prose writer, nephew of Seneca the Younger. *On the Civil War* (1st century AD).

4 Power can enable people to achieve, for themselves and for others, success, fortune, victory, the good life. But if power is the stuff of fantasies, it is also the stuff of nightmares.

> THOMAS L. QUICK, American consultant and author. *Power Plays* (Franklin Watts, New York, 1985).

5 There is a saying: 'Where power is, women are not'; but for God's sake, please remember the counter-argument to that: if you think you are powerless, you are. Women *must* be willing to be powerful. It is because we bear scars from the ways men have used their power over us that women often want no part of power.

> ANITA RODDICK, British businesswoman, co-founder and Chief Executive of The Body Shop International. In a foreword to Eileen Gillibrand & Jenny Mosley, *She Who Dares Wins* (Thorsons, London, 1995).

6 There is a homely adage which runs: 'Speak softly and carry a big stick; you will go far.'

> THEODORE ROOSEVELT (1858–1919), American soldier, statesman, and 26th President of the United States of America 1901–09. In a speech made at the Minnesota State Fair, 2 September 1901.

7 Despite the bad odour that clings to the very notion of power because of the misuses to which is has been put, power in itself is neither good nor bad. It is an inescapable aspect of every human relationship, and it influences everything from our sexual relations to the jobs we hold, the cars we drive, the television we watch, the hopes we pursue. To a greater degree than most imagine, we are the products of power.

> ALVIN TOFFLER, American scholar, lecturer and author. *Powershift* (Bantam, New York, 1990).

8 If you would be powerful, pretend to be powerful.

> HORNE TOOKE (1736–1812), British politician and writer. Quoted in Ralph Waldo Emerson, *The Conduct of Life* (1860).

74 practice
See also: training 103

1 The underlying principle of all development, is practice.

> JAMES ALLEN, American theologian and author. *The Mastery of Destiny* (Putnam, New York, 1909).

2 In any craft, practice is the only means to success.

> JOE GORES, American author. 'Should I Be a Writer?', in A. S. Burack (ed.), *The Writer's Handbook* (The Writer, Boston, 1978).

3 The barber learns his trade on the orphan's chin.

> ARABIC PROVERB.

4 Practice makes perfect.

> LATIN PROVERB.

75 praise
See also: criticism 18; human nature 39; incentive/s & rewards 43; motivation 63; people 70

1 Praise when it's due is as good as a raise when it's due.

> ANON.

2 The best way to knock the chip off someone's shoulder is to pat him on the back.

> ANON.

3 Praise generates energy, but only if it is justified. Receiving unmerited accolades can be an insult that reveals indifference on the part of the bestower.

> JAN CARLZON, Swedish business leader, former CEO of Scandinavian Airlines System, speaker and author. *Moments of Truth* (Ballinger, Cambridge,

4 In business one often receives neither praise nor criticism. I spent my initial years in a state of constant concern that my performance was so appalling that my services were about to be dispensed with. Above everything, individuals need a degree of assurance about the perception of their performance and this seems to me a not unreasonable requirement.

JOHN HARVEY-JONES, British business consultant, broadcaster, author and former Chairman of ICI Industries. *All Together Now* (William Heinemann, London, 1994). Reprinted by permission of The Peters Fraser and Dunlop Group Limited on behalf of John Harvey-Jones.

5 Unmerited abuse wounds, while unmerited praise has not the power to heal.

THOMAS JEFFERSON (1743–1826), American statesman, and 3rd President of the United States of America 1801–09. In a letter to Edward Rutledge, 27 December 1796.

6 A wise executive once told me that he liked to think of handing out praise as the same as handing out money to his employees. 'I can't always pay our people as much as I'd like to, so I pretend that praise is money. Whenever I tell one of my people that they did a wonderful job,' he said, 'it's like giving them a $100 bonus. Sure, they can't spend it on something nice. But they bank the praise in their mind – and they feel better about me and our company.' That may be the most compelling argument for praise: it will help you hang on to talented people when your money can't.

MARK H. McCORMACK, American sports marketing consultant, founder and CEO of International Marketing Group, and author. *McCormack on Managing* (Century, London, 1995).

7 Good reviews provide helium for the soul, of course, and they make a day about perfect, but I'm inclined to take the attitude of the oldtimer. Someone had praised him lavishly to the skies. He turned and said with a glint in his eyes, 'Well, mother, pin a rose on me!'

GREGORY PECK, American actor. *The Hollywood Reporter*, 11 October 1948.

8 Praise makes good men better and bad men worse.

ENGLISH PROVERB.

76 **presentation**

See also: creativity 17; image 41

1 A good presentation poses as many questions as it presents answers.

ANON.

2 Never judge a book by its cover.

ANON.

3 Customers focus on the solution, not the presentation of the solution, and if you are too good or too slick, they actually are less likely to believe or value the solution. This suggests that we should emphasise creativity and information over presentations.

RICHARD E. PLANK, American academic, Associate Professor of Marketing at Western Michigan University, and DAVID E. REID, American academic, Associate Professor of Marketing at the University of Toledo. 'Difference Between Success, Failure in Selling', *Marketing News* (American Marketing Association), 4 November 1996, page 14. Reprinted with permission.

priorities 77
See also: focus 31; getting started 35

1 Don't throw the baby out with the bath water.
   ANON.

2 First things first.
   ANON.

3 Let all things be done decently and in order.
   THE BIBLE. 1 Corinthians, 14:40.

4 Sometimes you don't have the luxury of choosing your battles; you have to fight each battle as it presents itself.
   JAMES CARVILLE, American political consultant and author, and Campaign Manager for Bill Clinton's 1992 US presidential campaign. Attrib. (1992).

5 In every affair consider what precedes and what follows, and then undertake it.
   EPICTETUS (2nd century AD), Greek philosopher. *Discourses* (2nd century AD).

6 While you're saving your face, you're losing your ass.
   LYNDON B. JOHNSON (1908–73), American statesman, and 36th President of the United States of America 1963–69. Attrib.

7 The time to repair the roof is when the sun is shining.
   JOHN F. KENNEDY (1917–63), American statesman, and 35th President of the United States of America 1961–63. His State of the Union message, 11 January 1962.

8 Ownership is optional, control is essential.
   ROBIN M. PRIEBE, Australian pastoralist. CWE, 25 May 1997.

78 problems & problem-solving

See also: decisions 20; leadership 51; limitations 53; obstacles 66; opportunity 68; responsibility & responsibilities 90; success 98

1 *Murphy's Laws*

Murphy's First Law – Nothing is as easy as it looks.

Murphy's Second Law – Everything takes longer than you think.

Murphy's Third Law – Anything that can go wrong will go wrong.

Murphy's Fourth Law – If there is a possibility of several things going wrong, at a minimum the one that causes the most damage will go wrong.

Murphy's Fifth Law – If it is impossible for something to go wrong, it will definitely go wrong.

Murphy's Sixth Law – Left to themselves, things will go from bad to worse.

Murphy's Seventh Law – If things seem to be going well, you have obviously overlooked something.

ANON.

2 That which does not kill us strengthens us.

ANON.

3 The man who can smile when things go wrong has thought of someone he can blame it on.

ANON.

4 There are no problems in life, only opportunities.

ANON.

5 A problem is simply the difference between what one has and what one wants. Any question poses a problem. Generating and solving problems is the basis of forward thinking and

progress. If description is a matter of looking back to see what one has then problem solving is a matter of looking forward to see what one can get.

EDWARD DE BONO, Maltese-born British scholar, teacher, lecturer and author. *Lateral Thinking* (Ward Lock Education, London, 1970).

6 The more you know about a problem, the easier it is to solve. Oh yes? The problem is, we can be so close to the problem we get bogged down with information and ignore things we already know, so we don't consider them. 'Everybody knows that!' Fortunately, if you allow uninformed people to help you generate ideas, you may find the occasional solution popping up that is so clear, you want to kick yourself. 'Of course! It's so obvious!' So when you're trying to solve a problem, by all means involve people who know a lot about the subject. And include one or two who know nothing.

TIMOTHY R. V. FOSTER, British video producer and presenter, author and consultant. *Positive Thinking: 101 Ways to Generate Great Ideas* (Kogan Page, UK, 1991; Wrightbooks, Victoria, 1992).

7 It's much easier to point out the problem than it is to say just how it should be solved.

JOHN KENNETH GALBRAITH, Canadian-born American economist, Emeritus Professor of Economics at Harvard University, former senior White House adviser, diplomat and author. *Capitalism, Communism and Coexistence* (Houghton Mifflin, New York, 1988). Copyright © 1988 by John Kenneth Galbraith. Reprinted by permission of Houghton Mifflin Company. All rights reserved.

8 Do yourself a favour when you have a personal or business problem, when you have an ailment, when you've taken a jolt from the school of hard knocks: don't tell anyone. Twenty per cent don't care, and eighty per cent are glad to hear about it. Don't give them the satisfaction. The only pleasure trouble can

give you is keeping it to yourself – at least you know something that no one else around the office knows.

> TOM HOPKINS, American sales trainer, motivator and author. *How to Master the Art of Selling* (Champion Press, Scottsdale, Arizona, 1982; republished HarperCollins, London, 1994).

9 Problems are only opportunities in work clothes.

> HENRY J. KAISER (1882–1967), American industrialist and founder of more than 100 companies, including Kaiser Steel and Kaiser Aluminium. Attrib.

10 Our problems are man-made, therefore they may be solved by man.

> JOHN F. KENNEDY (1917–63), American statesman, and 35th President of the United States of America 1961–63. In a speech made at The American University, Washington DC, 10 June 1963.

11 There are two ways to approach problems. You can sit down and say, 'Oh my God, I can't face this, it will destroy me.' Or you can stand up and look beyond it to see how it can make you grow.

> NICK NOLTE, American actor. *OK! Magazine*, May 1993.

12 Sometimes when you look at the world and all its problems and we're here worrying because our thighs are a bit flabby, it's ridiculous.

> DOLORES O'RIORDAN, Irish singer, songwriter and lead vocalist of The Cranberries. Quoted in Liz Evans (ed.), *Women, Sex and Rock 'n' Roll: In Their Own Words* (Pandora, London, 1994). Reprinted by permission of HarperCollins Publishers Limited.

13 At BrainReserve, we never work toward a solution – we always go past it. We push the problem all the way to the end, to the blackest future possibility. The extreme. Then we let the trends help us work back to the solution. It's an approach we call Extremism, and it works for any problem.

FAITH POPCORN, American business consultant, co-founder and CEO of BrainReserve, and author. *The Popcorn Report* (Doubleday, New York, 1991). Copyright 1991 by Faith Popcorn. Used by permission of Doubleday, a division of Bantam Doubleday Dell Publishing Group, Inc.

14 **A smooth sea never made a skilful mariner.**
    ENGLISH PROVERB.

15 **Every path has its puddle.**
    ENGLISH PROVERB.

16 **The dynamic interactions of motivation, learning, perception and problem solving are real and important.**
    ROBERT S. WOODWORTH (1869–1962), American psychologist, Professor of Psychology at Columbia University and author. *Dynamics of Behaviour* (Columbia University Press, New York, 1918; republished Methuen, London, 1958).

productivity 79

See also: incentive/s & rewards 43; motivation 63;
responsibility & responsibilities 90

1 **A worker who can envision the whole cathedral and who has been given responsibility for constructing his own portion of it is far more satisfied and productive than the worker who sees only the granite before him.**
    JAN CARLZON, Swedish business leader, former CEO of Scandinavian Airlines System, speaker and author. *Moments of Truth* (Ballinger, Cambridge, Massachusetts, 1987; revised edition Harper & Row, New York, 1989). Copyright © 1987 by Ballinger Publishing Company. Reprinted by permission of HarperCollins Publishers, Inc.

2 **It is beginning to dawn on leaders and management that there is a direct and powerful link between happiness and the**

bottom line. Happy, fulfilled people are more productive at all levels of the corporate structure.

AMANDA GORE, Australian corporate speaker and trainer. Quoted in Ruth Ostrow, 'The Taming of the Beast', *Weekend Australian*, 9 September 1995. © The Weekend Australian.

3 No man is so methodical as a complete idler, and none so scrupulous in measuring out his time as he whose time is worth nothing.

WASHINGTON IRVING (1783–1859), American historian, biographer and essayist. 'My French Neighbour', *Wolfert's Roost* (1855).

4 Where there is no desire, there will be no industry.

JOHN LOCKE (1632–1704), British philosopher. *Some Thoughts Concerning Education* (1693).

5 People are your resources, not your products or equipment. Taking care of people's needs is the key to productivity.

ROGER MEADE, American information systems developer and CEO of Scitor Corp. *Industry Week*, 18 October 1993. © Copyright Penton Publishing, Inc, Cleveland, Ohio. Reprinted with permission.

6 It is better to have loafed and lost than never to have loafed at all.

JAMES THURBER (1894–1961), American short-story writer, humorist and essayist. 'The Courtship of Arthur and Al', *Fables of Our Time* (1943).

80 products

See also: advertising 3; brands 6; marketing 58; selling 93; service 94

1 Our new customer-oriented perspective starts with the market instead of the product. Then the means of production is tailored to give the customer the best possible products.

JAN CARLZON, Swedish business leader, former CEO of Scandinavian Airlines System, speaker and author. *Moments of Truth* (Ballinger, Cambridge, Massachusetts, 1987; revised edition Harper & Row, New York, 1989). Copyright © 1987 by Ballinger Publishing Company. Reprinted by permission of HarperCollins Publishers, Inc.

2 A finished product is one that has already seen its better days.

> ART LINKLETTER, Canadian-born American radio and television personality. *A Child's Garden of Misinformation* (1965).

3 Bend your product around the trends and laugh your way straight to the bank.

> FAITH POPCORN, American business consultant, co-founder and CEO of BrainReserve, and author. *The Popcorn Report* (Doubleday, New York, 1991). Copyright 1991 by Faith Popcorn. Used by permission of Doubleday, a division of Bantam Doubleday Dell Publishing Group, Inc.

4 Far-shifting preferences, flowing out of and interacting with high-speed technological change, not only lead to frequent changes in the popularity of products and brands, but also shorten the life-cycle of products.

> ALVIN TOFFLER, American scholar, lecturer and author. *Future Shock* (The Bodley Head, London, 1970).

profits 81

See also: business ethics 7; economics & economists 26; marketing 58; money 62; responsibility & responsibilities 90; success 98

1 Whatever you make in business, if you don't make a profit, you won't make it for long.

> ANON.

2 My business school in America was wrong, I am now convinced. The principal purpose of a company is not to make a profit, full stop. It is to make a profit in order to continue to do things or make things, and to do so even better and more abundantly. To say that profit is a means to other ends and not an end in itself is not a semantic quibble, it is a serious moral point.

> CHARLES HANDY, British academic, business consultant and author. *The Age of Paradox* (Harvard Business School Press, Cambridge, Massachusetts, 1994).

3 The smell of profit is clean
And sweet, whatever the source.

> JUVENAL (Decimus Junius Juvenalis; c. AD 60 – c. AD 140), Roman poet and satirist. *Satires* (c. AD 100).

4 Even genius is tied to profit.

> PINDAR (c. 518/522 – c. 438/446 BC), Greek poet. *The Odes of Pindar* (5th century BC).

5 More men come to doom
through dirty profits than are kept by them.

> SOPHOCLES (496–406 BC), Greek playwright. *Antigone*, play (442–441 BC).

82 **progress**

See also: change 9; future, the 33; obstacles 66; opportunity 68; problems & problem-solving 78

1 Never mistake motion for progress.

> ANON.

2 All progress is based upon a universal innate desire on the part of every organism to live beyond its income.

> SAMUEL BUTLER (1835–1902), British scholar, translator and novelist. 'Lord, What is Man?' *Note-Books* (1912).

3 We have always been in error in our tendency to measure progress by the increase in the gross national product. I would like to see progress measured by the number of people who have a full, secure role in the society.

JOHN KENNETH GALBRAITH, Canadian-born American economist, Emeritus Professor of Economics at Harvard University, former senior White House adviser, diplomat and author. *Capitalism, Communism and Coexistence* (Houghton Mifflin, New York, 1988). Copyright © 1988 John Kenneth Galbraith. Reprinted by permission of Houghton Mifflin Company. All rights reserved.

4 Progress is man's ability to complicate simplicity.

THOR HEYERDAHL, Norwegian ethnologist, adventurer and author. Attrib.

5 There can be no progress if people have no faith in tomorrow.

JOHN F. KENNEDY (1917–63), American statesman, and 35th President of the United States of America 1961–63. In a speech made to the Inter-American Press Association, Miami Beach, Florida, 18 November 1963.

6 The desire to understand the world and the desire to reform it are the two great engines of progress, without which human society would stand still or retrogress.

BERTRAND RUSSELL (3rd Earl Russell; 1872–1970), British philosopher, mathematician, social reformer and writer. 'The Place of Sex Among Human Values', *Marriage and Morals* (1929).

7 The reasonable man adapts himself to the world; the unreasonable one persists in trying to adapt the world to himself. Therefore all progress depends on the unreasonable man.

GEORGE BERNARD SHAW (1856–1950), Irish playwright and critic, Nobel laureate 1925. 'Maxims for Revolutionists', *Man and Superman* (1903).

8 There are no gains without pains.

> ADLAI STEVENSON (1900–65), American politician, diplomat and ambassador to the United Nations 1960–65. In his speech accepting Presidential Nomination at the Democratic National Convention, 26 July 1952.

83 promises

See also: courtesy 16; customers 19; selling 93; service 94

1 To keep your customers, keep your promises.

> ANON.

2 In the best institutions, promises are kept no matter what the cost in agony and overtime.

> DAVID OGILVY, British-born American advertising expert, founder of Ogilvy & Mather international advertising group, New York, and author. *Confessions of an Advertising Man* (Atheneum, London, 1963; revised edition Pan, London, 1987).

3 With an explosion of competitors, many of them new and without track records, reliability, rather than overly aggressive promises, is the most valuable strategic edge, especially for the mid to long haul. While getting faster at responding to customers is imperative, living up to commitments has never been worth more.

> TOM PETERS, American academic, consultant, lecturer and author. *Thriving on Chaos* (Alfred A. Knopf, New York, 1987).

4 He that promises too much means nothing.

> ENGLISH PROVERB.

5 Vows made in storms are forgot in calms.

> ENGLISH PROVERB.

6 Who promises much and does little, dines a fool on hope.
   GERMAN PROVERB.

publicity 84

See also: advertising 3; image 41; marketing 58

1 Any publicity is good publicity.
   ANON.

2 Let the newspapers say what they like about you, just as long
   as they spell your name right.
   ANON.

3 There is no such thing as bad publicity.
   ANON.

4 To some people, publicity is vulgar. They think you should be in
   the newspaper just three times in your lifetime – when you are
   born, when you marry, and when you die.
   ANON.

5 In the first place, publicity is not a pursuit dedicated to the grab-
   bing of all the free space the traffic will bear. Publicity, I learned,
   is journalism, plus salesmanship, plus diplomacy, plus showman-
   ship. In the second place, the space itself does not mean a thing.
   In the third place, it is far better to never get one's name in the
   paper than to have whole columns which say the wrong thing.
   CAROLE LOMBARD, American actress. *The Hollywood Reporter,* 24 October
   1938.

6 We could only sit there shaking our heads at how fundamen-
   tally simple politics was – just as in show business, you kept
   your name in the paper no matter what.

ARTHUR MILLER, American playwright, screenwriter and author. *Timebends* (Methuen, London, 1987).

7 There is only one thing in the world worse than being talked about, and that is not being talked about.
OSCAR WILDE (1854–1900), Irish playwright, poet, author and wit. *The Picture of Dorian Gray* (1891).

85 punctuality

See also: efficiency 27; time management 102

1 Few things tend more to alienate friendship than a want of punctuality in our engagements.
WILLIAM HAZLITT (1788–1830), British critic, poet and essayist. 'On the Spirit of Obligations', *The Plain Speaker* (1826).

2 Timeliness is best in all matters.
HESIOD (8th century BC), Greek poet. *Works and Days* (8th century BC).

3 Punctuality is the politeness of kings.
LOUIS XVIII (1755–1824), French king. *Souvenirs de Lafitte* (1844). Attrib.; probably a proverb of earlier origin.

4 Punctuality is the soul of business.
ENGLISH PROVERB.

5 Time and tide wait for no man.
ENGLISH PROVERB.

6 Time is money.
ENGLISH PROVERB.

7 Men count up the faults of those who keep them waiting.
   FRENCH PROVERB.

8 Better late than never.
   GREEK PROVERB.

9 Better three hours too soon than a minute too late.
   WILLIAM SHAKESPEARE (1564–1616), British poet and playwright. *The Merry Wives of Windsor*, play (1597).

10 To arrive early is unfortunate, but to be late is the rudest thing imaginable. Sometimes I do not know whether I organise time or time organises me.
   KIRI TE KANAWA, New Zealand operatic soprano. Rolex watch magazine advertisement, 1996. Reprinted by permission of Montres Rolex S. A., Geneva.

purpose 86

See also: achieving 2; goals & goal-setting 36; success 98

1 Purpose is the keystone in the temple of achievement.
   JAMES ALLEN, American theologian and author. *The Mastery of Destiny* (Putnam, New York, 1909).

2 All things at last yield to the silent, irresistible, all-conquering energy of purpose.
   JAMES ALLEN, American theologian and author. *The Mastery of Destiny* (Putnam, New York, 1909).

3 The secret of success is constancy to purpose.
   BENJAMIN DISRAELI (1804–81), British statesman, novelist, and Prime Minister 1868 and 1874–80. In a speech, 24 June 1870.

'The future is out there in the world,
and the one place you won't find it is the
place where most people look for it.'
FAITH POPCORN

questions 88:6

See also: efficiency 27; marketing 58; products 80; service 94

1 In the pursuit of quality and excellence, it is a great asset when you decide to use exclusively the best fruit of the vineyard and select only the best 20 grapes out of a hundred.

> MICHEL DIETRICH, French-born Australian vintner, Quelltaler Winery, Clare Valley, South Australia. *Australian Tempo Libero*, 1987.

2 If you aren't tough, you just don't get quality. If you're soft and fuzzy, like our little characters, you become the skinny kid on the beach and people in this business don't mind kicking sand in your face.

> MICHAEL EISNER, American entertainment and media industry leader, and CEO of Disney Corporation. Reported by Robert Lusetich in the *Weekend Australian*, 11 December 1995. © The Weekend Australian.

3 Quality is remembered long after the price is forgotten.

> GUCCI FAMILY, Italian fashion industry dynasty. Family slogan.

4 One shining quality lends lustre to another, or hides some glaring defect.

> WILLIAM HAZLITT (1778–1830), British critic, poet and essayist. *Characteristics* (1823).

5 Quality is the minimum level of service that a firm chooses to provide in order to satisfy its target clientele. At the same time, it is the degree of consistency the firm can maintain in providing the predetermined level of service.

> JACQUES HOROVITZ, French business consultant and author. *Winning*

Ways, originally *Qualité de Service* (InterEditions, Paris, 1987; republished Productivity Press, Cambridge, Massachusetts, 1990).

6 **Everybody in an organisation has to believe their livelihood is based on the quality of the product they deliver.**

LEE IACOCCA, American automotive industry leader, former CEO of Chrysler Motors and director of several other auto manufacturing companies, and author. *Talking Straight* (Bantam, New York, 1988). Copyright © 1988 by Lee Iacocca. Used by permission of Bantam Books, a division of Bantam Doubleday Dell Publishing Group Inc.

7 **In Japan the commitment to quality is so ingrained it's almost like personal hygiene.**

LEE IACOCCA, American automotive industry leader, former CEO of Chrysler Motors and director of several other auto manufacturing companies, and author. *Talking Straight* (Bantam, New York, 1988). Copyright © 1988 by Lee Iacocca. Used by permission of Bantam Books, a division of Bantam Doubleday Dell Publishing Group Inc.

8 **The boss must be absolutely intolerant of any short cuts. If he gives lip service to quality – meaning he knows something's wrong but keeps building it anyway – then the word spreads like wildfire. Workers at every level will say: 'Well, if the boss doesn't give a damn, why should I?'**

LEE IACOCCA, American automotive industry leader, former CEO of Chrysler Motors and director of several other auto manufacturing companies, and author. *Talking Straight* (Bantam, New York, 1988). Copyright © 1988 by Lee Iacocca. Used by permission of Bantam Books, a division of Bantam Doubleday Dell Publishing Group Inc.

9 **Either dance well or quit the ballroom.**

GREEK PROVERB.

See also: advice 4; listening 54; negotiation 64;
presentation 76; selling 93

1 If you want answers, ask questions.
   ANON.

2 In a courtroom, a good lawyer never asks a witness a question
   to which he doesn't already know the answer.
   ANON.

3 Socrates, 'the gadfly of Athens,' was one of the greatest
   philosophers the world has ever known. He did something
   that only a handful of men in all history have been able to
   do: he sharply changed the whole course of human thought;
   and now, twenty-four centuries after his death, he is honoured as one of the wisest persuaders who ever influenced
   this wrangling world. His method? Did he tell people they
   were wrong? Oh, no, not Socrates. He was far too adroit for
   that. His whole technique, now called the 'Socratic method,'
   was based upon getting a 'yes, yes' response. He asked
   questions with which his opponent would have to agree. He
   kept on winning one admission after another until he had an
   armful of yeses. He kept on asking questions until finally,
   almost without realising it, his opponents found themselves
   embracing a conclusion they would have bitterly denied a
   few minutes previously. The next time we are tempted to tell
   someone he or she is wrong, let's remember old Socrates
   and ask a gentle question – a question that will get the 'yes,
   yes' response.
       DALE CARNEGIE (1888–1955), American educator, motivator and author.
       How to Win Friends and Influence People (Simon & Schuster, New York, 1937;
       revised edition 1981).

4 Examinations are formidable even to the best prepared, for the greatest fool may ask more than the wisest man can answer.

CHARLES CALEB COLTON (1780–1832), British clergyman and writer. *Lacon* (1825).

5 The important thing is not to stop questioning. Curiosity has its own reason for existing.

ALBERT EINSTEIN (1879–1955), German–Swiss–American physicist. Attrib.

6 I never stop myself from asking whomever I run into – cab-drivers, people at airports, moviegoers on line – what they think about cars or cookies or computers or whatever we're working on. The future is out there in the world, and the one place you won't find it is the place where most people look for it. It's not in your office.

FAITH POPCORN, American business consultant, co-founder and CEO of BrainReserve and author. *The Popcorn Report* (Doubleday, New York, 1991). Copyright 1991 by Faith Popcorn. Used by permission of Doubleday, a division of Bantam Doubleday Dell Publishing Group, Inc.

7 He who asks questions cannot avoid the answers.

CAMEROONIAN PROVERB.

8 Better ask questions twice than lose your way once.

DANISH PROVERB.

9 To question a wise man is the beginning of wisdom.

GERMAN PROVERB.

10 When managing people, one of the greatest time-savers is asking questions – more specifically, asking the *right* questions. In behavioural psychology we learn that everything is a result of something else. And when a problem arises, it is usually a clue

that a deeper problem lies beneath the surface. The best way to get to the bottom of things is to not jump to conclusions but to ask questions.

JIM ROHN, American business philosopher, lecturer and author. *Seven Strategies for Wealth and Happiness* (Brolga, Melbourne, 1994).

11 Thére aren't any embarrassing questions – just embarrassing answers.

CARL ROWAN, American diplomat and journalist. 'Ambassador, Talk of the Town', *The New Yorker*, 7 December 1963. Reprinted by permission. © 1963 The New Yorker Magazine, Inc.

12 I'm not pretending to know all the answers. In some cases I'm still learning what the questions are!

LANA TURNER (1920–95), American actress and author. Lana Turner & Hollis Alpert, *Lana: The Lady, the Legend, the Truth* (E. P. Dutton, New York, 1982). Copyright © 1982 by Eltee Productions and Hollis Alpert. Used by permission of Dutton Signet, a division of Penguin Books USA Inc.

r

'Life eventually boils down to a choice –
you either stand by your principles and
responsibilities, or you don't.'
PETE GOSS

responsibility & responsibilities 90:7

See also: getting started 35; money 62; training 103

1 Limited resources demand limited objectives.

   ANON.

2 The One Minute Manager's symbol – a one minute readout
   from the face of a modern digital watch – is intended to remind
   each of us to take a minute out of our day to look into the faces
   of the people we manage. And to realise that *they* are our most
   important resources.

   KENNETH BLANCHARD, American educator, management consultant,
   trainer and author, and SPENCER JOHNSON, American publisher, lecturer,
   communications consultant and author. *The One Minute Manager* (Collins,
   London, 1983). Reprinted by permission of HarperCollins Publishers.

3 In a sense, all fledgling business ventures involve pioneering.
   Every new product or service is initially an experiment. The
   smartest business gurus cannot flawlessly predict the future.
   Companies spend millions test-marketing products before
   offering them to the public. In spite of those efforts, many new
   products fail. The largest companies can ride out the failures,
   but most of us can't. This is the single biggest reason start-up
   businesses falter. It's not because some big company necessarily knows something they don't. Rather, the cost of trial and
   error eats up resources faster than revenues come in.

   LAURENCE A. CANTER and MARTHA S. SIEGEL, American lawyers
   and authors. *How to Make a Fortune on the Information Superhighway*
   (HarperCollins, London, 1995). Reprinted by permission of HarperCollins
   Publishers Limited.

4 The biggest wasters of their own resources are the people who don't know who they want to be or where they want to go.

> TOM HOPKINS, American sales trainer, motivator and author. *How to Master the Art of Selling* (Champion Press, Scottsdale, Arizona, 1982; republished HarperCollins, London, 1994).

5 We are taking a cat and painting it black and yellow and calling it a tiger . . . The fundamental problem is a lack of resources.

> DAVID MACGIBBON, Australian politician and federal senator. Comment made about budget cuts and their effect on equipping the Australian military. *The Bulletin*, 24 September 1996.

6 When absolute superiority is not attainable, you must produce a relative one at the decisive point by making use of what you have.

> CARL VON CLAUSEWITZ (1780–1831), Prussian general and strategist. *On War* (1852).

90 responsibility & responsibilities

See also: business ethics 7; corporate culture 15; employees 28; people 70

1 Compassionately accepting and taking responsibility for your present situation is the first and most important step in creating change. When you try to overcome a problem by pretending it doesn't exist, you are not taking responsibility for the problem – so you are not empowered to do anything about it.

> SUSAN M. CAMPBELL, American lecturer and author. *From Chaos to Confidence* (Simon & Schuster, New York, 1995).

2 An individual without information cannot take responsibility; an individual who is given information cannot help but take responsibility.

> JAN CARLZON, Swedish business leader, former CEO of Scandinavian

Airlines System, speaker and author. *Moments of Truth* (Ballinger, Cambridge, Massachusetts, 1987; revised edition Harper & Row, New York, 1989). Copyright © 1987 by Ballinger Publishing Company. Reprinted by permission of HarperCollins Publishers, Inc.

3 We desperately need, for the sake of our children, a national and global economy in which people act not only as consumers but as citizens, in which workers reassert responsibility for themselves and the success of their companies, and in which our businesses can do well *and* do good.

HILLARY RODHAM CLINTON, American lawyer, and First Lady of the United States of America 1993– . *It Takes a Village* (Simon & Schuster, New York, 1996).

4 I have talked about the responsibilities of individuals and institutions for the future of our children and the village they will inherit. No segment of society has a more significant influence on the nature of that legacy than business. We live in an era of what political scientist Edward Luttwak calls 'turbo-charged' capitalism, which is characterised by intense competition; breathtaking technological changes; global financial, information, and entertainment markets; constant corporate restructuring; and relatively less public control and influence over the private economy. This combination of changed circumstances poses new problems for families and communities, and for the children who grow up in them. Business affects us powerfully as consumers, as workers, as investors, and, more broadly, as citizens of the society it helps to create and as inhabitants of the environment it has a strong hand in shaping. Our circumstances therefore require new and thoughtful responses from every segment of society, particularly from business.

HILLARY RODHAM CLINTON, American lawyer, and First Lady of the United States of America 1993– . *It Takes a Village* (Simon & Schuster, New York, 1996).

5   I have respect for the person putting up the money. If they have enough faith in you to put up the money, whether it's personal or a bank or a distribution company like Warner Bros, you should have enough respect to watch their money as if it was your own. For them, you are a gamble. You should make sure they don't lose.

>   CLINT EASTWOOD, American film producer, director and actor. *OK! Magazine*, November 1994.

6   If you go over budget, you have to start asking people for money. And that means they have a right to an opinion about what you're shooting. You have to be financially responsible, or your independence gets taken away.

>   JODIE FOSTER, American film producer, director and actor. *Working Woman*, 1996; reprinted *Tatler*, September 1996.

7   Life eventually boils down to a choice – you either stand by your principles and responsibilities, or you don't.

>   PETE GOSS, British solo round-the-world yachtsman. Comment made about his decision to go to the rescue of a sinking French yachtsman in the storm-tossed Southern Ocean, Christmas 1996. 'My Best Christmas Present Ever', *Weekly Telegraph*, 8 January 1997.

8   A society that emphasises rights but neglects obligations can leave too much space for its citizens.

>   CHARLES HANDY, British academic, business consultant and author. *The Age of Paradox* (Harvard Business School Press, Cambridge, Massachusetts, 1994).

9   Businesses have core obligations to their shareholders, but their responsibilities go further. Finding the right balance between duty and a wider responsibility is a dilemma at the heart of capitalism.

>   CHARLES HANDY, British academic, business consultant and author. *The Age of Paradox* (Harvard Business School Press, Cambridge, Massachusetts, 1994).

10 The good modern organisation does not have job descriptions, but job responsibilities. A considerable amount of 'fuzz' is left around the organisation so that the freedom of action of the individual is not constrained.

> JOHN HARVEY-JONES, British business consultant, broadcaster, author and former Chairman of ICI Industries. *All Together Now* (William Heinemann, London, 1994). Reprinted by permission of The Peters Fraser and Dunlop Group Limited on behalf of John Harvey-Jones.

11 It was all a bit like being on the Moon: you moved forward because you were falling forward. The clear path is revealed later, looking back. Which doesn't mean that one disclaims responsibility for one's actions. We are what we have done; besides, we can't deny it without giving up our pride.

> CLIVE JAMES, Australian-born British broadcaster and author. *Falling Towards England* (Jonathan Cape, London, 1985).

12 Do your duty in all things. You cannot do more. You should never wish to do less.

> ROBERT E. LEE (1807–70), American soldier, and commanding general of the armies of the Confederate States of America 1861–65. Inscribed beneath his bust in the Hall of Fame for Great Americans, New York University.

13 Because we [the USA] have emerged as the only remaining superpower, we have an awesome responsibility both to ourselves as a nation and to the rest of the world. I don't know what that responsibility will mean to the future of our great country, but I shall always remain confident of the American people's ability to rise to *any* challenge.

> H. NORMAN SCHWARZKOPF, American soldier and general of the United States Army (retired), commander of the Coalition Forces in the Gulf War, 1991. *It Doesn't Take a Hero* (Bantam, New York, 1992).

14 Democracy depends upon active citizens who feel a sense of responsibility for their community. I therefore advise young people to take a share of this responsibility, at least in one area of activity. Whether one becomes involved in community work, supports environmental causes or helps promote international understanding, the question cannot be 'what are the interests of the individual?' but 'how much commitment does society demand of each of its citizens?'

> RITA SUSSMUTH, German professor, politician and President of the Bundestag (the German Parliament). CWE, 28 October 1996.

15 No one has absolute control over his or her destiny. The point is to control what you can. Far from being an idea that pertains only to members of the Business Roundtable, 'control your destiny or someone else will' is a philosophy of life basic enough to apply to anyone ... The meaning is simple: take responsibility. Whenever something's bothering you, whether it's a competitor stealing your customers or a bad habit you can't shake, you face a clear choice: either solve the problem yourself or accept a fate that you may not like. Considered from this perspective, the ethic of personal responsibility gains appeal.

> NOEL M. TICHY, American academic and author, and STRATFORD SHERMAN, American journalist and author. *Control Your Destiny or Someone Else Will* (Doubleday, New York, 1993). Copyright © 1993 by Noel M. Tichy and Stratford Sherman. Used by permission of Bantam Doubleday Dell Publishing Group, Inc.

16 In an ideal world, every living being would be everyone's responsibility. In a real, yet changing world, we are shyly edging toward such a distant possibility.

> PETER USTINOV, British actor, producer, playwright, university chancellor and author. 'Toward the Age of Common Sense', *1995 Britannica Book of the Year* (Encyclopaedia Britannica, Chicago, 1995). © 1995 Encyclopaedia Britannica Inc.

17 Taking control of ourselves means taking the responsibility for making the best use of what we have – our minds, our talents and developed abilities, and that precious little time we have to spend on living. The choice is ours and it is here that personal honesty and responsibility determine whether we will win or lose our own Superbowl of life.

DENIS WAITLEY, American personal development counsellor, lecturer and author. *The Psychology of Winning* (Nightingale-Conant, Chicago, 1979; republished Berkley, New York, 1984).

'A corporation without a strategy is like
an airplane weaving through stormy skies,
hurled up and down, slammed by the wind,
lost in the thunderheads.'
ALVIN TOFFLER

strategy 97:4

sacrifices 91
See also: incentive/s & rewards 43

1 The Servant knows that he will have no reward and that in the end he will sacrifice himself for his master. That is his reward.

ALISTAIR McALPINE (Lord McAlpine of West Green), British business leader, political figure and author. *The Servant* (Faber & Faber, London, 1992).

2 Drown thyself not to save a drowning man.

ENGLISH PROVERB.

3 I think it *cost* me to do this movie [Pulp Fiction]. Around $30 000. I wanted to stay in a different hotel, so I said, I'll add money to the per diem. But it was well worth it.

JOHN TRAVOLTA, American actor. *Vanity Fair*, July 1994. (The film went on to relaunch his career as a film star.)

self-consciousness 92

1 I always say I am a man of very few inner resources. I hate being by myself.

OSCAR DE LA RENTA, American fashion designer of Dominican origin. *Town & Country*, July 1996.

2 If you happen to have a wart on your nose or forehead, you cannot help imagining that no one in the world has anything else to do but stare at your wart, laugh at it, and condemn you for it, even if you have discovered America.

FYODOR DOSTOEVSKY (1821–81), Russian novelist. *The Idiot* (1868).

3 Those people who are uncomfortable in themselves are disagreeable to others.

> WILLIAM HAZLITT (1778–1830), British critic, poet and essayist. 'On Disagreeable People', *Sketches and Essays* (1839).

93 selling

See also: advertising 3; consumers 14; courtesy 16; customers 19; human nature 39; marketing 58; money 62; negotiation 64; products 80; profits 81

1 A good salesperson can sell anything, because in reality what they are selling is themselves.

> ANON.

2 Nothing happens unless someone sells something.

> ANON.

3 Anything can be sold on the Information Superhighway. As for how to go about it, you are limited only by your own imagination, and, in this early stage, where the newness of the medium makes even the most standard marketing practices controversial, acceptance of your role as a pioneer.

> LAURENCE A. CANTER and MARTHA S. SIEGEL, American lawyers and authors. *How to Make a Fortune on the Information Superhighway* (HarperCollins, London, 1995). Reprinted by permission of HarperCollins Publishers Limited.

4 Man does not only sell commodities, he sells himself and feels himself to be a commodity.

> ERIC FROMM (1900–80), German-born American psychoanalyst and philosopher. *Escape from Freedom* (1941).

5 To sell is what the honest writer wants to do, to sell to earn a living to feed his family, or even for the pure satisfaction of selling,

of having written something good enough to cause the largest number of people to reach into their pockets and give over money they have earned . . . To sell, it is only necessary to capture the human imagination and touch the human heart.

> PAUL GALLICO, American author. 'Aim for the Heart', in A. S. Burack (ed.), *The Writer's Handbook* (The Writer, Boston, 1978).

6 Ad writers forget they are salesmen and try to be performers. Instead of sales, they seek applause.

> CLAUDE HOPKINS (1867–1932), American advertising copywriter, senior advertising agency executive and author. *Scientific Advertising* (1928).

7 I learned a long time ago that selling is the highest-paid hard work – and the lowest-paid easy work – that I could find. And I also found out another exciting thing about selling – the choice was mine, all mine.

> TOM HOPKINS, American sales trainer, motivator and author. *How to Master the Art of Selling* (Champion Press, Scottsdale, Arizona, 1982; republished HarperCollins, London, 1994).

8 It's the winning score, the bottom line, the name of the game, the cutting edge, the point of it all . . . Prospecting, meeting people, building a flow of referrals, qualifying, presenting, demonstrating, overcoming objections . . . they're all important. But, unless you can close, you're like a football team that can't sustain a drive long enough to score. It's no good if you play your whole game in your own territory and never get across their goal line. So welcome to the delightful world of closing. If you don't love it now, start falling in love, because that's where the money is.

> TOM HOPKINS, American sales trainer, motivator and author. *How to Master the Art of Selling* (Champion Press, Scottsdale, Arizona, 1982; republished HarperCollins, London, 1994).

9 The role of front-line service delivery personnel in the selling effort is crucial. In many companies they sell service daily and can sell additional services, related services and more of a service. Often, front-line service delivery personnel, being at the lower end of the pay scale, view their company's products and services as beyond their own economic reach and thus show reluctance to actively sell. Good training can give these employees the confidence to proudly sell their company's products and services.

> LINDA M. LASH, British training and development counsellor and author. *The Complete Guide to Customer Service* (John Wiley & Sons, New York, 1989). Copyright © 1989 Linda M. Lash. Reprinted by permission of John Wiley & Sons.

10 The qualities that I believe make a good salesman:
- Believe in your product.
- Believe in yourself.
- See a lot of people.
- Pay attention to timing.
- Listen to the customer – but realise that what the customer wants is not necessarily what he or she is telling you.
- Develop a sense of humour.
- Knock on old doors.
- Ask everyone to buy.
- Follow up after the sale with the same aggressiveness you demonstrated before the sale.
- Use common sense.

I have no illusions that I'm breaking new ground with this list. These are essential, self-evident, universal qualities that all salespeople know in their heads – if not their hearts.

> MARK H. McCORMACK, American sports marketing consultant, founder and CEO of International Management Group, and author. *McCormack on Selling* (Century, London, 1995).

11 I've never bought anything from salespeople who didn't know their product and yet I have bought things I didn't know I needed from people who did.

MARK H. McCORMACK, American sports marketing consultant, founder and CEO of International Management Group, and author. *McCormack on Selling* (Century, London, 1995).

12 Creative power can promote an employee's progress in any phase of business, especially in salesmanship. A salesman has to use his imagination, deliberately and consciously, to think up just what little thing he can do to be helpful to each customer. Every case calls for different tactics. That fact helps explain why aptitude testers maintain that the two traits most needed for success in selling are an objective personality and creative imagination.

ALEX F. OSBORN (1888–1966), American academic and author. *Applied Imagination: Principles & Procedures of Creative Thinking* (Charles Scribner's Sons, New York, 1953).

13 A man without a smiling face must not open a shop.

CHINESE PROVERB.

14 The buyer needs a hundred eyes, the seller not one.

ITALIAN PROVERB.

15 It is no sin to sell dear, but a sin to give ill measure.

SCOTTISH PROVERB.

16 There is a finite amount of power in an organisation. It is not there for the taking; it is however there for the giving. People will cede power to you if they believe that it is in their interest to do so. You must sell them on the idea that it *is* in their interest. You are a salesperson. You have a product to sell – yourself – a plan, your talents. That is why it is so important for

you to know yourself, to know what you are selling. See yourself as selling much of the time. Most people do not admit that they engage in selling.

Occasionally, of course, when they want a raise, a favour, or approval from higher management, they grant the need to be cast in a selling role. But if you are pursuing power, you are selling almost all the time.

THOMAS L. QUICK, American consultant and author. *Power Plays* (Franklin Watts, Danbury, Connecticut, 1985).

17 Human nature being what it is, most people will take the easiest course of action. They will sell the products which are easiest to sell, and will work hardest for the people they like and who support them.

JOHN ROCK, Australian sales, marketing and management consultant and author. *Managing Key Accounts* (Longman Professional, Melbourne, 1994).

18 Buying and selling is good and necessary; it is very necessary and it may, possibly, be very good; but it cannot be the noblest work of man.

ANTHONY TROLLOPE (1815–82), British novelist. *Dr Thorne* (1858).

19 I was always brought up to believe that you should not knock somebody else's choice. If you're shoving motor cars and a fellow drives up in a Cadillac, you don't say, 'God, have *you* got a bag of worms, you should have a Rolls-Royce' – because straight away you've insulted the fellow's intelligence and his perspicacity.

GORDON WHITE, British-born American-based businessman, Chairman of Hanson Industries, New York. Quoted in Alan Whicker, *Whicker's New World* (Weidenfeld & Nicolson, London, 1985).

service 94

1 *The Key Rules of Superior Service*
Rule #1: The Customer is always right.
Rule #2: If the Customer is ever wrong, refer to Rule #1.

> ANON.

2 If, as a customer, you find the service you receive less than you deserve, it's probably more a reflection of leadership than front line competency. Skills training is critical but nothing will ever replace a great example.

> BOB ASHFORD, Australian tourism industry executive, National Manager of the AussieHost Program of the Inbound Tourism Organisation of Australia. *AussieHost News*, August 1995.

3 If McDonald's did not ensure repeat business, we would be out of business in just two days. The basis for bringing our customer back is giving them great service, unmatched by our competitors and building a trusting relationship with everyone who visits us for a meal.

> CHARLIE BELL, Australian business leader and CEO of McDonald's Australia. In a foreword to Stephen Dando-Collins, *The Customer Care Revolution* (Pitman, Melbourne, 1996).

4 We are at an historic crossroad where the age of customer orientation has arrived, even for businesses that have never before viewed themselves as service businesses.

> JAN CARLZON, Swedish business leader, former CEO of Scandinavian Airlines System, speaker and author. *Moments of Truth* (Ballinger, Cambridge, Massachusetts, 1987; revised edition Harper & Row, New York, 1989).

5 The necessity of measuring results [of customer service programs] is particularly crucial for those employees who affect customer service through their work but who don't have face-to-face contact with the customer.

JAN CARLZON, Swedish business leader, former CEO of Scandinavian Airlines System, speaker and author. *Moments of Truth* (Ballinger, Cambridge, Massachusetts, 1987; revised edition Harper & Row, New York, 1989). Copyright © 1987 by Ballinger Publishing Company. Reprinted by permission of HarperCollins Publishers, Inc.

6 We have often confused service with subservience and viewed jobs in the service sector as stepping stones to a 'real' job. But, we can no longer afford the misplaced arrogance of looking at service in this light.

CATHERINE DEVRYE, Australian lecturer, motivator, author and 1993–94 Australian Executive Woman of the Year. 'She'll Be Right Approach Not Good Enough', *AussieHost News*, February 1997.

7 Organisations that figure out how to offer – and deliver – guaranteed, breakthrough service will have tapped into a powerful source of competitive advantage. Doing so is no mean feat, of course, which is precisely why the opportunity to build a competitive advantage exists. Though the task is difficult, it is clearly not impossible, and the service guarantee can play a fundamental role in the process.

CHRISTOPHER W. L. HART, American academic at Harvard Business School. 'The Power of Unconditional Service', *Harvard Business Review*, July–August 1988, page 62. Copyright © 1988 by the President and Fellows of Harvard College. All rights reserved.

8 Render more and better service than you are paid for, and sooner or later you will receive compound interest from your investment. It is inevitable that every seed of useful service you sow will sprout and reward you with an abundant harvest.

NAPOLEON HILL (d. 1970), American motivator and author. Matthew Sartwell (ed.), *Napoleon Hill's Keys to Success* (Dutton, New York, 1994). Copyright © 1994 by The Napoleon Hill Foundation. Used by permission of Dutton Signet, a division of Penguin Books USA Inc.

9 Service is the virtue that distinguishes the great of all times and which they will be remembered by. It places a mark of nobility upon its disciples. It is the dividing line which separates the two great groups of the world – those who help and those who hinder, those who lift and those who lean, those who contribute and those who only consume.

BRYANT S. HINCKLEY, American pioneer of the 19th-century Wild West and writer. *Not by Bread Alone* (Bookcraft, Salt Lake City, 1955).

10 The noblest service comes from nameless hands,
And the best servant does his work unseen.

OLIVER WENDELL HOLMES SNR (1809–94), American physician, humorist, poet and author. *The Poet at the Breakfast Table* (1872).

11 In the world of services, quality does not necessarily mean luxury, supremacy, or 'top of the line.' Management must first identify the level of service to which the company will aspire. A service reaches the required degree of excellence when it meets the expectations of its target clientele, regardless of how that clientele is defined.

JACQUES HOROVITZ, French business consultant and author. *Winning Ways*, originally *Qualité de Service* (InterEditions, Paris, 1987; republished Productivity Press, Cambridge, Massachusetts, 1990).

12 Service brings to mind my Rotary Club days. Their slogan was 'Service above self.' If we understand what true service means, either toward others or commercially speaking, we will provide that service to someone else before we think of ourselves.

JON M. HUNTSMAN, American business executive, Chairman and CEO of Huntsman Corp, Utah. *Services Marketing Today* (American Marketing Association), August 1996.

13 Superior service companies sell service rather than price or product, and customers often buy service rather than price or product.

LINDA M. LASH, British training and development counsellor and author. *The Complete Guide to Customer Service* (John Wiley & Sons, New York, 1989). Copyright © 1989 Linda M. Lash. Reproduced by permission of John Wiley & Sons Inc.

14 Public service means service to the public, not services the public has to put up with.

JOHN MAJOR, British statesman, and Prime Minister 1990–97. 'Trust My Instincts', *Weekly Telegraph*, 8 January 1997.

15 If the customer is faced with two equivalent products, the reason he usually chooses one over the other is service. The promise of excellent service is how you win new customers and clients. What many of us forget, however, is that the continued delivery of that service is how you keep clients. It's good business. In the long run, it costs a lot less to hold onto existing clients than to find new ones.

MARK H. McCORMACK, American sports marketing consultant, founder and CEO of International Management Group, and author. *McCormack on Selling* (Century, London, 1995).

16 The old processes were production, inventory control, and marketing. The new process is customer service. This is not the old

customer service notion of trying to placate customers after they have been let down. This is a new notion of proactive customer service – to see that they are not let down in the first place.

> KEN PARRY, Australian academic, leadership consultant and author. *Transformational Leadership* (Pitman, Melbourne, 1996).

17 The line between selling and service is blurring.

> FAITH POPCORN, American business consultant, co-founder and CEO of BrainReserve, and author. *The Popcorn Report* (Doubleday, New York, 1991). Copyright 1991 by Faith Popcorn. Used by permission of Doubleday, a division of Bantam Doubleday Dell Publishing Group, Inc.

18 If you want good service, serve yourself.

> SPANISH PROVERB.

19 Providing high-quality service is a mind-set. Unfortunately, so is servitude. In the US, marketers have long used service to differentiate their products. In Europe, however, recognition of customer service to accomplish that goal is just emerging as a strategic option. Partly because of cultural differences and the European sense of privacy, current [European] approaches to service are impersonal.

> ALLYSON L. STEWART-ALLEN, British marketing consultant, director of International Marketing Partners, London. 'Customer Care', *Marketing News* (American Marketing Association), 18 November 1996, page 17. Reprinted with permission.

sincerity 95

See also: courtesy 16; negotiation 64; selling 93; service 94

1 Say what you mean, and mean what you say.

> ANON.

2 Civility is not a sign of weakness, and sincerity is always subject to proof.

> JOHN F. KENNEDY (1917–63), American statesman, and 35th President of the United States of America 1961–63. In his inaugural address, 20 January 1961.

3 Practise what you preach.

> ENGLISH PROVERB.

4 The way I see it, it doesn't matter what you believe just so you're sincere.

> CHARLES M. SCHULZ, American cartoonist and creator of *Peanuts*, Charlie Brown and Snoopy. *Go Fly a Kite, Charlie Brown* (1963).

5 A little sincerity is a dangerous thing, and a great deal of it is absolutely fatal.

> OSCAR WILDE (1854–1900), Irish playwright, poet, author and wit. 'Intentions', *The Critic as Artist* (1891).

96 statistics

See also: economics & economists 26; marketing 58; money 62

1 Figures never lie; only the figurers do.

> ANON.

2 In any collection of data, the figure most obviously correct, beyond all need of checking, is the mistake.

> Corollary #1: No-one you ask for help will spot the mistake.
> Corollary #2: Anyone who stops by with unsought advice – especially a superior – will spot the mistake immediately.
> ANON.

3 Statistics are like ventriloquists' dolls – experts can make them say whatever they want them to say.

ANON.

4 There are three kinds of lies – lies, damned lies, and statistics.

BENJAMIN DISRAELI (1804–81), British statesman, novelist, and Prime Minister 1868 and 1874–80. Quoted in Mark Twain, *Autobiography* (1924), but also variously attributed to others, including Twain himself.

5 Russia's [1996] presidential election is over and a Kremlin aide breaks the news to Boris Yeltsin: 'Communist Gennardy Zyuganov won 55 per cent of the vote.' Yeltsin looks shocked. 'Don't worry,' says the aide. 'You got 65 per cent.'

LEONID KUCHMA, Ukrainian statesman and President of the Republic of the Ukraine. Story reported to have been told by Kuchma to Aleksander Kwasniewski, President of Poland. Reuters, 10 June 1996.

6 He uses statistics as a drunken man uses lamp-posts – for support rather than illumination.

ANDREW LANG (1844–1912), British scholar, translator, critic and author. Quoted in A. L. Mackay (ed.), *A Dictionary of Scientific Quotations*.

7 You and I are forever at the mercy of the census-taker and the census-maker. That impertinent fellow who goes from house to house is one of the real masters of the statistical situation. The other is the man who organises the results.

WALTER LIPPMANN (1889–1974), American editor, columnist and author. 'The Golden Rule and After', *A Preface to Politics* (1914).

8 I want a society that cherishes the dignity and self-respect of the individual . . . It must be a society in which individuals are much more than statistics to be patronised, sorted, and ground down by impersonal state bureaucracies.

JOHN MAJOR, British statesman, and Prime Minister 1990–97. 'Trust My Instincts', *Weekly Telegraph*, 8 January 1997.

97 **strategy**

See also: corporate culture 15; decisions 20; goals & goal-setting 36; leadership 51; marketing 58

1 Attempt easy tasks as if they were difficult, and difficult as if they were easy.

> BALTASAR GRACIAN (1601–58), Spanish Jesuit priest and author. *The Art of Worldly Wisdom* (1647).

2 Much of life now looks like [a] doughnut. Organisations as well as individuals have come to realise that they have an essential core, a core of necessary jobs and necessary people, a core which is surrounded by an open flexible space, which they fill with flexible workers and flexible supply contracts. The strategic issue for organisations, nowadays, is to decide what activities and which people to put in which space. It is not always obvious.

> CHARLES HANDY, British academic, business consultant and author. *The Age of Paradox* (Harvard Business School Press, Cambridge, Massachusetts, 1994).

3 Great strategies, like great works of art or great scientific discoveries, call for technical mastery in the working out but originate in insights that are beyond the reach of conscious analysis.

> KENICHI OHMAE, Japanese management consultant. *The Mind of the Strategist* (McGraw-Hill, New York, 1982).

4 A corporation without a strategy is like an airplane weaving through stormy skies, hurled up and down, slammed by the wind, lost in the thunderheads. If lightning or crushing winds don't destroy it, it will simply run out of gas.

ALVIN TOFFLER, American scholar, lecturer and author. *The Adaptive Corporation* (Gower, Aldershot, Hampshire, 1985).

1 We cannot ensure success, but we can deserve it.
> JOHN ADAMS (1735–1826), American statesman, and 2nd President of the United States of America 1797–1801. In a letter, February 1776.

2 All successful men are men of purpose. They hold fast to an idea, a project, a plan, and will not let it go . . . The intensity of the purpose increases with the growing magnitude of the obstacles encountered.
> JAMES ALLEN, American theologian and author. *The Mastery of Destiny* (Putnam, New York, 1909).

3 I wanted to be successful for my father because I never got the doctorate in music, which is what he wanted me to do. But I wanted to do it on my own terms and I fell on my face. It was the biggest gift though, because then I started to see pretty much everything for what it was in the whole music world.
> TORI AMOS, American singer and songwriter. Quoted in Liz Evans (ed.), *Women, Sex and Rock 'n' Roll: In Their Own Words* (Pandora, London, 1994). Reprinted by permission of HarperCollins Publishers Limited.

4 Getting to the top isn't difficult. Staying there is the hard part.
> ANON.

5 If at first you don't succeed, blame someone else.
> ANON.

6 If at first you don't succeed, destroy all evidence that you tried.
ANON.

7 If success were easy, there would be no such thing as failure.
ANON.

8 Success is getting up one more time than you fall down.
ANON.

9 Success is the flip side of failure.
ANON.

10 Success requires no apologies; failure permits no alibis.
ANON.

11 The rules of success won't work unless you do.
ANON.

12 The toughest thing about success is that you've got to keep on being a success.
IRVING BERLIN (real name Israel Baline; 1888–1989), Russian-born American composer. *Theatre Arts*, February 1958.

13 Success is precise and prompt obedience to the call of circumstance.
LEON BLUM (1872–1950), French statesman and critic. Attrib.

14 I started smoking cigars at the age of eight, because I wanted to look successful. That's important when you're eight years old.
GEORGE BURNS (1897–1996), American comic, actor and entertainer. Quoted in Tichi Wilkerson & Marcia Borie, *Hollywood Legends* (Tale Weaver, Los Angeles, 1988).

15 I felt that anything so wonderful must have been a cosmic

mistake and braced myself for its removal. Dreams that do come true can be as unsettling as those that don't.

BRETT BUTLER, American comedienne, actress and author. *Knee Deep in Paradise* (Hyperion, New York, 1996; Transworld, Sydney, 1996). Reproduced by permission of the publisher.

16 Almost every day, we hear of women and men who started this adventure [i.e. business] with no obvious advantages but are now leaders in their community, industry or profession. Sometimes, they have a special insight into the needs of a particular group. Elsewhere, they recognise a trend. More often, they are determined to succeed regardless of the barriers they face and in spite of early or apparent failure.

TOM CANNON, British academic, visiting professor, business consultant, broadcaster and author. *How to Get Ahead in Business* (Virgin, London, 1993).

17 The deciding element in her success, leaving aside the fact that she'd married a great Newport name, was the duchess. Ann realised something that only the cleverest social climbers ever do. If you want to ride swiftly and safely from the depths to the surface, the surest way is to single out a shark and attach yourself to it like a pilot fish.

TRUMAN CAPOTE (1924–84), American author, screenwriter and playwright. *Answered Prayers* (Hamish Hamilton, London, 1986).

18 Some people are better than others at anticipating the response of a complex environment, and it is people with this ability that are likely, in the long run, to be most successful.

MARK CASSON, British academic, author and Professor of Economics at the University of Reading. In an introduction to *Entrepreneurship* (Edward Elgar, Aldershot, Hampshire, 1990).

19 It is truly said, 'Success is the sweetest revenge.' I myself have lists of people that I have to give credit to for motivating me

along the path to success through their ruthless actions toward me. Now that I have left them behind in the dust of my victories, they are no longer a threat to me.

CHIN-NING CHU, Chinese-born American lecturer, corporate trainer and author, President of Asian Marketing Consultants Inc. *Thick Face, Black Heart* (AMC, Beavertown, Oregon, 1992). Reprinted by permission of Warner Books, Inc. Copyright © 1992 by Chin-Ning Chu. All rights reserved.

20 Success means accomplishments as a result of our own efforts and abilities. Proper preparation is the key to our success. Our acts can be no wiser than our thoughts. Our thinking can be no wiser than our thoughts. Our thinking can be no wiser than our understanding.

GEORGE S. CLASON, American publisher and author. *The Richest Man in Babylon* (1955; republished Signet, New York, 1988). Copyright © 1955 by George S. Clason, renewed © 1983 by Clyde Cason. Used by permission of Dutton Signet, a division of Penguin Books USA Inc.

21 He or she who approaches customer care with a determination to profit from change will succeed.

STEPHEN DANDO-COLLINS, Australian author and editor. *The Customer Care Revolution* (Pitman, Melbourne, 1996).

22 Man owes his success to his creativity. No one doubts the need for it. It is most useful in good times and essential in bad.

EDWARD DE BONO, Maltese-born British scholar, teacher, lecturer and author. *Lateral Thinking for Management* (McGraw-Hill, London, 1971).

23 Success in business would seem to depend much less on native talent and a lot more on thinking and personality factors. Certainly success in business often seems spurred by a desire to make things happen.

EDWARD DE BONO, Maltese-born British scholar, teacher, lecturer and author. *Tactics: The Art and Science of Success* (Collins, London, 1985). Reprinted by permission of HarperCollins Publishers Limited.

24 Successful people are very often very single-minded and determined. Indeed, it would be possible to pick this out as the one characteristic common to almost all successful people. It can take the form of drive: if you want something hard enough, you will get it. It can take the form of ruthlessness: let nothing stand between you and your goal. It can take the form of a strong sense of purpose: know exactly where you want to go and get there. It can take the form of determination and persistence: accept failure only as a step on the path to success.

EDWARD DE BONO, Maltese-born British scholar, teacher, lecturer and author. *Tactics: The Art and Science of Success* (Collins, London, 1985). Reprinted by permission of HarperCollins Publishers Limited.

25 If, in order to succeed in an enterprise, I were obliged to choose between fifty deer commanded by a lion, and fifty lions commanded by a deer, I should consider myself more certain of success with the first group than with the second.

SAINT VINCENT DE PAUL (1576–1660), French Roman Catholic priest and co-founder of the order that bears his name. Attrib.

26 To laugh often and much;
To win the respect of intelligent people
   and the affection of children;
To earn the appreciation of honest critics
   and endure the betrayal of false friends;
To appreciate beauty;
To find the best in others;
To leave the world a bit better,
   whether by a healthy child,
   a garden patch or a redeemed social condition;

To know even one life has breathed
  easier because you have lived;
This is to have succeeded.

> RALPH WALDO EMERSON (1803–82), American philosopher, poet and essayist. *What is Success?*

27 Nothing is more humiliating than to see idiots succeed in enterprises we have failed in.

> GUSTAVE FLAUBERT (1821–80), French novelist. *Sentimental Education* (1869).

28 Risk-taking is an integral and intrinsic part of success or living a full life. You can spend your life with regrets, saying, 'Gee, if I had done this instead of that.' It's a waste of time. You didn't.

> MALCOLM FORBES, American publisher. Quoted in Edward de Bono, *Tactics: The Art and Science of Success* (Collins, London, 1985).

29 Developing your potential is an exciting adventure. It is time that women started to realise that they too can be daring, courageous and adventurous in their efforts to succeed.

> EILEEN GILLIBRAND and JENNY MOSLEY, British counsellors, trainers and authors. *She Who Dares Wins* (Thorsons, London, 1995).

30 Business is becoming more and more akin to intellectual sumo wrestling. Business success is based ever more directly and speedily on the abilities of the people in the business to change, foresee trends, take acceptable risks, be more in tune with tomorrow's needs of today's customers and to set their stalls out for the myriad economic and social changes which are occurring. To seize advantage in these ways is not a matter of brute force, but one of finely honed intelligence, coupled with genuine qualities of character and a continuous dedication to staying ahead in the race.

> JOHN HARVEY-JONES, British business consultant, broadcaster, author and former Chairman of ICI Industries. *All Together Now* (William

Heinemann, London, 1994). Reprinted by permission of The Peters Fraser and Dunlop Group Limited on behalf of John Harvey-Jones.

31 The way to secure success is to be more anxious about obtaining than about deserving it.

> WILLIAM HAZLITT (1778–1830), British critic, poet and essayist. 'On the Qualifications Necessary to Success in Life', *The Plain Speaker* (1826).

32 'Tis a lesson you should heed,
Try, try again.
If at first you don't succeed,
Try, try again.

> WILLIAM EDWARD HICKSON (1803–70), British clergyman and poet. *Try and Try Again*.

33 Friendship is tested in the thick years of success rather than in the thin years of struggle.

> BARRY HUMPHRIES, Australian humorist. Attrib.

34 I looked out my [car] window. A creeping civilisation on wheels surrounded me. To the left a man ate yoghurt out of a container, anxiously stirring some kind of fruit from the bottom. I thought of the dancer's guilt I used to feel when I went over my calorie quota by doing the same thing. I would have been better off with plain yoghurt. Denial was necessary to success somehow.

> SHIRLEY MACLAINE, American actress, dancer, singer and author. *Dance While You Can* (Bantam, New York, 1991).

35 The Servant must give credit for his rise as often as he can to others, and attribute any successes he may have to these men. Often they will be men of little account, so the Servant will construct legends about them to advance their prestige.

> ALISTAIR McALPINE (Lord McAlpine of West Green), British business leader, political figure and author. *The Servant* (Faber & Faber, London, 1992).

36 What I've learned from life – success and failure – is to follow my instinct.

> BETTE MIDLER, American singer and actress. *Hello!*, 16 October 1993.

37 I would have sworn that I had not changed, only the public perception of me had, but this is merely fame's first illusion. The fact, as it took much more time to appreciate, is that such an order of recognition imprints its touch of arrogance, quite as though one has control of a new power, a power to make real everything one is capable of imagining. And it can open a voraciousness for life and an impatience with old friends who persist in remaining ineffectual . . . There were weighty interviews and even pronouncements, and worst of all, a newly won rank to defend against the inevitable snipers. The crab who manages to climb up out of the bucket causes a lot of the other crabs to try to pull him back down where he belongs. That's what crabs do.

> ARTHUR MILLER, American playwright, screenwriter and author.
> Comments made in reference to the success of his play, *Death of a Salesman*.
> *Timebends* (Methuen, London, 1987).

38 The world around me has its own idea of my successes and failures which is sometimes independent of my own idea.

> HELEN MIRREN, British actress. *Hello!*, 25 February 1995.

39 From the beginning, I would assess people who were successful and wonder how they got where they are. What is it about them? How do they handle this? And then I would try it on like a suit of clothes and see if it would work for me.

> DEMI MOORE, American actress. *OK! Magazine*, March 1996.

40 There's a terrific division between popular fiction and the Booker Prize. I think that is unhealthy because the great novelists appealed to everybody: Dickens, Thackeray, Trollope, P. G.

Wodehouse. They told stories, but now you're either a pop novelist or a Booker novelist. I hope I cross that great divide but I'm only reluctantly accepted by the literati; being successful in England is a dangerous occupation.

JOHN MORTIMER, British lawyer, screenplay writer, playwright and author. In an interview with Graham Lord, *Weekly Telegraph*, 9 June 1993. Reprinted by permission of the Peters Fraser & Dunlop Group Ltd.

41 After the war [World War II], like many others, 'Tam' [Hugh Williams] found his place had been filled while he had been away and that he was largely forgotten as an actor. He went bankrupt and then emerged triumphant as one of the most successful playwrights that London has seen.

DAVID NIVEN (1909–83), British actor and author. *The Moon's a Balloon* (Hamish Hamilton, London, 1971).

42 To be successful, keep looking tanned, live in an elegant building – even if you're in the cellar – be seen in smart restaurants – even if you nurse one drink – and if you borrow, borrow big.

ARISTOTLE ONASSIS (1906–75), Greek shipping magnate. Attrib.

43 There are any number of people who can go out and fly a jumbo jet, but there's a very elite group of people who can design it and make it work, and my father was a designer and a person who could make things work. If I've had any success it's because I was able to fly the plane he built; but I couldn't have built it.

KERRY PACKER, Australian media proprietor. Quoted in Terry Lane, *As the Twig is Bent* (Dove, Victoria, 1979).

44 The secret of a better and more successful life is to cast out those old dead, unhealthy thoughts. Substitute for them new vital, dynamic faith thoughts. You can depend upon it – an inflow of new thoughts will remake you and your life.

NORMAN VINCENT PEALE, American theologian and author. *The Power of Positive Thinking* (The World's Work, UK; Simon & Schuster, New York, 1953).

45 One must be sure of success to the very end, for without that there is no hope.

CAMILLE PISSARRO (1830–1903), French artist. Attrib.

46 He who would climb the ladder must begin at the bottom.

ENGLISH PROVERB.

47 Nothing succeeds like success.

ENGLISH PROVERB.

48 Labour is the father of fame.

GREEK PROVERB.

49 The only place where success comes before work is in the dictionary.

VIDAL SASSOON, British hair stylist. Attrib.

50 Overlooking the little failures brings the big successes. Watch out for the hidden enemy that waits in every corner. Don't be eager to taste its dull poison – the poison of negative thinking.

CHARMAINE SAUNDERS, Australian psychologist, lecturer, broadcaster, columnist and author. *Women & Stress* (Angus & Robertson, Sydney, 1990). Reprinted by permission of HarperCollins Publishers.

51 The business of movie making is capital intensive, like oil exploration. You dig a lot of dry holes before you hit a gusher.

JOHN SAYLES, American film director, producer, and screenwriter. In an interview with Mary Colbert, *Age*, 14 February 1997.

52 It's something that I decided from the very beginning – that I would never do nudity. I wanted to become a success without showing, you know, private things. I'm not saying that other girls who've done topless things or nude things are wrong to do that. It's just not my thing.

CLAUDIA SCHIFFER, German model. *Vanity Fair*, January 1993.

53 *Dick Smith's C.A.S.H.E.D Philosophy for Success*

Communicate – It is incredibly important for a boss – for an entrepreneur – to communicate clearly to staff and customers . . .

Ask – Ask the advice of others and copy the success of others. People love to be asked.

Simple – Use common sense and keep everything simple.

Honesty – I believe that if you want to be successful, you've got to surround yourself with other capable people, and in that case, you've got to be absolutely honest. Otherwise, if they see you're dishonest, they'll be dishonest to you – which is understandable.

Enthusiasm – You've got to be enthusiastic if you're going to motivate your customers to buy more from you.

Discipline – You've got to put incredibly hard work in, especially in the early days. Eighty to ninety hours a week . . . But have a goal. Don't do it forever.

DICK SMITH, Australian entrepreneur, publisher and adventurer. Quoted in Emma Alberici, *The Small Business Book* (Penguin, Victoria, 1995).

54 There is no success without hardship.

SOPHOCLES (c. 496–406 BC), Greek playwright. *Electra* (418–414 BC).

55 To travel hopefully is a better thing than to arrive, and the true success is to labour.

ROBERT LOUIS STEVENSON (1850–94), British author. 'El Dorado', *Virginibus Puerisque* (1881).

56 There is no one, in my opinion, who is successful today that has done the whole thing on their own . . . Really successful people have always seen who are most valuable to them and who they must trust. They must make sure that other people recognise the degree of confidence that has been put upon them.

> JACKIE STEWART, British racing-car driver, Formula One world champion, media commentator, and racing-team manager. Quoted in Edward de Bono, *Tactics: The Art and Science of Success* (Collins, London, 1985). Reprinted by permission of HarperCollins Publishers Limited.

57 My dad never raised me to believe that being a woman inhibited any of my choices or possibilities to succeed.

> SHARON STONE, American actor. *Vanity Fair*, April 1993.

58 I like thinking big. I always have. To me it's very simple: if you're going to be thinking anyway, you might as well think big. Most people think small, because most people are afraid of success, afraid of making decisions, afraid of winning.

> DONALD TRUMP, American entrepreneur, developer and author. *Trump: The Art of the Deal* (Century Hutchinson, London, 1988).

59 Early to bed,
Early to rise,
Work like hell,
And advertise.

> TED TURNER, American media proprietor, CEO of Turner Broadcasting. His response to Barbara Walters when asked the secret of his success. *20–20*, an ABC television news program, first aired 23 February 1990 in the USA.

60 These success encourages: they can because they think they can.

> VIRGIL (Publius Vergilius Maro; 70–19 BC), Roman poet. *Aeneid* (30–19 BC).

61 If you want to succeed, double your failure rate.

>THOMAS J. WATSON (1874–1956), American industrialist, founder of IBM. Attrib.

62 Success is on the far side of failure.

>THOMAS J. WATSON (1874–1956), American industrialist, founder of IBM. Quoted in Stephen R. Covey, *The 7 Habits of Highly Effective People* (Simon & Schuster, New York, 1989).

63 Nothing great is easy.

>MATTHEW WEBB (1848–83), British long-distance swimmer and the first person to swim the English Channel, 25 August 1875. His personal motto, which is preserved on a memorial at Dawley, England.

64 We are realising that what drives you can drive you over the edge. Success in the 90s is about balance.

>PAUL WEST, Australian business executive and Manager of Sulzer Medical. Quoted in Ruth Ostrow, 'The Taming of the Beast', *Weekend Australian*, 9 September 1995. © The Weekend Australian.

65 The motive of success is not enough. It produces a short-sighted world which destroys the sources of its own prosperity. The cycles of trade depression which afflict the world warn us that business relations are infected through and through with the disease of short-sighted motives. The robber barons did not conduce to the prosperity of Europe in the Middle Ages, though some of them died prosperously in their beds. Their example is a warning to our civilisation.

>A. N. WHITEHEAD (1861–1947), British mathematician, philosopher, Professor of Philosophy at Harvard University and author. *Adventures of Ideas* (Harvard University Press, Cambridge, Massachusetts, 1933; reprinted Penguin, London 1942).

66 Nothing succeeds like excess.

> OSCAR WILDE (1854–1900), Irish playwright, poet, author and wit. *The Importance of Being Earnest*, play (1895).

67 It doesn't matter if it is a black cat or a white cat as long as it catches the mouse.

> DENG XIAOPING (1904–97), Chinese Communist leader. Attrib.

68 If you have a product, you need to understand that you cannot spend more money than you have – you have to budget. It is important to make a profit. If you continue with those principles you will have success and you will grow.

> CARLA ZAMPATTI, Australian fashion designer. *Sydney Morning Herald*, 7 December 1996.

t

'Twenty people in a room doesn't make a team.'
ROBERT KRIEGEL and DAVID BRANDT

teams & teamwork 100:7

99 **talent**

See also: creativity 17; genius 34; innovation 45;
inspiration 46; originality 69; success 98

1 To do easily what is difficult for others is the mark of talent.

> HENRI FRÉDÉRIC AMIEL (1821–81), Swiss philosopher and poet. *Journal*, 17 December 1856.

2 Lack of talent never stood in the way of success.

> ANON.

3 It took me fifteen years to discover that I had no talent for writing, but I couldn't give it up because by that time I was too famous.

> ROBERT BENCHLEY (1889–1945), American actor, drama critic, humorous writer, father of Nathaniel Benchley (author of *Sail a Crooked Ship*), and grandfather of Peter Benchley (author of *Jaws*). Attrib.

4 Mediocrity knows nothing higher than itself, but talent instantly recognises genius.

> ARTHUR CONAN DOYLE (1859–1930), British physician and author. *The Valley of Fear* (1915).

5 The world is always ready to receive talent with open arms. Very often it does not know what to do with genius.

> OLIVER WENDELL HOLMES SNR (1809–94), American physician, humorist, poet and author. 'Iris, Her Book', *The Professor at the Breakfast Table* (1860).

6 I have put my genius into my life; all I've put into my works is my talent.

OSCAR WILDE (1854–1900), Irish playwright, poet, author and wit. Spoken to André Gide, and quoted in Gide's *Oscar Wilde: In Memoriam* (1900).

teams & teamwork 100

1 Self-managing teams are becoming the basic building blocks of America's largest organisations. Such teams are empowered to solve problems and implement decisions with little or no intervention by management. If a self-managing team is to do its job, team members need to be able to build consensus out of disagreement. Members are expected to set aside personal agendas in favour of the group mission. Yet conflicts must be aired and honoured. Teamwork is a constant balancing act between self-interest and group interest.

SUSAN M. CAMPBELL, American lecturer and author. *From Chaos to Confidence* (Simon & Schuster, New York, 1995).

2 We must all lean the same way to get around corners.

STEPHEN DANDO-COLLINS, Australian author and editor. *The Customer Care Revolution* (Pitman, Melbourne, 1996).

3 Joint undertakings stand a better chance
When they benefit both sides.

EURIPIDES (480–405 BC), Greek playwright. *Iphigenia in Tauris* (c. 414–412 BC).

4 Being self-employed is exciting because it all rests on your shoulders. I see it as the difference between doing an individual sport and a team sport. With an individual sport, you

still need a lot of support, but ultimately the buck stops with you.

> JANE FLEMMING, Australian track and field athlete, and Olympic gold medallist. *Sydney Morning Herald*, 4 January 1997.

5 In Hong Kong and Japan a considerate supervisor would discuss a worker's personal problems with other members of the group because they are collectivist cultures ... In the USA and Britain, on the other hand, a considerate supervisor would not discuss a worker's personal problems with other members of the group. Because they are individualist cultures.

> DAVID J. HICKSON, British academic, editor, author and Professor of International Management and Organisation at the University of Bradford Management Centre, and DEREK S. PUGH, British academic, author and Professor of International Management at the Open University Business School. *Worldwide Management: The Impact of Societal Culture on Organisations Around the Globe* (Penguin, London, 1995). Copyright © David J. Hickson and Derek S. Pugh, 1995.

6 The environment we set up at Mac assumes that this special, hand-picked team is the best in the world at what they do – there is none better ... a small band of people doing some great work, really great work that will go down in history. Rather than joining an organisation, where there's a lot more process, many more layers, and more of a guarantee you'll make something good, but almost a guarantee that it won't be great. It means you can fail, but because you're really great you're willing to take on that risk.

> STEVE JOBS, American computer technology pioneer and founder of Apple Computers. Quoted in Steven Levy, *Insanely Great: The Life and Times of Macintosh, the Computer that Changed Everything* (Viking, New York and London, 1994; revised edition Penguin, 1995). Copyright © Steven Levy, 1994, 1995.

7 Twenty people in a room doesn't make a team. Teams don't just happen. They have to be developed, facilitated, and motivated.

> ROBERT KRIEGEL, American business consultant, speaker and author, and DAVID BRANDT, American clinical psychologist, organisational consultant, executive coach and author. *Sacred Cows Make the Best Burgers* (Warner, New York, 1996).

8 Teams are the Ferraris of work design. They're high performance, but high maintenance and expensive.

> EDWARD LAWLER, American academic, management professor at the University of Southern California. *Fortune*, 5 September 1994. © 1994 Time Inc. All rights reserved.

9 When people are in harmony, they will fight on their own initiative, without exhortation.

> ZHUGE LIANG (2nd century AD), Chinese general of the Han dynasty. *Mastering the Art of War: The Way of the General.*

10 The boat won't go if we all don't row.

> HARVEY MACKAY, American business executive, CEO of Mackay Envelope Company, motivator and author. In a speech made at the DCI Field & Sales Force Automation Conference, Boston, October 1996. 'Sales Pro Emphasises the Personal Touch', *Marketing News* (American Marketing Association), 4 November 1996, page 8. Reprinted with permission.

11 How can one individual solve the problems of the world? Problems can only be solved if one is part of a team.

> NELSON MANDELA, South African leader, and President of the Republic of South Africa 1994– . *Life*, April 1990.

12 Form a team, not a committee.

> MARK H. McCORMACK, American sports marketing consultant, founder and CEO of International Management Group, and author. *McCormack on Managing* (Century, London, 1995).

13 It may sound obvious, but a team of ten people can get something done a lot faster than one person working alone. Of course, if it's obvious, why are there so many solo acts in most organisations and so few teams?

> MARK H. McCORMACK, American sports marketing consultant, founder and CEO of International Management Group, and author. *McCormack on Managing* (Century, London, 1995).

14 When spider webs unite, they can tie up a lion.

> ETHIOPIAN PROVERB.

15 A single arrow is easily broken, but not ten in a bundle.

> JAPANESE PROVERB.

16 Clapping with the right hand only will not produce a noise.

> MALAY PROVERB.

17 Teamwork isn't simple. In fact, it can be a frustrating, elusive commodity . . . Teamwork doesn't appear magically just because someone mouths the words. It doesn't thrive just because of the presence of talent or ambition. It doesn't flourish simply because a team has tasted success.

> PAT RILEY, American basketball coach, who coached the Los Angeles Lakers to four NBA championships. *The Winner Within* (Berkley, New York, 1994).

18 As in any organisation, Attila had to periodically reiterate the long-term vision. He knew what the Huns could achieve working together, and he wanted his plan for the Great Conquest to survive his own death.

> WESS ROBERTS, American author. *Victory Secrets of Attila the Hun* (Bantam, London, 1993).

technology 101

See also: change 9; communication & communicating 11;
computers 13; future, the 33; innovation 45

1 If the human race wants to go to hell in a basket, technology
   can help it get there by jet. It won't change the desire or the
   direction, but it can greatly speed the passage.

   CHARLES M. ALLEN, American educator. In a speech ('Unity in a
   University') made at Wake Forest University, Winston–Salem, North Carolina,
   25 April 1967.

2 I think man is a transitional species, to be supplanted by some
   new life form that includes computer technology.

   ARTHUR C. CLARKE, British author. Quoted in Neil McAleer, *Odyssey:
   The Authorised Biography of Arthur C. Clarke* (Victor Gollancz, London,
   1992).

3 The connecting of . . . computers has been compared to
   another massive project: the gridding of the country with inter-
   state highways, which began during the Eisenhower era. This is
   why the new network was dubbed the 'information superhighway.' The term was popularised by then-senator [subsequently
   Vice President] Al Gore, whose father sponsored the 1956
   Federal Aid Highway Act. This highway metaphor isn't quite
   right though. The phrase suggests landscape and geography, a
   distance between points, and embodies the implication that
   you have to travel to get from one place to another. In fact, one
   of the most remarkable aspects of this new communications
   technology is that it will eliminate distance . . .

   The term 'highway' also suggests that everyone is driving
   and following the same route. This network is more like a lot
   of country lanes where everyone can look at or do whatever
   his individual interests suggest. Another implication is that
   perhaps it should be built by the government, which I think

would be a major mistake in most countries. But the real problem is that the metaphor emphasises the infrastructure of the endeavour rather than its applications. At Microsoft we talk about 'Information At Your Fingertips,' which spotlights a benefit rather than the network itself. A different metaphor that I think comes closer to describing a lot of the activities that will take place is that of the ultimate market. Markets from trading floors to malls are fundamental to human society, and I believe this one will eventually be the world's central department store . . . When you hear the phrase 'information highway,' rather than seeing a road, imagine a marketplace or an exchange . . . Many transactions will involve money, tendered in digital form rather than currency. Digital information of all kinds, not just as money, will be the medium of exchange in this market.

BILL GATES, American information technology pioneer, founder and CEO of Microsoft Corporation, and author. *The Road Ahead* (Viking Penguin, New York, 1995). Copyright © 1995 by William H. Gates III. Used by permission of Viking Penguin, a division of Penguin Books USA Inc.

4 Far from replacing the human element in business, the growth of information technology places an even higher premium upon human skills. Even if it were possible to draw up computer programs to take ethical or market decisions, somebody would still have to define the limits of such decisions.

JOHN HARVEY-JONES, British business consultant, broadcaster, author, and former Chairman, ICI Industries. *All Together Now* (William Heinemann, London, 1994). Reprinted by permission of The Peters Fraser and Dunlop Group Limited on behalf of John Harvey-Jones.

5 The sum total of all the 'little' improvements in technology, regardless of the industry, have likely contributed to a greater increase in organisational productivity than all the great inventors and their inventions.

JAMES M. KOUZES and BARRY Z. POSNER, American educators, management and training consultants, and authors. *The Leadership Challenge* (Jossey-Bass, San Francisco, 1995).

6 **Technology made large populations possible; large populations now make technology indispensable.**

JOSEPH WOOD KRUTCH (1893–1970), American essayist, teacher and critic. 'The Nemesis of Power', *Human Nature and the Human Condition* (1959).

7 **Technology is important but not a solution unto itself. It offers different things to different people. Individual users want technology to make their jobs easier. Managers want technology to make their staffs more productive. Corporate officers want technology to make them more competitive and improve their own technology. None of these people want technology for technology's sake.**

G. A. 'ANDY' MARKEN, American marketing consultant, President of Marken Communications, Santa Clara, California. 'PR's Biggest Challenge: Translation', *Marketing News* (American Marketing Association), 11 March 1996, page 4. Reprinted with permission.

8 **For tribal man space was the uncontrollable mystery. For technological man it is time that occupies the same role.**

MARSHALL McLUHAN (1911–80), Canadian communications theorist, university professor and author. 'Magic that Changes Mood', *The Mechanical Bride* (1951).

9 **The new electronic interdependence recreates the world in the image of a global village.**

MARSHALL McLUHAN (1911–80), Canadian communications theorist, university professor and author. *The Gutenberg Galaxy* (University of Toronto Press, Toronto, 1962).

10 The battle for sustainable development will be won only if industry is in the front lines. Significant gains can come from conservation; but technological development is critical. The main consumers of fossil fuels today are technologies – steam and the internal combustion engine – that have their origins in the 19th century. If we get our market signals right, private companies will prove to be among our most effective environmentalists; only they have the capacity to bring environmentally sound products to market, cleaner new fuels and processes and the next generation of engines.

> BRIAN MULRONEY, Canadian statesman, and Prime Minister 1984–93. 'The Future Has Started', *1990 Britannica Book of the Year* (Encyclopaedia Britannica, Chicago, 1990). © 1990 Encyclopaedia Britannica Inc.

11 Technology is like a bus. If it goes in the direction you want to go, you take it.

> RENZO PIANO, Italian architect. *The 7.30 Report*, ABC-TV Australia, 12 December 1996.

12 'Travel substitution' is shorthand for the hope that ever more capable telecommunications technologies – videoconferencing among them – will allow us to substitute electrons and video screens for air miles and in-the-flesh meetings.

> PAUL SAFFO, American researcher, fellow of the Institute of the Future. *Fortune*, Autumn 1993. © 1993 Time Inc. All rights reserved.

13 The high velocity of change can be traced to many factors. Population growth, urbanisation, the shifting proportions of young and old – all play their part. Yet technological advance is clearly a critical node in the network of causes; indeed, it may be the node that activates the entire net. One powerful strategy in the battle to prevent mass future shock, therefore, involves the conscious regulation of technological advance. We cannot and must not turn off the switch of technological progress.

Only romantic fools babble about returning to a 'state of nature.' . . . To turn our back on technology would not only be stupid but immoral.

ALVIN TOFFLER, American scholar, lecturer and author. *Future Shock* (The Bodley Head, London, 1970).

14 ˙One cannot but wonder what sort of world we would be living in today if the leading edge of technology was not a moving target.

BOB WHITE, Australian banker, former CEO of Westpac Banking Corporation, and CECELIA CLARKE, Australian author. *Cheques and Balances* (Viking, Victoria, 1995).

15 The effect of new technologies on the sites of cities, and on transformations of cities, is one of the fundamental problems which must enter into all sociological theories, including the forecasting of business relations.

A. N. WHITEHEAD (1861–1947), British mathematician, philosopher, Professor of Philosophy at Harvard University and author. *Adventures of Ideas* (Harvard University Press, Cambridge, Massachusetts, 1933; reprinted Penguin, London, 1942).

time management 102

See also: do it now 25; efficiency 27; focus 31; goals & goal-setting 36; priorities 77

1 If you can't manage your own time well, how can you expect to manage others'?

ANON.

2 While we do control our choice of action, we cannot control the consequences of our choices. Universal laws or principles do. Thus, we are not in control of our lives; *principles* are. We

suggest that this idea provides key insight into the frustration people have had with the traditional 'time management' approach to life.

> STEPHEN R. COVEY, American educator, leadership consultant, author and former Professor of Business Management at Brigham Young University; A. ROGER MERRILL, American management and leadership consultant and author; and REBECCA R. MERRILL, American author. *First Things First* (Fireside/Simon & Schuster, New York, 1994).

3 Those who make the worst use of their time are the first to complain of its brevity.

> JEAN DE LA BRUYÈRE (1645–96), French writer. *Characters* (1688).

4 I see these coaches who say that coaching is their vocation, their avocation, and their vacation. I don't think I'd enjoy that.

> BOBBY KNIGHT, American college basketball coach, University of Indiana. *Profiles,* March 1993.

5 Organise for the next day at the end of the previous day. This is what gives me peace of mind at night, a feeling that I am on top of things, and a real excitement about coming into work the next morning. Simply by arranging the next day – defining on paper what I want to accomplish – I feel that I have a head start.

> MARK H. McCORMACK, American sports marketing consultant, founder and CEO of International Management Group, and author. *What They Don't Teach You at Harvard Business School* (Collins, London, 1984).

6 People in organisations are all boss-watchers, especially when external conditions are ambiguous. For better or worse, what you spend your *time* on – not what you sermonise about – will become the organisation's preoccupation.

> TOM PETERS, American academic, consultant, lecturer and author. *Thriving on Chaos* (Alfred A. Knopf, New York, 1987).

training 103

See also: employees 28; focus 31; learning 52; people 70; service 94; teams & teamwork 100

1 How do you raise the commitment of every employee? Training is obviously fundamental to achieving genuine customer service which isn't forced and which comes from the heart. Apart from the clear efficiency and product quality gains, employees who are well trained will be more confident and agreeable on the job. Their approach to tasks and customers will be far different to [that of] an undertrained person who will visibly show signs of stress and anxiety.

> CHARLIE BELL, Australian business leader, CEO of McDonald's Australia. In a foreword to Stephen Dando-Collins, *The Customer Care Revolution* (Pitman, Melbourne, 1996).

2 Sending men to war without training is like abandoning them.

> CONFUCIUS (c. 551 – c. 479 BC), Chinese teacher, philosopher and political theorist. *Analects* (6th century BC).

3 Training is an ongoing process. It doesn't begin and end with a solitary training session. All staff should undergo a refresher course at least once every twelve months. And those refresher courses should be updated so that staff learn something new every time. The economy will have changed in one way or another within twelve months. Governments may have changed. Business will have changed. Customer expectations may have changed. Technology will certainly have changed. Your organisation will have changed. Staff will have changed. Priorities may have changed. Hopefully, customer care targets and goals may have been achieved or even exceeded, requiring modified targets. All these factors will influence the customer care training that you will need to employ in twelve months' time.

STEPHEN DANDO-COLLINS, Australian author and editor. *The Customer Care Revolution* (Pitman, Melbourne, 1996).

4 Government training programs should concentrate not just on the jobless but on upgrading the skills of those already at work.

ROBERT F. KENNEDY (1925–68), American politician, US senator, US Attorney General and presidential candidate. In a speech made in Indianapolis, 4 April 1968.

5 Employees should be trained in the services they are expected to provide to customers. They need technical skills training to know how to operate computer terminals, to process material services, to follow administrative procedures, and so on. They need behavioural skills training to know what to say to customers and how to say it in line with the company's service strategy. And they need conceptual skills training to know how their jobs fit into the overall goals of the organisation. Training enables employees to satisfy customers – to meet or exceed customers' expectations. Many service companies excel in initial training but fail to establish a good ongoing method for communicating changes and new service offerings to employees.

LINDA M. LASH, British training and development counsellor and author. *The Complete Guide to Customer Service* (John Wiley & Sons, New York, 1989). Copyright 1989 Linda M. Lash. Reprinted by permission of John Wiley & Sons Inc.

6 Common sense is unteachable only in the sense that it isn't learned overnight. A fool doesn't wake up one morning a sage. But even the most foolish person over time can become significantly less foolish.

MARK H. McCORMACK, American sports marketing consultant, founder and CEO of International Management Group, and author. *McCormack on Selling* (Century, London, 1995).

7 A young branch takes on all the bends that one gives it.
   CHINESE PROVERB.

8 Give a man a fish, and you feed him for a day. Teach him to fish,
   and you feed him for a lifetime.
   CHINESE PROVERB.

9 During training, too much importance is given to the physical
   aspect, which surely gives the players great stamina and resistance, but Soccer is more than just physical strength. It is, most
   importantly, intelligence and initiative – being able to anticipate your opponent's next move. It is, in one word, tactics.
   RALE RASIC, Australian soccer coach and coach of the Australian World
   Cup team, 1974. *Australian Tempo Libero*, 1987.

10 The best form of 'welfare' for the troops is a sound training.
   ERWIN ROMMEL (1891–1944), German field marshal. *Infantry Tactics*
   (1937).

11 Training should be seen, by employers and employees, as an
   essential investment with rich returns for both when it is prop-
   erly focused.
   ALLEN SHEPPARD, British business leader, Chairman and Group Chief
   Executive of Grand Metropolitan. In a foreword to Jeremy G. Thorn,
   Developing Your Career in Management (Mercury, London, 1992).

12 Regardless of what you manage, wherever there are goals to be
   achieved by organising and directing the resources and efforts
   of others, your watchword must still be professionalism. This
   requires skill, experience and training, for effective managers
   are not born, they need to be trained and developed. This
   investment in training is like any other: if it is made wisely it
   will pay rich dividends; and it should never stop, for no one can
   know it all.

JEREMY G. THORN, British business executive, CEO of an engineering company and author. *Developing Your Career in Management* (Mercury, London, 1992).

13 Over the past 15 years, I have seen a gradual evolution in the area of training. First it was: 'Training? No-one does any training in retail.' Then we progressed to: 'What if I train my staff and they leave?' To which the only response is: 'What if you don't train them and they stay?'

DEBRA TEMPLAR, Australian business executive, Training and Development Manager of the Retail Traders Association of Victoria. 'Retail Shoe on Other Foot', *AussieHost News*, October 1997.

14 A man can seldom – very, very seldom – fight a winning fight against his training: the odds are too great.

MARK TWAIN (real name Samuel Clemens; 1835–1910), American journalist, editor and author. *As Regards Patriotism* (1923).

15 Once we are destined to live out our lives in the prison of our mind, our one duty is to furnish it well.

PETER USTINOV, British actor, producer, playwright, university chancellor and author. *Dear Me* (William Heinemann, London, 1977).

16 The 'sage on stage' mode of teaching is being replaced by a new model: 'the guide on the side.' In this role, professors minimise the lecture component of their classroom presentations and devote the majority of sessions to innovative, nontraditional marketing education. Among the supplemental approaches that work effectively are case studies; computer-based applications such as simulations, data disks and templates, and supplemental instructional materials; marketing practitioners as guest speakers; in-class exercises such as focus groups, sales role plays, customer retention plans; independent studies, student internships, and class or team projects; and videos or slide shows.

ART WEINSTEIN, American academic, Associate Professor of Marketing at Nova Southeastern University, Fort Lauderdale, Florida. *Marketing News* (American Marketing Association), 12 August 1996, page 12. Reprinted with permission.

17 Companies can't promise lifetime employment, but by constant training and education we may be able to guarantee lifetime employability.

JACK WELCH, American industrialist, CEO of General Electric Company. Quoted in Noel M. Tichy & Stratford Sherman, *Control Your Destiny or Someone Else Will* (Doubleday, New York, 1993).

'A faulty computer will produce rubbish.
A computer working flawlessly will also
produce rubbish if the input is rubbish.'
EDWARD DE BONO

value 104:3

value 104

See also: customers 19; money 62; profits 81; service 94;
values 105

1 The value you add comes from the values you hold.

> ANON.

2 That which cost little is less valued.

> MIGUEL DE CERVANTES (1547–1616), Spanish novelist, dramatist and
> poet. *Don Quixote* (1605–15).

3 The value of any conclusion depends on both the validity of the
logic and also the validity of the starting perceptions and values. A faulty computer will produce rubbish. A computer working flawlessly will also produce rubbish if the input is rubbish.

> EDWARD DE BONO, Maltese-born British scholar, teacher, lecturer and
> author. *I Am Right – You Are Wrong* (Viking, London, 1990). Copyright ©
> Mica Management Resources Inc, 1990.

4 Stop for a moment and consider just how valuable customers
are. They alone make it possible for you to earn your livelihood
in the way that you do. Treat them well and satisfied customers
will be your best source of advertising and marketing. Give
them good value and they will continue to reward you with
their dollars year after year.

> MICHAEL LEBOEUF, American business consultant, speaker and author,
> Professor of Management at the University of New Orleans. *How to Win
> Customers and Keep Them for Life* (Putnam, New York, 1987). Reprinted by
> permission of The Putnam Publishing Group. Copyright © 1987 by Michael
> LeBoeuf, Ph.D.

5 Price setting is at the heart of every business strategy, and getting the price strategy right requires a deep understanding of a business's products, customers and competitors. A business that does not understand the forces that limit and create its pricing options does not understand its business. To such a business 'quality' and 'customer satisfaction' are labels used to dignify otherwise meaningless activities. Only when a business understands how it delivers value, and how it receives value in return, can it begin to take serious steps to increase both factors. A business that delivers high value can demand it, and satisfied customers and profitable trading patterns develop together.

JOHN LEGGE, Australian business consultant, author and lecturer in innovation and entrepreneurship at Swinburne University of Technology, Victoria. *Pricing Strategy and Profit* (Longman Professional, Melbourne, 1993).

6 The real price of everything, what everything really costs to the man who wants to acquire it, is the toil and trouble of acquiring it.

ADAM SMITH (1723–90), British economist and philosopher. *The Wealth of Nations* (1776).

7 There is no such thing as absolute value in this world. You can only estimate what a thing is worth to *you*.

CHARLES DUDLEY WARNER (1829–1900), American novelist, editor and essayist. 'Sixteenth Week', *My Summer in a Garden* (1871).

8 [A cynic is] A man who knows the price of everything and the value of nothing.

OSCAR WILDE (1854–1900), Irish playwright, poet, author and wit. *Lady Windermere's Fan*, play, (1892).

105 **values**

See also: business ethics 7; corporate culture 15; value 104

1 In every era, society must strike the right balance between the freedom businesses need to compete for a market share and to make profits and the preservation of family and community values. If either is undermined, the consequences will end up costing us all more in the long term, materially and otherwise, than we can possibly gain in the short term.

> HILLARY RODHAM CLINTON, American lawyer, and First Lady of the United States of America 1993– . *It Takes a Village* (Simon & Schuster, New York, 1996).

2 Values are determined by systems, contexts and circumstances.

> EDWARD DE BONO, Maltese-born British scholar, teacher, lecturer and author. *Parallel Thinking: From Socratic to de Bono Thinking* (Viking, London, 1994). Copyright © McQuaig Group Inc, 1994.

3 It's value versus values. We had all the necessary values inherent in our brand, but we only touted the low fares. And an onrush of look-alikes made us think that the low-fare ladder was getting too crowded.

> JOYCE ROGGE, American airline executive and Vice President of Advertising and Promotions at Southwest Airlines. Ian P. Murphy, 'Southwest Emphasises Brand as Others Follow the Low-Fare Leader', *Marketing News* (American Marketing Association), 4 November 1996, page 1. Reprinted with permission.

4 There is something between the gross specialised values of the mere practical man, and the thin specialised values of the mere scholar. Both types have missed something; and if you add together the two sets of values, you do not obtain the missing elements.

> A. N. WHITEHEAD (1861–1947), British mathematician, philosopher, Professor of Philosophy at Harvard University and author. *Science and the Modern World* (1925).

'Every man who ever created anything
was a gambler.'
KERRY PACKER

winners & winning 106:18

winners & winning 106

See also: achieving 2; leadership 51; persistence &
perseverance 71; success 98

1 It's not how you win or lose, it's how you place the blame.
   ANON.

2 Victory is like fine wine. Years in the making, moments in the
   tasting.
   ANON.

3 Who dares wins.
   ANON. (Motto of the Special Air Service Regiments of the British, New
   Zealand and Australian armies.)

4 Winners are grinners. Losers can please themselves.
   ANON.

5 Winners make things happen. Losers let things happen.
   ANON.

6 Face it, it's about penis size and winning. We as men have been
   trained since little boys to win, to win, win, win, win. Winning is
   everything. I've come to realise that life is about other things
   than just winning . . . But maybe not.
   MARTY BAUER, American talent agent and President of the United Talent
   Agency, Los Angeles. *Vanity Fair*, January 1993.

7 Everyone is a potential winner. Some people are disguised as
   losers, don't let their appearances fool you.

KENNETH BLANCHARD, American educator, management consultant, trainer and author, and SPENCER JOHNSON, American publisher, lecturer, communications consultant and author. *The One Minute Manager* (Collins, London, 1983). Reprinted by permission of HarperCollins Publishers Limited.

8 To win without risk is to triumph without glory.

PIERRE CORNEILLE (1606–84), French poet and dramatist. *The Cid* (1637).

9 If I see a good footballer, I like one of those guys who goes in hard for the ball and plays it all the time. Guys who stand on the sidelines, the receivers, are not the ones who will win.

JOHN ELLIOTT, Australian businessman and President of the Carlton Australian Rules Football Club. Quoted in Peter Denton, *Elliott: A Biography of John D Elliott* (Little Hills Press, Bedford, UK, & Crows Nest NSW, 1986).

10 In a traditional competitive, male world the image of 'winning' is often associated with a single person bursting through the ranks and leaving others behind. Let's have a different understanding of the word 'winning.' Winning for women should mean working effectively, confidently and quickly within a network of supportive people, sharing their aspirations and hopes. Any true definition of 'winning' highlights the sense of fulfilment that results from personal efforts. It emphasises the success that comes from disentangling or liberating oneself. Personal liberation can only come from understanding yourself and knowing what you need to fight for.

EILEEN GILLIBRAND and JENNY MOSLEY, British counsellors, trainers and authors. *She Who Dares Wins* (Thorsons, London, 1995).

11 Just as athletics demonstrate continuously that it is the frame of mind of the athlete, rather than the sheer physical power, which is the decisive factor in winning, so it is with business.

JOHN HARVEY-JONES, British business consultant, broadcaster, author and former Chairman of ICI Industries. *All Together Now* (William Heinemann, London, 1994). Reprinted by permission of The Peters Fraser and Dunlop Group Limited on behalf of John Harvey-Jones.

12 The job of businessmen and women is to win – to create, lead, inspire and motivate teams of people who, by their creativity, speed of reaction, dedication and relevance to the needs of tomorrow, will ensure that their business gets in front and stays there.

JOHN HARVEY-JONES, British business consultant, broadcaster, author and former Chairman of ICI Industries. *All Together Now* (William Heinemann, London, 1994). Reprinted by permission of The Peters Fraser and Dunlop Group Limited on behalf of John Harvey-Jones.

13 If you think you can win, you can win. Faith is necessary to victory.

WILLIAM HAZLITT (1778–1830), British critic, poet and essayist. 'On Great and Little Things', *Literary Remains* (1836).

14 The next time someone in your office has a disaster, notice how people react to it. The losers will hurry over to get the whole story in all its grimy detail. Then they'll tell a few sad tales of their own, and before you know it a royal banquet of bad news is in full swing. Winners handle someone else's trouble differently. With silence. Or they may offer a few quick words of encouragement. There's none of the loving analysis of catastrophe that losers insist on. When someone has a great success, the same split between winners and losers shows up. This time it's the winners who are crowding around to hear every detail, and perhaps share a success story or two of their own. Now it's the losers who are too busy to talk to you.

TOM HOPKINS, American sales trainer, motivator and author. *How to Master the Art of Selling* (Champion Press, Scottsdale, Arizona, 1982; republished HarperCollins, London, 1994).

15 He who would greatly deserve must greatly dare, for brilliant victory is only achieved at the risk of disastrous defeat, and those laurels are even brighter that are gathered in the very track of danger.

> WASHINGTON IRVING (1783–1859), American historian, biographer and essayist. Comment made about Captain James Lawrence in a report on the loss of the USS *Chesapeake* in the War of 1812 (1813).

16 Winners and losers in the 21st century will be defined not so much by technological wizardry but by the simple ability of technology to disseminate information where and when it is needed.

> JOHN NAISBITT, American social forecaster, visiting professor, speaker and author. *Global Paradox* (William Morrow, New York, 1994).

17 He who does not hope to win has already lost.

> JOSÉ JOAQUIN OLMEDO (1780–1847), Ecuadorian statesman and poet. Attrib.

18 Every man who ever created anything was a gambler.

> KERRY PACKER, Australian media proprietor. Quoted in Terry Lane, *As the Twig is Bent* (Dove, Victoria, 1979).

19 If you want to be a film producer, quite simply start doing it . . . You may attract fame, make money, go broke or find yourself, but you will know you are alive. If you believe strongly enough in yourself, your team and your project, you will win through.

> DAMIEN PARER, Australian film producer and author, son of World War Two photographer Damien Parer. *Film Business* (AFTRS, New South Wales, 1989).

20 For when the One Great Scorer comes to write against your name,
He marks – not that you won or lost – but how you played the game.

> GRANTLAND RICE (1880–1954), American sportsman and author. Attrib.

21 I realised what 'winning' is for women today. It's about remaining a full-service feeling, reacting, sexy, sensual woman, not just a career-oriented machine. It's about achieving your goals without letting your balls get busted – and without letting your boobs get busted either.

> KAREN SALMONSOHN, American author. *How to Succeed in Business Without a Penis* (Harmony, New York, 1996).

22 When you give in, give in all the way. And when you win, try to win all the way so that the responsibility to make it work rests squarely on you.

> ROBERT TOWNSEND, American business executive, CEO of Avis car rental group, and author. *Further up the Organisation* (Alfred A. Knopf, New York, 1970; revised edition Michael Joseph, London, 1984).

23 The winners in life begin by fantasising their own 'scripts,' as if their lives were a magnificent, epic motion picture for which they had been chosen as writer, producer, director and star.

> DENIS WAITLEY, American personal development counsellor, lecturer, and author. *The Psychology of Winning* (Nightingale-Conant, Chicago, 1979; republished Berkley, New York, 1984).

women in business 107

1 Real women don't have flushes, they have power surges.

> SANDRA CABOT, Australian physician, lecturer and author. Attrib.

2 Issues affecting women are not soft or marginal, but are central to decisions involving all nations.

HILLARY RODHAM CLINTON, American lawyer, and First Lady of the United States of America 1993– . In a speech at the Sydney Opera House, 21 November 1996.

3 The definition of having it all is having a family, having a man in your life, having a successful business. I think there are very few men who can tolerate women who move at the same speed as they move . . . I really believe that women are never allowed on a team, anyway. One is allowed to function as a satellite around the sun, but you're never actually allowed on the team. You can shine, you can be a star, but stars always have to perform all the time.

JANE DEKNATEL, British-born American-based film and television producer. Quoted in Alan Whicker, *Whicker's New World* (Weidenfeld & Nicolson, London, 1985)

4 When a woman takes her will and forces it onto a group of men, they react by saying, 'This person is a bitch.' There's a force in them which is very frightened of the true feminine spirit.

MARIANNE FAITHFULL, British singer and songwriter. Quoted in Liz Evans (ed.), *Women, Sex and Rock 'n' Roll: In Their Own Words* (Pandora, London, 1994). Reprinted by permission of HarperCollins Publishers Limited.

5 When I started as a bank trainee, there was more prejudice toward me as a woman than as a Jew. Later, when I had two master's degrees and was a ranking officer, I was considered a valuable statistic; I helped fill minority quotas. At one bank I was the only Jewish woman among several hundred vice presidents. Now, there are many more than a dozen Jewish female vice presidents.

SUSAN FISHER, American banker. Quoted in Diane Bletter & Lori Grinker, *The Invisible Thread* (Jewish Publication Society, Philadelphia, 1989).

6 Women are savvy, but very conservative – we don't tend to take high risks. It's a good starting point, but we have to be careful that we don't end up taking no risks at all.

VIVIENNE JAMES, Australian investment banker, Executive Vice President of Bankers Trust Australia and author. *Qantas Club*, November 1996.

7 Many people say that business is a man's world. And many women think that to succeed in business they have to be like men, or how they perceive men to be – aggressive, dominant, competitive. All of us, both men and women, must realise that women can bring their own unique strengths to the business world. We can nurture and mentor, build trust and create partnerships. We can give someone a hug and talk about what's really bothering them. You don't have to be strong. What you need to be is a team player.

SHERRY LANSING, American entertainment industry leader and Chairman of Motion Picture Group of Paramount Pictures. CWE, 30 October 1996.

8 Another reason for the less-than-could-be participation of women in the hundreds of thousands of new businesses started every year is the much harsher penalty society imposes on a woman running a business that fails to achieve the desired results. For a man it is so much easier, as it is generally believed that he 'can always come back again in another company.' Many seem to take the view that the woman who failed in business did so because she shouldn't have been there in the first place. It is wrong, unfair and stupid.

ARTHUR LIPPER III, American businessman. In a foreword to Russel R. Taylor, *Exceptional Entrepreneurial Women* (Praeger, New York, 1988).

9 In the first decades of the third millennium we and our children will look back at the later half of the 20th century and remark on how quaint were the days when women were excluded from

the top echelons of business and political leadership, much as we today recall when women could not vote. How naive were the men and women of the 1980s, we will say, those people who believed in something called a 'glass ceiling' and thought it would forever exclude women from the top.

> JOHN NAISBITT and PATRICIA ABURDENE, American social forecasters, academics and authors. *Megatrends 2000* (William Morrow, New York, 1990).

10 Women and the information society – which celebrates brain over brawn – are a partnership made in heaven. And wherever the information society is flourishing, women are entering the labour force. Wherever the information revolution has spread, women have flocked into the work force. Even in Japan, a culture so traditional that the word 'wife' means 'inside the house,' 40 per cent of the work force is female . . . In Japan all this change necessitated the invention of a new word, *soto san*, to describe a wife who is active outside the house.

> JOHN NAISBITT and PATRICIA ABURDENE, American social forecasters, academics and authors. *Megatrends 2000* (William Morrow, New York, 1990).

11 Perhaps his most valuable innovation was to be the first to employ women as copywriters, starting with his wife. They were housed in a separate department and had to wear hats in the office.

> DAVID OGILVY, British-born American advertising expert, founder of Ogilvy & Mather international advertising agency group, New York, and author. Referring to Stanley Resor, head of the J. Walter Thompson advertising agency group in New York for 45 years. *Ogilvy on Advertising* (Pan, London, 1983).

12 A woman is like a teabag. Only in hot water do you realise how strong she is.

> NANCY REAGAN, American political figure, and First Lady of the United States of America 1981–89. Attrib.

13 I am constantly asked why there are so few women at the top.
I will tell you why: women do not know how exceptional they
are and they lack confidence. However, any woman lacking confidence should remember this: if you can figure out which one
gets the last toffee, the four year old or the six year old, you can
negotiate any contract in the world!

> ANITA RODDICK, British businesswoman, co-founder and Chief Executive
> of The Body Shop International. In a foreword to Eileen Gillibrand & Jenny
> Mosley, *She Who Dares Wins* (Thorsons, London, 1995).

14 Corporations as we know them have been created by men for
men, often influenced by the military model. Hierarchical struc-
tures built on authority remain the same. The only way I could
challenge this was to set up my own business. But here we are
eighteen years later and it is still far easier for any woman to go
to a bank and secure a loan for a new kitchen or fitted
wardrobe, than it is to get them to agree to lend her money to
start a business.

> ANITA RODDICK, British businesswoman, co-founder and Chief Executive
> of The Body Shop International. In a foreword to Eileen Gillibrand & Jenny
> Mosley, *She Who Dares Wins* (Thorsons, London, 1995).

15 Today's models . . . are well aware of their own value . . .
They're entrepreneurs who know the value of their own image
and talent perfectly well. Back in 1923, when the first modelling
agency opened in New York, models were paid $5 a day to
'keep smiling and keep quiet.'

> OLIVIER ROYANT, French journalist. *Paris Match*, 1995; reprinted in *Hello!*,
> 22 April 1995.

16 A woman doesn't need a penis in business. Just balls.

> KAREN SALMONSOHN, American author. *How to Succeed in Business
> Without a Penis* (Harmony, New York, 1996).

17 Until women love who they are and stop trying to compete with men as if males belong to a different species, they cannot expect to make the best of themselves. Women have a right to equal opportunities to prove themselves, such as in the workplace, but beyond that equality is a myth. Are all men equal? Of course they are not, nor women, nor any two people. So, in my opinion women should stop playing semantics and get on with the business of being the best individuals they can.

> CHARMAINE SAUNDERS, Australian psychologist, lecturer, broadcaster, columnist and author. *Women & Stress* (Angus & Robertson, Sydney, 1990). Reprinted by permission of HarperCollins Publishers.

18 Education is an important instrument for increasing and bettering the chances of women's employability and empowering women to think for themselves, become confident and also develop the capability of recognising more accurately the area of exploitation. In spite of inadequacies, education has made a definite impact. It opens up an arena in which women can compete with men and prove their independent identity.

> KAMLA SINGH, Indian women's advocate, academic and author. *Women Entrepreneurs* (Ashish, New Delhi, 1992).

19 As a Jewish woman in the public eye, I feel that I must set some kind of example. So to keep the balance, I strive to be a politically and socially aware person with really great nails.

> ARLENE SORKIN, American actress. Quoted in Diane Bletter & Lori Grinker, *The Invisible Thread* (Jewish Publication Society, Philadelphia,1989).

20 Men's salaries are preposterous. If actresses had parity, you couldn't make a movie. Men pay men more. Period.

> MERYL STREEP, American actress. *OK! Magazine*, March 1994.

21 Women's liberation has acquired a bad name since it was taken over by sour-faced, embittered women with a grudge against

the male sex, but at its best, in encouraging women to use their femininity to achieve greater freedom and fulfilment, it marks one of the great achievements of the century.

AUBERON WAUGH, British columnist and author. *Weekly Telegraph*, 8 January 1997. © Telegraph Group Limited, London, 1997.

Index (by source)

How to use these indexes

These indexes do not make reference to page numbers. The first number in each reference denotes the section in which a quotation is to be found. The second number denotes the item number within that section. For example, 98:17 refers to section 98, item 17.

index

index

index

index

index

WHITE, Gordon 15:15, 54:10,
93:19
WHITEHEAD, A. N. 7:10, 10:7, 10:8,
33:34, 33:35, 40:22, 49:21, 49:22,
98:65, 101:15, 105:4
WHITEHEAD, Rowland 11:12, 35:13
WHITLAM, Gough 66:11
WIENER, Norbert 44:10
WILDE, Oscar 34:10, 41:11, 48:9,
52:8, 56:7, 61:19, 61:20, 62:36,
67:14, 84:7, 95:5, 98:66, 99:6,
104:8
WILKERSON, Tichi 33:36
WILLIAMS, Sara 30:32
WOODWORTH, Robert S. 17:12,
63:12, 69:13, 78:16
WRISTON, Walter 30:33

X

XIAOPING, Deng 98:67

y

YATES, Paula 48:10
YEW, Lee Kuan 9:43
YOUNG, Edward 25:23
YOUNG, Lewis H. 19:25

Z

ZAMPATTI, Carla 61:21, 98:68
ZENO of Citium 54:11
ZIGARMI, Drea 51:10
ZIGARMI, Patricia 51:10
ZIGLAR, Zig 56:8, 63:13

Index (by key word)

a

index

index

index

Index

d

e

f

g

index

i

index

index

m

index

index

O

index

index

index

index

index

y